Going to War

Also by Philip Towle

DEMOCRACY AND PEACEMAKING: Negotiations and Debates, 1815–1973

ENFORCED DISARMAMENT FROM THE NAPOLEONIC CAMPAIGNS TO THE GULF WAR

FROM ALLY TO ENEMY: Anglo-Japanese Military Relations, 1904–45

TEMPTATIONS OF POWER: The United States in Global Politics after 9/11 (*With Robert J. Jackson*)

Going to War

British Debates from Wilberforce to Blair

Philip Towle

Centre of International Studies, University of Cambridge, UK

First published in hardback 2009 and this paperback edition 2010 by
PALGRAVE MACMILLAN

Palgrave Macmillan in the UK is an imprint of Macmillan Publishers Limited, registered in England, company number 785998, of Houndmills, Basingstoke, Hampshire RG21 6XS.

Palgrave Macmillan in the US is a division of St Martin's Press LLC, 175 Fifth Avenue, New York, NY 10010.

Palgrave Macmillan is the global academic imprint of the above companies and has companies and representatives throughout the world.

Palgrave® and Macmillan® are registered trademarks in the United States, the United Kingdom, Europe and other countries.

ISBN 978–0–230–57334–5 hardback
ISBN 978–0–230–23793–3 paperback

This book is printed on paper suitable for recycling and made from fully managed and sustained forest sources. Logging, pulping and manufacturing processes are expected to conform to the environmental regulations of the country of origin.

A catalogue record for this book is available from the British Library.

Library of Congress Cataloging-in-Publication Data
Towle, Philip, 1945–
   Going to war : British debates from Wilberforce to Blair / Philip Towle.
      p.   cm.
   Includes bibliographical references and index.
   ISBN 978–0–230–57334–5 (cloth)   978–0–230–23793–3 (pbk)
   1. Great Britain—Military policy—Public opinion.   2. War—Public opinion—Great Britain—History.   3. War and society—Great Britain—History.   4. Civil–military relations—Great Britain—History.
   5. Public opinion—Great Britain—History.   I. Title.
   UA647.T68 2009
   355′.033541—dc22   2008053018

10   9   8   7   6   5   4   3   2   1
19   18   17   16   15   14   13   12   11   10

Printed and bound in Great Britain by
CPI Antony Rowe, Chippenham and Eastbourne

To those who first inspired my interest in history: D. J. Porritt,
D. Dupree, D. S. Heesom and S. D. Londsborough.

Contents

Preface   viii

Abbreviations   ix

Introduction   1

  1 Culture and Circumstance   11

  2 The Anglican Church and War   24

  3 Civil Society   40

  4 The Media and War   56

  5 War and Literature   68

  6 The Rise of the Armchair Strategists   80

  7 The Professional Military   102

  8 Parliament and War   116

  9 The Public Debate   132

10 Iraq and Afghanistan   142

11 Do Debates on War Matter?   156

Notes   166

Chronology   194

Selected Biographies   198

Bibliography   207

Index   222

Preface

I am extremely grateful to the following colleagues for information and advice; John Freeman, Helen James, Arthur Williamson, the late Richard Edes, Lord Harries of Pentregarth, Geoffrey Williams, Charles Jones, Yusaku Horiuchi and the anonymous readers at Palgrave Macmillan. Veronica, as always, gave me unstinted support. I owe a great deal to my students at the Centre of International Studies in Cambridge for their responses to my ideas and to those who provided me with the opportunity to present some of my arguments at their various institutions: Brian Bond at the University of London, Ralph Pettman at the University of Melbourne, Jean Gardini at the University of Bath, Richard King at the Royal Naval College, Dartmouth, the Pavate Fellowship in New Delhi, the members of the British International History Group and Murielle Cozette and Bill Tow at the Australian National University in Canberra. Naturally, all the mistakes and misjudgements are my own.

Abbreviations

CND	Campaign for Nuclear Disarmament
GDP	Gross Domestic Product
HoC	House of Commons
HoL	House of Lords
NATO	North Atlantic Treaty Organisation
NGO	Non-Governmental Organisation
WLIPF	Women's League for International Peace and Freedom

Introduction

Critics of British foreign policy have always focused on the contrast between its protestations of peaceful, benevolent intentions and the frequency with which it has chosen to intervene in other countries' affairs and go to war. In March 1939 one German headline read, 'Forty-Two Wars in Eighty Years: A Balance Sheet of British "Peacefulness"'.[1] The writer was part of a general Nazi campaign to expose British hypocrisy, highlighting the contrast between Britain's complaints about the German treatment of the Jews and its own repression of the Indians and Palestinians. Methodical, statistical studies have also shown that, whether or not Britain is the most belligerent country, it has certainly been involved in more wars than most.[2] This propensity still provides critics with plenty of ammunition; in the last quarter of a century Britain chose to fight against Argentina in 1982, against Iraq in 1991 and again from 2003, against Serbia in 1999, against the Taleban in Afghanistan from 2001, to say nothing of smaller UN peacekeeping or peacemaking operations.

After a millennium in which it was itself the victim of repeated invasions and occupations, England and its successor Great Britain learnt to protect themselves by maintaining a powerful navy and intervening on the European continent to sustain a balance between competing powers. They also found that trade and discovery brought increasing wealth and control of rich areas beyond Europe. After the battle of Trafalgar in 1805 the Royal Navy dominated the seas vastly enhancing Britain's ability to intervene abroad. The British justified these interventions to themselves and, often less effectively, to foreigners on the grounds that they were beneficial to other peoples, helping small European states to keep their independence, spreading Western civilisation beyond Europe and increasing the wealth of those who lived under their rule. As a British historian confidently asserted after the First World War,   ·

> A great part of the world's area is inhabited by peoples who are still in a condition of barbarism.... For such peoples the only chance of improvement was that they should pass under the dominion of more highly developed peoples; and to them a European Empire brought, for the first time, not merely law and justice, but even the rudiments of the only kind of liberty which is worth having, the liberty which rests upon law.[3]

Modern commentators often regard imperialism as racist but, as the historian's comments suggest, the official view was 'culturist' in the sense that Western, and particularly British, political culture was regarded as the ideal.

The moralistic tone of such pronouncements explains the reference in the subtitle of this book to William Wilberforce, the most famous of the Evangelicals who struggled to end the slave trade at the end of the 18th Century. The campaign against slavery was the first mass pressure group which set the pattern for the dozens of humanitarian pressure groups that were subsequently founded in Britain. It led to the use of British warships to interdict slave ships and to the establishment of Sierra Leone, the first British colony in Africa, where freed slaves were settled. The subtitle also refers to Tony Blair, the most idealistic of Britain's recent prime ministers, who believed firmly that armed force could and should be used after the end of the Cold War to correct wrongs and spread democracy.

Analysts have often commented on the stability of ideas; now we can measure this stability via opinion polls.[4] In the British case, so strong was the synergy between national self-interest and faith in the virtues of spreading national culture that it has survived through the transformations of British society brought by industrialisation and democratisation, through a series of world wars and the disappearance of the British Empire in the 1960s. If the post-Trafalgar era of British dominance passed away between 1914 and 1939, US military power provided Britain with an Indian summer in which it could continue to exercise influence in distant regions when this did not conflict with US policies.[5] The 1996 Defence White Paper rephrased the historian's comment quoted above in a more diplomatic language, according to which Britain wanted to promote:

An international framework that favours freedom and democratic institutions and open trading relationships, and that allows people everywhere to pursue and enhance their well-being, in the belief that this will not only be to our benefit, including our greater security, but also to the benefit of the international community as a whole.[6]

These sentiments were enthusiastically endorsed by Tony Blair's Labour government, which came into office in 1997, and explain why, at the beginning of 2008, under Blair's successor, Gordon Brown, 7398 British servicemen were operating in Afghanistan, 6371 in Iraq and nearly 3000 in Cyprus,[7] and why so many humanitarian Non-Governmental Organisations (NGOs) were founded in Britain and continue to be based there.

The First World War administered the most severe shock to this interventionist culture. In some ways this was surprising, Britain lost almost the same proportion of its population in the French Wars between 1793 and 1815 as in the First World War,[8] but the victories in the French Wars were commemorated in the names given to Trafalgar Square and Waterloo station, there was no annual day of mourning and few memorials scattered around the villages. The wars were followed by the greatest period of expansion in British history, when they conquered vast areas of Asia and Africa. Nevertheless, the perspective in Britain changed between 1815 and 1918. During these years Britain became less hierarchical so that for the first time the death of anyone, whatever their rank in society, was considered more important than it had been in the past, the peacetime mortality and birth rates declined, making the sudden deaths of large numbers of young people more shocking.[9] At the same time, the spread of education, the growth of the media and the proximity of the battlefields made people aware of the nature of the fighting in the First World War. After the American Civil War in the 1860s writers had struggled to find an unromantic, graphic way of describing combat; this fundamental cultural change was completed between 1914 and 1918 so that it is no longer the accounts by national leaders or by generals which matter to the public as a whole, it accounts by civilians of their wartime struggles to survive and the soldier's view from the frontline.[10]

After the shock of that war the British elite re-examined their strategic culture and many became convinced that, in future, they should rely on the League of Nations to maintain peace, keep out of European affairs so that they could focus on imperial affairs and reduce their military spending so that war debts could be repaid.[11] This new synthesis fell apart in the 1930s under threats from the Axis, and after 1945 the country again contributed to maintaining the balance of power and what it believed was the common good through the North Atlantic Treaty Organisation (NATO) alliance. But, as Britain now became more committed to European defence than it had ever been in peacetime, its propensity to intervene militarily outside Europe weakened in the face of a temporary loss of confidence and the growing demand for independence amongst the peoples of Asia and Africa.[12] As colonialism declined in moral and military authority, its demise encouraged an increase in the number of humanitarian NGOs; it was in these years that organisations like Oxfam, Amnesty International and a host of others grew up in Britain and were emulated elsewhere. Alongside the media, with which they have a symbiotic relationship, they have replaced colonialism as the spearhead of Western cultural interference overseas. Military interventionism, in the forms of peacekeeping or peacemaking, revived after the end of the Cold War when the UN Security Council was unfrozen and television brought pictures into homes of the chaos in the Third World. In 2008, despite the continuation of guerrilla operations mounted by Afghans and Iraqis against the presence of British and other Western forces in their countries, there is continued pressure from commentators in the media for Britain to intervene in Myanmar, Zimbabwe and Sudan and to impose Western political culture.

Because of the British propensity to send military forces overseas and the controversy that it has caused, the country has a particularly rich literature devoted to the subject. This is a study of the debates initiated by the pressure groups and people who have struggled to shape or weaken the interventionist culture over the last 200 years. It tries to modify the conventional wisdom by showing how open Parliamentary debates at the onset of war only began to include the military prospects during the Falklands campaign in 1982; how the emphasis in the media has moved from the heroism of the troops and the skill of the generals to the impact of conflict on civilians; how often governments have tried to avoid receiving professional military advice on the onset of war; how deeply divided the pressure groups have always been between the humanitarian and the anti-war movements and how prescient some of the poets, novelists and armchair strategists have been about the shape of future wars.

Above all, it shows how the pollsters and political analysts have revolutionised our view of public opinion and proved that the mass of people often show more understanding of what an impending war might mean than governments, media commentators and the chattering classes in general. The wider public are aware of both the problems in

other parts of the world which impel the government towards intervention and the increasing difficulties which military intervention of any
sort is likely to encounter. Although the upper classes dismissed poorer
groups as fickle and jingoistic before 1914, the public as a whole have
shown before the Second World War, during the Suez Crisis in 1956 and
again before the invasion of Iraq in March 2003, that their judgements
are often as good or better than the government's and that, while they
broadly accept the interventionist culture, their support is conditional.[13]

As the pace of change began to increase in the 19th Century, so
people became more concerned about the future. Traditional utopias,
which satirised existing policies towards war and peace, such as *Gulliver's
Travels*, were supplemented by warnings, not only about existing practice, but also about what would happen if existing trends continued or
the wrong policies were followed. Alfred Tennyson's hero in his poem
'Locksley Hall', published in 1842, foresaw not only aerial commerce
and warfare and the use of chemical weapons but also, as a correction,
the evolution of international organisations to hold the 'fretful realms'
in awe. At the start of the 20th Century the popular novelist H. G. Wells
forecast the development of tanks and nuclear weapons; Nevil Shute
imagined the impact which aerial bombardment would have on ordinary British families in the 1930s and predicted in the 1950s that life
would be destroyed in a nuclear war.

By 1900 civilian or armchair strategists had begun to analyse international security. Government ministers and senior officers could have
learnt as much or more about what was impending from studying the
War of the Future published by the Polish banker Ivan Bloch in 1898,
The Great Pacific War written by the British journalist Hector Bywater in
1925 or *The Military Strength of the Powers* by the Russian economist Max
Werner, published in 1939, as they would have done by poring over the
most highly classified documents. In the 1920s the Royal Institute of
International Affairs joined the earlier Royal United Services Institution
as a 'think tank' studying international affairs, while the first professorships of International Relations were founded at the University of Wales
in Aberystwyth and the London School of Economics. Their publications vastly increased the information available on the risks involved
in each military intervention overseas and conversely the threats to
which British isolationism would expose Europe and the rest of the
world.

Even if the armed forces were discouraged by convention from partic-
ipating in public debates, one would have expected their commanders
to play a major part in a government's decision to go to war. However,

when the outbreak of a great war threatened, the leaders of the armed forces had to struggle to make their advice heard by ministers. In both 1914 and 1939 politicians tried to exclude military voices from deliberations because they were primarily concerned with their political objectives, they did not want to hear about the difficulty of achieving victory. But, once war broke out, the relative influence of the different institutions was transformed. Senior officers became more important, while politicians and civil servants receded into the background. The permanent under-secretary at the Foreign Office confided in his diary during the Second World War that he might be more useful growing onions.[14] The power of ministers waned in comparison with that wielded by the commanders of the armed forces, though the authority of the prime minister shrank much less than others. The armed forces could no longer be moved around like chessman, as the younger Pitt had done so incompetently in the French Wars.[15] The new balance of power within the government inevitably produced friction. There were bitter arguments between Lloyd George and his military advisers in the First World War, and between Winston Churchill and the commanders of the armed forces two decades later.[16] Such friction can be creative, however, painful for those involved; strong wartime prime ministers sometimes forced the heads of the armed forces to rethink or, at least, to justify their strategic and tactical plans. After the war publicity about these arguments affected the standing and influence of the armed forces, and attitudes amongst the elite towards future interventions.[17]

The aristocrats who ruled Britain in the 19th Century gave ground reluctantly to interested groups and to popular demands for some say on how the country was run. They preferred a situation in which the masses could not influence debates because of their illiteracy and lack of knowledge about politics, war and foreign affairs. They also learnt during the anti-slavery campaign how powerful informed opinion could become when exercised about some moral issue and they had no interest in encouraging the emergence of such groups. Nevertheless, because of the strength of popular demands, the electorate was expanded to include the middle classes in 1832 and 1867 but it was only in the 1920s that universal adult suffrage was conceded. Although some 70 per cent of the population was illiterate or semi-literate, it was not until 1870 that the government made a real effort to educate the whole population. Governments were less repressive than they had been in previous centuries, but they still imposed taxes on newspapers to prevent the poor reading about politics. It was when the Advertisement Duty was dropped in 1853, the Newspaper Stamp Duty in 1855 and the Paper

Duty in 1861, and when higher speed presses were introduced that the mass circulation newspapers could blossom.[18]

Every time that another profession or group has begun to participate in the national debate on security in general and overseas intervention in particular, politicians have met their efforts with disdain. By and large Members of Parliament (MPs) have supported government attempts to retain control of the debate, after all, they could hope to become ministers themselves one day. It was not until the beginning of the Falklands War in 1982 that the government provided Parliament with information on the British forces being deployed and that MPs openly debated the interaction between strategy and politics. Before that, open Parliamentary debates at the onset of war had been almost entirely confined to politics and morality, and the revolution which occurred in the 1980s did not go unopposed; retired military officers now serving as MPs, led by Denis Healey and Paddy Ashdown, disputed the right and ability of other MPs without military experience to participate in subsequent debates. Healey solemnly told the House of Commons on 6th September 1990, 'nobody who has not fought in a war has much right to talk about what would happen if a war takes place.'[19] Rarely has the fear of democracy and discussion been more succinctly expressed.

Thus ministers and their supporters have derided and dismissed the challengers; during the Boer War radical commentators led by J. A. Hobson propagated the notion that the working classes were jingoistic xenophobes not to be trusted with high politics and particularly with decisions about going to war[20]; after the First World War the Prime Minister Lloyd George fostered the myth that the armed forces were led by half-witted aristocrats,[21] while other commentators attacked the intervention in strategic debates by the Anglican Church.[22] Many of these myths linger on; press commentators sometimes claim that less-educated people are naturally more interventionist than their better-educated compatriots, even when opinion polls suggest exactly the opposite[23]; the idea that all British generals of the First World War were peculiarly stupid is still the conventional wisdom.[24] The real issue was less the generals' competence, though this was certainly very mixed, but the intense pressure under which they laboured from public and politicians alike to break through the German lines and end the war quickly. They could only try to do so by staging great offensives and suffering heavy casualties. The alternative to these offensives on the Western Front was to remain on the defensive until the British naval blockade began to starve the Central Powers and to weaken their resolve. But that was politically unacceptable; Herbert Asquith, the first wartime prime minister, was forced to resign for not pushing the war effort ahead more effectively. Wartime impatience is only too often followed by peacetime lamentations over the consequences.[25]

In recent years politicians have tried to start other hares. Once international lawyers began to participate more actively in debates on the onset of war, they also came under attack. On 17 March 2003, Lord Goodhart introduced a debate in the House of Lords on the legality of the pending attack by the United States and Britain on Iraq. This was the first time that the legality of a war had been publicly debated at such length in Parliament before the war began. On cue the representatives of the two main political parties – Baroness Ramsay and Lord Howell – stood up to disparage international law and lawyers, arguing that they always disagree amongst themselves and that they were just using a legal cover for their political prejudices.[26] In fact, the real problem with international law is that it is apolitical. Treaties apply equally to all parties but all countries do not represent the same threat to peace; Axis foreign policy was not comparable to democratic foreign policy in the 1930s. Status quo and non-status quo powers are fundamentally different.

This book concentrates mainly on pre-war debates because once great wars have begun, rational, wide-ranging discussions are rare.[27] The national 'herd' replaces many of the smaller groups because the public's instinct is to rally round the government. People become more cautious than they are in peacetime about openly criticising national policy because they are afraid of appearing unpatriotic and encouraging their country's foreign critics. Those who break this taboo are usually subject to vituperation. Asked in November 1944 whether they backed the use of chemical weapons against Japan, the very crude opinion polls available seemed to show that 71 per cent of Americans, who offered an opinion, turned the proposal down,[28] but once the incomparably more destructive nuclear weapons had been dropped on Hiroshima and Nagasaki, defensiveness about their government's policy and overwhelming relief that the war had ended overcame such hesitations. In August 1945, 85 per cent of Americans and 72 per cent of Britons appeared to approve of dropping the bombs.[29] Similarly, because they were unsure about the justice of the cause, the great majority of Britons opposed an attack on Iraq without UN support in February 2003, but as soon as the government had launched its offensive, public opinion rallied to its support, though this backing eroded when the campaign bogged down in guerrilla warfare.[30] The tendency to endorse government policy in wartime is understandable and gratifying to the armed forces in the short term, because they want to feel that their sacrifices are appreciated. But it has the grave, long-term disadvantage that it discourages wartime debates and politicians now know from opinion polls that they can rely on support, particularly from the educated classes, in a total war or a short, limited conflict. Thus, governments are much less afraid of public opinion today, when they intervene overseas, than they were in the 1930s.

Of course, by no means every section of opinion has accepted the interventionist consensus described above – thereby undermining the determinist views, discussed in Chapter 11, which maintain that biological or economic factors cause the outbreak of war. There has been opposition amongst the elite on political and ethical grounds to Britain's participation in every war for the last 200 years; from the Whigs led by Charles James Fox during the French Revolutionary Wars, from the Cobdenite liberals during the Crimean War, from much of the Liberal Party and the Nonconformist Churches during the Boer War, from sections of the Labour and Liberal parties during the First World War, from pacifists, like George Lansbury, in the Second World War and from radicals and communists during the Cold War against the Soviet Union. Thus, however narrow the number of participants, opponents of the war have always raised the questions whether it was justified, whether the means employed to achieve victory were proportionate and whether it has a reasonable chance of success.

In the 19th Century both pressure to exercise British power and criticism of war increased. The free traders argued that wars were not only wrong but wasteful and archaic, thus challenging the basis of the interventionist consensus. On the other side, enthusiastic imperial governors spread the frontiers of the empire across India and Africa, while the Social Darwinists propagated the notion that nations were not merely destined to fight but that they needed to do so in order to avoid decadence by ensuring that only the fittest survived.[31] This was much more radical, and belligerent, than the traditional British view that intervention in Europe was sometimes necessary to preserve the balance of power and that intervention elsewhere was of benefit to both Britain and the colonial peoples. The First World War largely eradicated Social Darwinist ideas from the British debate, partly because it was so obvious that, if death was not wholly random in the trenches, it was the brave who were more likely to be killed,[32] and partly because the League of Nations was established to replace the struggle for survival amongst the nations. When collective security failed in the 1930s, the elite reluctantly concluded that the country would have to reaffirm the interventionist ethic, ally with the French and persuade the United States to emerge from isolation. During the Cold War the debate focused on the morality and efficacy of trying to deter the outbreak of an East–West war by the threat to employ nuclear weapons on a horrific scale. Once the Cold War ended with the collapse of Soviet power, the West was in a position to wage a series of conventional wars in former Yugoslavia, in Afghanistan and in Iraq, each of which opened a new debate on interventionism and led to increased reliance on the traditional *jus ad bellum* criteria for evaluating the justice of war.

This is then a study of the way in which British ideas about warfare and other forms of intervention have evolved over the last two centuries when Britain and then the United States have been the dominant world powers. It is also a study of how the various interested groups and the people as a whole have overcome political opposition and misunderstanding to establish their right and ability to participate responsibly in debates about whether Britain should intervene with military forces in Europe and elsewhere. Before the Anglo-American invasion of Iraq in 2003 the debate covered the legitimacy of operating without a specific UN mandate, the ability of precision-guided munitions to minimise civilian casualties, the efficiency of allied forces at countering insurgency, the ability of US and British forces to re-establish an Iraqi government and the impact of the attack on Muslim opinion across the world. This was a much wider discussion than those held 200 years before about the French Revolution or of 100 years before about the Boer War in Southern Africa. However, there has been no similar widening within government and thus, as we shall see in Chapter 10, after the intervention in Afghanistan in 2001 and Iraq in 2003, a new debate began about the ways in which governmental authority to launch the country into war might be limited and the public debate given greater weight.

1
Culture and Circumstance

When people ask why governments took the decisions which led to war and why people supported them, they usually mean what reasons did they give or what motives did they hide? But our conscious and articulated motives are like the visible part of the iceberg; the assumptions and feelings, which make up our culture, lie behind the decisions we take, even if they are hidden from us. As one commentator put it, 'continuity is no accident. Social customs, like personal habit, economise human effort. They store knowledge, pre-arrange decisions, save us the trouble of weighing every choice afresh.'[1] They become particularly important in an intense crisis which may lead to intervention in a major war; Sir Edward Grey, the British foreign secretary, who more than any other carried the burden of the British decision to go to war in 1914, recalled afterwards:

> It is not always easy for a man to trace the inward path and steps by which he reaches his conclusions; so much of the working of the mind is subconscious rather than conscious. It is difficult to be sure of one's own mind, one can only guess at the processes in others.[2]

Usually this means that a statesman feels highly constrained by circumstances but believes that foreign decision makers have more latitude in a crisis to change their policy and avoid the recourse to arms, while the successful resolution of the conflict requires the opposite perceptions.[3] The leaders' ideas or preconceptions have been formed over generations and passed down through families, books and institutions such as schools, Churches or the media.[4] Yet conventions also change; over the last 200 years institutions and ideas have altered with the vast social and economic transformation brought by the industrial revolution, democratisation and education, and by the four great wars in which Britain has been involved, against France from 1793 to 1815, against Germany from 1914 to 1918 and from 1939 to 1945 and the Cold War with the Soviet Union from 1945 to 1990. The national culture has thus not only evolved but also proved strong enough to absorb generations of immigrants from France, the Netherlands, Eastern Europe and now from the Third World.

Each country's culture shapes its attitude towards warfare. Thus, even though educated Japanese read widely in Western literature in the early 20th century and Japan emulated Western economic and political methods, Japanese had a very different attitude towards the sacrifices which war demanded, the reasons for fighting and the way in which wars should be conducted in the 1930s and 1940s.[5] Similarly, as China met few Great Power challengers for hundreds of years, traditional Chinese stressed psychological warfare over brute force and regarded warriors with some disdain, though they also put great weight on maintaining the Empire's prestige and supported the use of their army when this seemed unavoidable.[6] In the Muslim world the Koran has shaped attitudes towards warfare and international affairs because it makes no distinction between religion and politics. Even so, there can be considerable differences of interpretation about the tactics which are permissible and the relationship between the Muslim and the non-Muslim world.[7]

It is sometimes easier to say which factors did not shape such attitudes, rather than the reverse, and, in the British case, the mass of literature on warfare dating from antiquity was clearly inaccessible to most of our ancestors. British society at the beginning of the 19th century and before was divided by the chasm separating those who had been educated from the illiterate or semi-literate.[8] Nor was their direct experience a substitute for lack of literary knowledge; the illiterate majority can have had only a folk memory of the civil wars, which had ended half a century before. The army raised by the Stuart Pretender to the British throne marched in 1745 from Scotland to Derby but, while it lived off the countryside, its effects were geographically limited. The civil war in the mid-17th century and the Wars of the Roses in the 15th century affected the lives of far more people, although memories would have been attenuated as the generations passed.

Overseas campaigns in the Americas, India or against Napoleon no doubt had considerable impact in garrison towns and ports to which old soldiers and sailors returned with tales of strange lands and distant battles. But the number returning to the inland villages would have been smaller and their impact would have varied with their ability to describe events which were so remote from the villagers' experience.[9] Many of our ancestors must never have seen a warship and only occasionally met soldiers. Families might also move from one village to a neighbouring one and so widen peoples' knowledge and experience but the villages had only perhaps 200–400 inhabitants and the collective experience was still very limited.[10]

If they were unschooled and had no direct experience of warfare and only infrequent contact with those who had, where did our ancestors derive their view of war? Conflict is built into the structure of any society, between brothers and sisters, parents and children, and between the adults living in the village; children of all social classes gain their first lessons about the way people interact from what they observe around them and they would have seen plenty of trouble. A 19th-century historian summarised the disputes brought before the court during the 15th century in the little textile-producing and farming village of Castle Combe in Wiltshire; 'affrays, assaults, blood-shedding, tippling in alehouses, eaves-dropping or night-walking, keeping bad houses, gaming or playing at forbidden games, barratry or disturbing the peace by false reports and quarrels'.[11] No doubt, most villages would have had 'rebels' determined to challenge the authorities, like John Rayner, discovered by the historian of the village of Foxton south of Cambridge, who was repeatedly fined over several decades for various offences from trespass to failure to keep his fences in order and encroaching on other people's land.[12] From such events and from interacting with other children, our ancestors would have learnt about quarrels and fights, and recent studies of childhood have found that 'children, particularly during middle childhood, refer to various aspects of peer relationships when they are asked to verbalise their understanding of peace and war'.[13] Beyond this understanding of local conflict, the uneducated must have learnt about the more ferocious violence of warfare itself from their village church and the lessons they heard on a Sunday.

We will discuss Anglican teaching at length in the next chapter, but *The Old Testament* provided all Christians with a rare and powerful insight into the struggles for survival typical of primitive tribes. It described the periodic enslavement of the Jewish people by powerful empires and their attempts, in turn, to establish a secure homeland by expelling, enslaving or killing the members of rival tribes and their leaders.[14] The *New Testament* told the story of the birth, the brief life and execution of Jesus of Nazareth after Israel had been conquered once again and become part of the mighty Roman Empire. The Roman centurions or officers were generally not represented as enemies, nevertheless, the threats of war, riot and insurrection were ever present. The overt political message in the *New Testament* was quietist; Jesus advised the Jews to 'render to Caesar the things which are Caesar's', in other words to respect the demands made by political leaders and to separate religion and politics. At the same time, the personal message was activist; in one of his parables Jesus praised a Samaritan who looked after a Jew attacked by robbers. There has, thus, always been a tension in Christianity between trying to help other people and avoiding violence because, on the street or in international politics, going to the help of someone who has been attacked always risks involvement in conflict.[15]

The *Old Testament* account of the Jews' epic struggles for survival over the centuries would have familiarised everyone with the frequency of war and the threats to the weak. The way in which Christian 'soft power' gradually infiltrated the Roman Empire until Constantine 1 made it the official religion in 324 would have been less salient. As indeed would the way in which the Jews' religion gave them a unique sense of belonging and cohesion during the centuries when they were dispersed across the world after the Romans savagely repressed their rebellion in 70. The Cathaginians who were similarly dispersed disappeared from history, the Jews survived, despite centuries of persecution and pogroms, to retake Palestine from the people living there after the Second World War.

The educated classes would have listened to the same religious stories but their understanding of them would have been potentially deeper and their world-view wider than those of their illiterate neighbours because written culture is more likely to be cumulative. As John Stuart Mill pointed out, education is 'the culture which each generation purposely gives to those who are to be its successors, in order to qualify them for at least keeping up, and if possible raising, the level of improvement which has been attained'.[16] On the other hand, this sort of culture is less grounded in immediate fact and thus more open to serious errors of judgement than the culture of the illiterate or semi-literate which, as pointed out above, was shaped, not by theory, but by cooperation and conflict in the family and the village. Elite culture has thus varied considerably over the ages; the bawdy stories told by the illiterate characters in Geoffrey Chaucer's *Canterbury Tales*, written towards the end of the 14th century, differ little from those told by modern comedians; on the other hand, the ideas put into the mouths of the more highly educated are sometimes barely comprehensible to modern readers. Elites experiment with new ideas, most of which turn out to be wrong but without which mankind would not progress. The majority suffer the consequences of the mistakes and benefit from the advances.

In traditional society mothers often provided wealthier children with basic education in literacy and religion before they began their schooling.[17] Later, boys would have gone to the grammar schools, which spread in the 16th and 17th centuries, where they were taught Latin grammar and familiarised with the classical texts of Greece and Rome. Like the *Old Testament*, these would have shown them the pervasive nature of warfare and the struggle for survival in which the weak were swept aside by the strong. They would also have gained some knowledge of their own country's history, of the repeated invasions between Caesar's arrival in 55 BC and that of William 1 in 1066, of the various civil wars and of Britain's intervention in the Hundred Years War and other continental campaigns. Personal experience, religious instruction, classical education and national history shaped beliefs about the causes of wars, their impact and the qualities which armies, leaders and nations needed to survive and prosper.[18]

The leading 17th-century poet John Milton suggested in one of the most influential essays on education that 'a complete and generous education [is one] which fits a man to perform justly, skilfully and magnanimously all the offices, both private and public, of peace and war'.[19] What makes this comment distinctive is the equal emphasis it puts on preparation for peace *and* war, and the stress it places on justice and magnanimity. The first separates it from modern commentary on education, which would usually ignore wartime requirements because we think of peace as the norm and war as an unfortunate interlude rather than a normal part of life, while the second separates it from the purposes of education in those societies, such as Japan and Germany in the 1930s, where speaking about magnanimity and justice in the same context as warfare would have been regarded as an oxymoron.[20] In Milton's ideal school, where 130 students would be housed from childhood until their early 20s, they would practise fencing and wrestling 'which, being tempered with seasonable lectures and precepts to them of true fortitude and patience, will turn into a native and heroic valour, and make them hate the cowardice of wrong doing'. They would also study military science and learn how to march and to ride as cavalry. Here then was the greatest poet of the age and a man with experience of civil war and governmental service, trying to combine learning, moral principle and practical military application in a detailed educational syllabus.

Christian thinkers from Augustine to Aquinas had built on the classical principles of the just war, developed by Aristotle and Cicero, so that, while the Church recognised that warfare was inevitable in the circumstances, its doctrine tried to prevent the brutal struggles for survival of the type described in the *Old Testament* breaking out between Christian nations by restricting both the number of occasions when war occurred and the methods then employed to achieve victory.[21] The age when poets could laud King Harold Hardrada of Norway for the plunder and repression of his own and other peoples faded as Europe became more settled.[22] In the 16th century, military writers still dismissed civilian suffering and boasted of their brutality but there were competing accounts and arguments which took a very different view.[23] Blaise Pascal, the French mathematician, inventor and Jansenist, who was a contemporary of Milton, lashed the Jesuits for inventing bogus justifications for ignoring Christian ethics and weakening restraints on violence.[24] A century later, Lord Chesterfield advised his son that it was better to die in warfare than to do 'a base or criminal action' such as poisoning the enemy.[25] All this underpinned the movement to develop international law from the time of the 17th-century Dutch jurist Hugo Grotius to his 18th-century Swiss successor Emmerich de Vattel. Again, educated men were familiar with this evolution and it was not unusual for Vattel to be quoted both inside and outside Parliament.[26]

In the 17th and 18th centuries, the rich had their minds broadened by the vogue for sending young gentlemen abroad to learn foreign languages and manners, and to appreciate art and architecture. At home or abroad, they could hardly have avoided knowing something about the ideas which have come to be called the Enlightenment. The movement's main contribution to international affairs was to popularise the notion that warfare could best be limited by collective efforts, and perhaps even federations, between nations.[27] This contrasted with the traditional religious belief that peace would grow from below when people's attitudes were changed. But monarchs, enlightened or not, continued to regard warfare as an extension of politics and the great powers were at war for over half of the 18th century, sometimes to expand their territory in Europe and overseas, sometimes out of fear that another state might acquire so much territory that the balance of power would be upset.[28] Preparing his son for a career in diplomacy, Lord Chesterfield sent him abroad to admire the customs and manners of foreign countries, and he also encouraged him to pay close attention to the strength of the countries he visited to assess their value as allies and the threat they might present to the balance of power.[29]

Although the radical essayist William Hazlitt grumbled about London's café society in the early 19th century for its addiction to discussing ephemeral news, educated men had the time to give prolonged consideration to the writers of the Enlightenment and other serious contemporary issues.[30] The August 1809 edition of the conservative *Quarterly Review*, for example, contained amongst other articles, 23 pages on the problems of the West Indian planters after the ending of the slave trade, 37 pages on the missionaries in the Pacific, 25 pages on mental illness, 14 pages on mineralogy, 14 pages on sermons and 30 pages on the war in the Iberian Peninsula. Such publications spread across the English-speaking world from the United States to Tasmania; they were not read just by a tiny British minority.[31] As Milton hoped, some of the educated clearly had a wide range of interests – scientific, religious, military and humanistic. Speeches in Parliament were replete with learned illusions and shaped by the rules of classical rhetoric; however, there was a vast gap separating this articulate elite from the uneducated masses, not necessarily in terms of principles, but in their knowledge of the world. And, although this gap is much narrower today, members of the educated elite in Britain and other English-speaking countries are more likely to favour overseas intervention; they know, or think they know, more about events elsewhere and are more readily tempted to believe that other countries will benefit from their intervention.[32]

The establishment of charitable religious schools in the 18th and 19th centuries very gradually widened the provision of education even before the 1870 Elementary Education Act made it free and universal, and attendance was compulsory from 1880. Numbers of schoolchildren then quadrupled from 1.2 million to 4.7 million.[33] Before that it was calculated that only two out of five children between six and ten years old ever attended school and only a third between the ages of ten and twelve.[34] Most of the rest expected to work from the moment they could provide useful labour on the farms, in the factories or in the great houses of the aristocracy. After the Education Acts the numbers with education and, therefore, the ability to read newspapers and gain some knowledge of political life widened dramatically and school teachers, pressure groups and the media began to influence their ideas in ways which would have been impossible before. As one political scientist rightly pointed out, 'the educational revolution which made the state responsible for child-life was comparable in its sphere to the Industrial Revolution in economics and the French Revolution in politics'.[35]

And so were the rapid changes in communications. One commentator noted in 1826:

We, who live in an age and country in which the means of locomotion and communication have been facilitated by all the power of human ingenuity and science, can scarcely imagine to ourselves the difficulties of obtaining intelligence in those regions where news-papers are unknown and whose peaceful solitudes have never been disturbed by the bugle of the mail-coach guard. Destitute of these aids even bad news does not fly apace; and the details of passing events, which in the course of eight and forty hours are transmitted from the Channel to the border, could scarcely cover the same distance in a twelvemonth, when Fame was compelled to limp with her despatches along the primitive ruts, and patriarchal bridle-paths of Watling Street and Ikenild Street, and the other renowned highways.[36]

The writer was about to witness the coming of the railway era which would make the age of canals and stagecoaches a relic of the past. Each age marvels at developments in communications and, in each, improve-ments in communications transform the speed with which news of events and ideas are transmitted and thus their impact on society. This, in turn, changes the balance of influence between institutions, so that, in the 19th century, the military had to pay more attention to news-papers whose war correspondents could rapidly transmit reports by telegraph over hundreds of miles to their editor's desk, and the popu-lar writer could sometimes evoke fears of invasion amongst hundreds of thousands who would never before have troubled themselves about affairs of state.

The most important of these affairs over the last 200 years included the wars against France from 1793 to 1815, against Germany from 1914 to 1918 and from 1939 to 1945, and the Cold War confrontation with the Soviet Union from 1945 to 1990. In the French Revolution-ary and Napoleonic Wars 210,000 British servicemen were killed out of a population of some 12 million in 1811 or one in every 57 people, and, of course, a much higher proportion of young males.[37] Materially, the French Wars cost £1500 millions in loans and taxes.[38] The annual expenditure on the war rose from about £22 millions in the 1790s to £84 million in 1815 and, by the end of the war, the national debt had grown from £290 million in 1788 to £862 million, leaving Britain the most heavily taxed state in Europe.[39] The country was spared a test on the same scale for 100 years, though Britain lost 23,000 men in the Cri-mea between 1854 and 1856 and the campaign cost some £50 million.[40]

During the First World War 730,000 servicemen were killed or one in 56 of its 41 million people over less than a quarter of the time occu-pied by the French Wars. During the French wars people seem to have accepted casualties more philosophically when the death of young peo-ple from disease or accident was so much more common. At the same time, the birth rate was very high and so, despite the deaths from disease and war, the population grew by 2,146,000 or 28 per cent from 1791 to 1811.[41] To put it in another way, death in childhood or early adulthood was less frequent before the First World War than it had been 100 years earlier. The size of the family was also declining and the loss of an only son was felt all the more keenly, as the death of Rudyard Kipling's son and tens of thousands of others demonstrated clearly. Certainly, if one examines the diaries kept by educated people, or their letters, there is no comparison between the impact of the French wars and the First World War; in the first case, they appear to have continued relatively unperturbed with their ordinary lives, in the second, their whole world was transformed and their minds constantly troubled by the news from France and the returning casualties.[42] As a total conflict, the First World War taxed Britain's industrial and financial resources to the utmost, and again the Exchequer was left deeply burdened with debts because only 7 per cent of military expenditure had been covered by taxation in the early stages of the war, though this had risen to a quarter by the time the Armistice was signed. Most of the debt was to British citizens but the debt to the United States (had it not lapsed in the 1930s) would not have been repaid until 1984.[43]

Britain may have suffered about half as many military casualties in the Second World War as in the First World War (360,000 civilian and military) out of a larger population of 46 million, but it faced a series of humiliating defeats in France, Singapore, Burma and Greece; its towns suffered much greater damage from bombers and missiles, and it could carry on fighting only because of US' financial, industrial and military support. This time the whole country was mobilised and half of the costs were raised through taxation. The government took care in this and other wars that the greatest burden fell on those most able to bear it. Income tax was raised for the first time during the wars against France, while in the 1920s the national debt was repaid by income and super tax payers, and by those estates rich enough to pay death duties. In the Second World War again the government tried to equalise the burden through food rationing and through heavy direct taxation.[44] The country was also saved by the US policy of 'lend-lease' of weaponry worth some $21,000 million, but it still had to sell £1118 million in capital assets and borrow £2879 million from external creditors, leaving it weaker than ever before in modern history.[45]

The Cold War gradually developed after the Second World War came to a close. Over the four decades that it lasted, the confrontation with the Soviet Union forced the country to spend a higher proportion of its GDP on defence than it had done during the heyday of its Empire; the cost per head in 1900 prices was £3.3, against £7.6 in 1952.[46] Britain had 902,000 men in its armed forces in 1953, compared with 695,000 mobilised by France, none by West Germany and 119,000 by Japan. It was only in the later 1950s that the manpower balance altered as Britain led the way in phasing out conscription. But replacing conscripts with wholly professional armed forces was expensive; in 1972 Britain was spending 4.9 per cent of its GDP on defence against 3.4 per cent in France, 3.1 per cent in Germany and 2.9 per cent in Italy, and high defence expenditure was often blamed at the time for the comparatively slow rate of British economic growth.[47] The burden was important because it was one reason why governments were tempted to rely on deterrence to reduce costs, despite the protests of the Campaign for Nuclear Disarmament (CND).

Prolonged tension and the threat of a greater disaster than any Britain had faced before in its history taxed the nerves more than other conflicts. The *Statement on Defence Estimates* for 1956 asserted bluntly that:

> To give full protection to everyone from sickness or death from the hazard of radioactivity alone would involve physical preparations on a vast scale and to make such preparations against all the hazards of a thermonuclear attack on this country would place a crippling burden on the national resources.

The White Paper concluded, 'whatever the preparations made, an attack on this country would involve loss of life and destruction on an unparalleled scale'.[48] The assessment was truthful enough but it was hardly surprising that it fostered the CND, whose members felt that it was better to abandon NATO and retreat into isolation rather than live for decades under such a threat. Some of the ablest and best informed commentators, including the leading US columnist, Walter Lippmann, believed that long years of confrontation might be too much for the democracies: 'A policy of shifts and manoeuvres may be suited to the Soviet system of government, which...is animated by patient persistence. It is not suited to the American system of government.'[49] Given the way democracies vent such fears in public, it was not surprising that Lippmann thought as he did, even if events in the last decade of the 20th century were to prove him wrong.

As his fears about the Cold War remind us, victory in these wars was never certain; when Britain's continental allies were defeated, the country became largely impotent against Napoleon's Empire. Pitt could send British armies to the Caribbean and South Africa to take over enemy colonies but even this was only achieved at the expense of immense sacrifice in lives and resources largely because of the yellow fever and other diseases to which they fell victim. It was not until Wellington found an effective way of deploying the British army in coordination with Spanish guerrillas, when Napoleon's armies were weakened by defeat in Russia and when British subsidies finally brought together an effective coalition of Russian, Austrian and Prussian forces, that the tide was turned.[50] The First World War was far shorter but by 1917 the various allied armies were bogged down, Russia was gradually collapsing into revolution and France had been weakened by attrition at Verdun and by the subsequent mutiny in its army. Losses of merchant ships to submarines increased dramatically and the Royal Navy had failed to destroy Germany's High Seas Fleet. It was only when Germany's final offensive ground to a halt in the Spring of 1918, when food short-ages undermined Austria–Hungary and when the tide of fresh US rein-forcements began to demoralise the Central Powers, that victory came into sight. The equivalent low point in the Second World War stretched from the Spring of 1940 to the Spring of 1942. The whole of West-ern Europe fell in the summer of 1940, the Royal Navy was defending merchant ships in the Atlantic against German submarines, RAF fighter aircraft were battling against the Luftwaffe over London, and the army was struggling to protect Egypt and the precious oil resources of the Mid-dle East. The situation became even more difficult once the Japanese had entered the war in December 1941 and quickly overran Malaya, Singapore and Burma. Only as the Soviet defences steadied against the Nazis' onslaught and the immense resources of the United States began to come into play did it become obvious that the Axis were doomed and Britain was safe, albeit gravely weakened financially and emotionally.

The Cold War was made up of a series of confrontations and skir-mishes around the world from Berlin to Cuba, and Korea to Mozam-bique. At the same time, British troops were embroiled in insurgencies from Malaya to Aden in which Soviet support for the guerrillas was suspected. Looking back it might seem clear that the West would be victorious over communism in such an economic, political and mili-tary test, but this was not so; during the 1960s and early 1970s it was the West which was most troubled. The United States was sapped by the guerrilla war in Vietnam, anti-war demonstrations, race riots in the cities and the demoralising assassinations of President John Kennedy, his brother, Robert and the civil rights leader, Martin Luther King.[51] Britain seemed to be in terminal decline after the strains of the World Wars and the loss of Empire, with its GDP per head falling for the first time in modern history below many of the other developed states including France, and the City of London facing one Sterling crisis after another.[52] It was only as the 1970s wore on that it became clear that liberal capitalism was triumphing across East Asia, that Western Europe was stabilised and that the Soviet economy was in disarray, thereby ceasing to be a model for Third World States and for disaffected Western intellectuals.[53] It was not until the 1980s and 1990s that Britain overcame its own demons and that the widespread assumption of the country's inevitable decline was dissipated. And the tradition of extra-European military interventionism revived.

In great military conflicts governments have become steadily more confident about popular support. Because the whole nation was insufficiently educated to join the political community and the ruling elite knew less about the opinions of the masses, Pitt's government feared the disaffection of the poor more than any of his successors were to do.[54] Thus governmental repression of dissent was greater during the French Wars than it was ever to be again. Conscientious objectors were persecuted during the First World War, refugees from Germany were, for a time, rusticated to the Isle of Man during the Second World War, fascist sympathisers were interned and traitors, like L. S. Amery's son, John or the propagandist William Joyce were hanged at the end of the conflict. In both the World Wars there was more anxiety about German spies operating in Britain than was justified by the threat they represented and national fears led to a number of miscarriages of justice, but repression was much less than it had been in the 1790s and there was no serious challenge to political stability.

The Cold War brought different problems because, as in the 1790s, those who wanted radical reforms could be easily confused in the tensions and anxieties of the moment with the handful who actually spied for the enemy. The fears were all the greater because of the seniority of the spies, who worked for the Soviet Union in the 1940s; Kim Philby was the liaison officer between MI6 and the CIA, Donald Maclean ran the American Department of the Foreign Office, Anthony Blunt was Keeper of the Queens' pictures and Klaus Fuchs worked in the Manhattan project to produce nuclear weapons, the most secret of all the Second World War programmes. Collectively, they were the most dangerous spies working for an enemy of the British state for 400 years. The government responded by tightening security procedures for entrants to official employment and the threat declined in parallel with the Soviet Union's attraction to disaffected Western intellectuals but it never disappeared until the Soviet Union itself collapsed.

The communist spies were, however, an aberration. Governments have become more confident in the 20th century about the nation's cohesiveness in wartime even though sensitivities over casualties and costs have increased as people have become more aware of them. Indeed the real problem is that debate is stifled to such a large extent in great wars that it becomes impossible to have a public discussion about the options.[55] In November 1916 the former Viceroy of India and Foreign Secretary Lord Lansdowne circulated a memorandum to the cabinet on Britain's prospects which, after examining Britain's resources and the losses so far, concluded:

> It is...our duty to consider, after a careful review of the facts, what our plight and the plight of the civilised world will be after another year, or, as we are sometimes told, two or three more years of a struggle as exhausting as that in which we are engaged.... Our own casualties already amount to over 1,100,000....We are slowly but surely killing all the best of the male populations of these islands.... Generations will have to come and go before this country recovers from the loss which it has sustained in human beings, and from the financial ruin and the destruction of the means of production which are taking place.[56]

The cabinet then tried to balance the losses against the objectives but, when Lansdowne broke his public silence by writing a letter to the *Daily Telegraph* in 1917 calling for a compromise peace, he was bitterly attacked on the grounds that he had improved enemy morale by giving the impression that Britain was on the verge of defeat.

In peacetime, by contrast, the national debate on warfare has become livelier, as more institutions and individuals have become involved, and the public has had a greater say, but, because of opinion polling, governments expect the public to become less excited than they did in the first half of the 20th century. A well-informed German observer commented on the British political scene in the 1930s, 'once the British get warmed up politically, they take a long time to cool down. All who know this, from the Prime Minister downwards, tread warily when the political temper of the people is roused.'[57] As we shall see in Chapter 9, subsequent opinion polling showed that the public as a whole were more phlegmatic than such comments suggested. It is to the individuals and institutions, which have both reflected and tried to change public attitudes that we turn in the next chapters.

2
The Anglican Church and War

After Britain and the United States invaded Iraq in March 2003, Tony Blair invited George W. Bush to Britain. The organisers did their best to avoid demonstrations against the war. President Bush only gave one speech and that was not announced beforehand. This meant that potential demonstrators had no opportunity to gather in London. Subsequently, Blair took Bush to his Sedgefield constituency in the north of England. There people had advance warning and the Anglican vicar led his flock in a peaceful demonstration against the war outside the inn where Bush and Blair were lunching. The demonstration was reported but commentators did not remark the change which it represented in the behaviour of the established Church. In the 19th century, the bishops never intervened in debates on warfare and leading a hostile demonstration against the prime minister would never have occurred to Anglican clergy. But it was in those years that the forces were taking shape which would overturn the modus vivendi between Church and state, based on the distinction between civil and foreign wars, that had lasted since the 16th century and which had left the government to decide when the country should intervene overseas. In 2003, the vicar of Sedgefield had the sympathy and support of the Archbishop of Canterbury Rowan Williams. The Churches had now become only the most cautious and conditional supporters of intervention abroad.

It was in the First World War that the Anglican hierarchy under Randall Davidson began for the first time to participate in the three crucial political debates about any conflict, the justification for intervening in the first place, the methods used in the fighting and the subsequent peace terms.[1] It was only when the Second World War broke out that an archbishop of Canterbury spoke on behalf of the Christian community in the House of Lords and that some clergy, led by Bishop George Bell of Chichester, began openly to criticise the strategies being employed to defeat the enemy on the grounds that they were immoral, caused unnecessary suffering to civilians and would lead to permanent bitterness between the belligerents.[2] It was only after the Second World War that the Church of England began again to use the traditional doctrine of the Just War to analyse the doctrine of deterrence and the conflicts in which governments chose to involve the country.

Western societies in general and British society in particular have become steadily more secular.[3] Fifty-seven per cent of British people told pollsters in 1993 that they lacked confidence in the Church against only 23 per cent who lacked confidence in the police.[4] Out of a population of 58 million in 1992 the Anglican Church had 1.81 million members and the total membership of Trinitarian Christian Churches was about 6.7 million.[5] But in Britain and the United States, we expect clergymen to agonise over political and social issues, to support humanitarian causes, to deplore violence in general and war in particular. We expect them to emphasise the contrast between the sometimes ruthless or, at best, insensitive behaviour of national leaders with the teachings of the Christian Gospels and to focus public attention both on the ends for which governments use force and the means they propose to employ. Many people assume that the clergy have always voiced concerns over international wars. But history was more complex.

As we have seen in the previous chapter, British society was shaped by its religion and its religion, in turn, reflected its culture. During the Reformation in the 16th century, England broke from the Roman Catholic hierarchy and established a national Church. Over the centuries there were dissenters, Quakers, Roman Catholics and others, but the Anglican Church was the major formative influence in England until the 18th century when Nonconformists grew in numbers.[6] It cooperated with Henry V111 and his successors to prevent the sort of ravages inflicted by the Wars of the Roses in the 15th century. The Church's attitude towards warfare was of vital importance to the country's military strategy and foreign policy because, as we have seen in the previous chapter, in the pulpit the Church had the most effective, indeed virtually the only, means of communicating regularly with the illiterate majority.

The new Church published a set of *Homilies* in 1547 which were supposed to be read every Sunday particularly by clergy who 'had not the gift of preaching'. The political message propagated by the *Homilies* was of the vital importance of order and obedience.[7] The authors argued that the people should not rebel even against a bad government since rebels would be tempted into 'envy, wrath, murder and desire of blood'[8] and civil war would devastate the countryside. The rebels would gather together and bring famine and plague.[9] The authors spoke from experience, sickness usually caused far more casualties than the fighting itself and armies spread pestilence and famine as they moved through the countryside seizing the food on which the peasants depended for survival.[10] The problem for the authors was that their warnings against the results of rebellion and civil war could be applied as easily to foreign conflicts. The Church emphasised the fallibility of human nature, all warfare exposed men to temptation. However, Tudor monarchs could not afford to damn international wars since they had to defend their country from external attack and to preserve the European balance of power. Thus the *Homilies* went on to distinguish the two types of struggle: those who fought in foreign wars 'die in good conscience for serving God, their Prince, and their country, and be children of eternal salvation', while rebels 'be rewarded with shameful deaths, their hands and carcasses set upon poles, and hanged in chains, eaten with kites and crows, judged unworthy the honour of burial'.[11]

The authors may be criticised for their complicity with the state, and yet it would have been unrealistic for them to believe that they could transform the nature of international relations. Dean Colet, the founder of St Paul's School, could preach before Henry V111 and denounce war as unchristian; Erasmus, the theologian and Biblical translator, could write to him praising his attempts to secure peace and complain to his other correspondents that 'the justest war can hardly approve itself to any reasonable person', but Henry went to war from time to time nonetheless, because of his ambitions, typical of a King of the period, and because he thought that it was necessary to secure his country's interests.[12] In England, where they had influence, the Anglican hierarchy did their best to warn of war's dangers and the distress which conflicts would bring. Their simple rural audiences undoubtedly missed the learned, classical allusions in the *Homilies* but they could hardly have misunderstood the drift of the political advice. Church and state were united in condemning rebellion, those who ignored such warnings would suffer appallingly in this world and be damned in the next. The mural above the chancel arch showing the Last Judgement when the good would be sent to paradise and the bad prodded by smiling devils into the boiling inferno of hell rammed the point home.

Of course, however often the *Homilies* were read in churches throughout the land, they could not prevent rebellion, particularly if the Church itself appeared to be under threat. The distinguished lawyer Francis Bacon listed 'innovation in religion' as the first of his ten causes and motives of sedition in the collection of his essays published in 1625. And so it was under Charles 1 and James 11 when the English Reformation seemed to be menaced by monarchs determined to restore Roman Catholicism. The clergy of all persuasions excited their followers to participate, provoking a contemporary historian of the rebellion, to complain that 'no good Christian can without horror think of those Ministers of the church who, by their function being messengers of peace, are the only trumpets of war and incendiaries of rebellion'.[13] The clergy were again stirred into action to support the 'Glorious Revolution' against James 11 in 1688 and at the end of the 18th century when they came to regard the French Revolution as a threat to all religion. Parsons referred to the revolutionaries as the 'Apocalyptic Beast' and Napoleon as the 'Anti-Christ', although there was also a widespread view that Providence was punishing France for its sins. Of course, by no means all were in favour of British participation in the war against France, pointing out the damage which wars would cause and the need for forgiving enemies. But the majority stoutly supported the government in what they clearly believed was a righteous conflict against the forces of evil.[14]

When the 19th century opened the Anglican Church had, thus, provided the country's official ideology for 250 years and maintained a symbiotic relationship with the state. Yet the tide of change was already beginning to flow, the diary of a Somerset clergyman like William Holland, shows that he was already being affected by the competition from the new Methodist Church and influenced by the newspapers he received. As the Century wore on, the Anglicans were challenged intellectually by Darwinism, by the growth of industrial cities and by the education of the mass of people. A more egalitarian, open and pluralistic society was developing, though it remained suffused with Christian values. In regard to warfare, for a time, the old cooperation between Church and state survived, but its days were numbered.

The surviving diaries and sermons written by 19th-century clergy show a spectrum from muscular, belligerent Christianity to support for pacifism as an ideal to be realised as society progressed.[15] J. B. Mozley, the Regius Professor of Divinity at Oxford, admitted that it was, at first sight, shocking that Christian nations should fight each other using weapons which they had taken years to perfect.[16] Mozley condemned the sins which led to war and the excesses of some of those involved, but he did not find these sins worse than the sins committed in everyday life; 'who can say that more sin is not committed every day in every capital of Europe than on the largest field of battle?'[17] It was only later, when, thanks largely to the media and the proximity of the battlefields,

British people were able to imagine the struggles in the trenches of the Somme, in a way that they had not visualised the losses in San Domingo and Spain during the French Wars, that such comparisons between the sins of peace and the excesses of war would come to strike clergy and laity alike as unfeeling and even bizarre.

Political leaders had established the convention, which continues to the present, of appealing to morality rather than interest, when they defended their decision to go to war. Although there were hard-headed strategic reasons for preserving the balance of power and, thus, going to war in 1793, 1854, 1914 and 1939, politicians chose to put less stress on these, when they justified their decisions, than on the defensive nature of the war or the infamy of their enemies.[18] This reflected the absorption of Christianity in the national culture and was more likely to inspire military and civilian commitment than cold-blooded and apparently abstract strategic or economic interests. In any case, politicians did not distinguish between a policy from which their country would benefit and one which they thought was for the general good. In 1793 the Prime Minister William Pitt argued that the government was not responsible for the French declaration of war and that the revolutionaries had already been waging 'at our very doors a war which aimed at an object no less destructive than the total ruin of the freedom and independence of this country'.[19] On 31 March 1854 the Foreign Secretary, the Earl of Clarendon defended the 'generous and high-minded people of this country, who detest aggression, whatever form it may assume, and who are always ready to protect the weak against the strong ... it was [out of] a sense of national honour, a sense of duty' that people and government had determined to stand up for Turkey against Russian aggression.[20] The Foreign Secretary Edward Grey told the House of Commons on 3 August 1914, 'we have consistently worked with a single mind and with all the earnestness in our power to preserve peace'.[21] The government's papers would make it clear when published, 'how strenuous and genuine and whole-hearted our efforts for peace were'.

Following these political reassurances, the 19th-century bishops made little or no contribution to debates on war in the House of Lords. The Archbishop's only input during the Crimean War was to support the proposal to set aside a day for 'humiliation and prayer'.[22] The Church of England apparently accepted the justice of the intervention. Nor had the situation apparently much changed during the Boer War. It was left to 5000 Nonconformist ministers to sign a petition against Britain's methods of dealing with the Boer guerrillas which involved burning their farms and 'concentrating' their families in unhealthy camps.[23] The silence or the support of the bishops over Britain's wartime policies was in marked contrast to the vociferous objections to successive wars from some of the political parties.[24] The Church leaders were very close to the country's political elite and either trusted that elite to make correct moral and political judgements on international affairs or regarded it as inappropriate to intervene in mundane matters.

But the situation was changing radically. The introduction of free and universal education meant that the mass of people, including the clergy, could now derive their political ideas from their teachers and from newspapers. The central position of the Church in society was thus threatened; the influence, stipends and status of the Anglican clergy declined, while the importance and income of the teachers grew.[25] The Darwinian revolution undermined traditional Christian teaching about the age of the Earth and man's relationship with the natural world.[26] In its Social Darwinist form it also suggested that war was in itself a good because it winnowed out the weak, the very opposite of the principles enunciated in the *New Testament*. Charles Darwin himself was humane; he loathed slavery and deplored the impact of European peoples on the inhabitants of Argentina, New Zealand and Australia. But his descriptions of this impact gave credence to the notion that there was an inevitable struggle for survival amongst human tribes just as much as there was between animal species.[27]

The Church hierarchy was now squeezed between the Social Darwinists who deplored Christian pacifism and the liberal critics of war who despised the Church for not denouncing all violent conflicts. The radical economist J. A. Hobson typified the second tendency. During the Boer War he demanded:

> When has a Christian nation ever entered on a war which has not been regarded by the official priesthood as a sacred war? In England the State Church has never permitted the spirit of the Prince of Peace to interfere when statesmen and soldiers appealed to the passions of race-lust, conquest and revenge. Wars, the most insane in origin, the most barbarous in execution, the most fruitless in results, have never failed to get the sanction of the Christian Churches.[28]

The Church's silence on warfare thus shocked an increasing number of its own members who pressed it to drop its neutrality. Just before and during the First World War this change became visible.[29] While it was confronted with a multitude of smaller issues, there were three basic problems in August 1914 and during the war years; first, whether to support the national cause, then, as the scale of the conflict became apparent and the mass of ordinary people began to look at war afresh, the theological problem of explaining God's willingness to allow such suffering, and, finally, how far to interfere in strategic decisions? Given that the hierarchy had accepted intervention in previous wars, its support in this conflict might be taken for granted. But this was not so, Percival, the bishop of Hereford, was, for example, discussing on 2 August 1914 whether the clergy should not encourage parishioners to lobby the government in favour of maintaining Britain's neutrality. He had already protested against the 'jingo' press and encouraged the clergy to pray for peace. But for him and many others the German invasion of Belgium in violation of the treaties laying down its neutrality and despite Belgium's total irrelevance to the argument between the Central Powers and the Entente transformed the situation. Ten days later Percival's letter appeared in *The Times* supporting the government's decision to go to war in the face of Germany's 'shameful, cynical and flagrant disregard of all moral considerations'.[30] The position taken by Randall Davidson, the archbishop of Canterbury, was crucial.[31] He was in close touch with the Prime Minister Herbert Asquith and was persuaded by Asquith on 31 July 1914 that protests by the Church, of the type that Percival was then meditating, would only give the impression that Britain was determined on neutrality and remove the incentives for the Central Powers to moderate their behaviour. Davidson was subsequently convinced that the government's decision to declare war was justified.

Belgium was the third small country that the Central Powers appeared to be menacing; Austria–Hungary had made humiliating demands on Serbia after the assassination of the Archduke Franz Ferdinand in Sarajevo by a nationalist fanatic and had subsequently rejected Serbia's grovelling reply; Luxemburg was to be overrun by Germany, despite the international guarantee of its neutral status and now Belgium was threatened. The point of the balance of power was not just to preserve peace but the independence of small states, Berlin appeared to be bent on proving the need to uphold it. Furthermore, the Low Countries had always been a special case because of their pivotal strategic position to Britain, France and other powers. In the 18th century they had been protected under international agreement by a series of fortifications and, after the French wars, the barrier against French expansion was strengthened using the indemnity imposed on France.[32] In 1830 Belgium asserted its independence from the Netherlands, and in November 1831 and April 1839 Belgium's status as a perpetually neutral state was guaranteed by the Great Powers. This status was reinforced during the Franco-Prussian War when Britain signed separate treaties with France and Prussia guaranteeing to come into the conflict, but only to protect Belgium, if its neutrality was threatened by either of the belligerents.[33] It was hard to conceive of a firmer guarantee and, if it were set aside, then the whole of international law could be dismissed to suit strategic convenience. It was no wonder that the British government ignored Germany's offer to withdraw its army and restore Belgium's neutrality after the war.[34] In later years the reasons for Britain's declaration of war in 1914 have often been forgotten and there are some who characterise its abandonment of Czechoslovakia to the Nazis at the Munich conference in 1938 as a national disgrace, while dismissing the reasons for attempting to protect a country in 1914 whose neutrality had been repeatedly guaranteed by the major belligerents.

If Davidson and most of the Church accepted this view in 1914, the Archbishop subsequently separated Church from state in a way that none of his predecessors had done. He was particularly exercised about the conditions of prisoners of war and of the foreign civilians who had been interned. While he supported the visits by representatives of the International Red Cross to POW camps in Britain, he worried about the condition of British prisoners in German camps, an anxiety shared by US diplomats in Germany.[35] He pressed the government to come to an agreement with the Germans so that interned civilians could be returned to their homeland. He publicised the Turkish massacres of the Armenians and urged the government to protest more vigorously.[36] The Archbishop asserted the right of the Primate to interfere privately in the conduct of war by opposing the use of poisonous gas in retaliation for the initiation of chemical warfare by the German army. He wrote first to the King's secretary, Lord Stamfordham, in May 1915 when he heard that retaliation was impending. When Stamfordham told him that the soldiers were becoming angry that they could not respond to German chemical attacks, he wrote to Asquith, 'if anyone had suggested a few months ago that the British Army would use poisonous gases for creating fatal disease among its enemies, the notion would have been scouted as preposterous'.[37] He went on to argue that international agreements would be dishonoured by retaliation and that Britain would subsequently be ashamed of its actions. The use of shells containing poisonous chemicals had been prohibited by the Hague Peace Conference in 1899, though the Germans could claim that they released such chemicals from cylinders rather than shells, thus not breaching the letter of the agreement. What Davidson did not try to do was to discuss the issue in military terms, indeed he expressly disclaimed military expertise. He needed to press Asquith on whether retaliation was really vital and whether it outweighed the damage to international law and to Britain's reputation if it resorted to 'German' methods. He might, otherwise, in theory, have been asking Britain to eschew a decisive weapon and to lose the war. Unfortunately, Bishop Bell, Davidson's biographer, did not analyse the issue in any detail though he faced the same dilemma in relation to strategic bombing in the Second World War. How great a sacrifice, if any, should a country make in its strategic policy in the middle of a total war, or rather should it ask its servicemen to make, in order to uphold Christian principles and both the letter and spirit of international law?

The autopsy on the First World War held by the Church in the 1920s showed that the national culture was now deeply fractured on interventionism and that the Anglican Church's traditional position as the unquestioning supporter of the state's foreign policy had been swept away. Davidson tried to heal the breaches in the Church by his passionate support for the League of Nations. 'Its key-note', he said in a highly emotional and deeply felt sermon in Geneva in September 1922, 'vibrates in harmony with the key-note of the Christian Faith itself, and the Christian Faith lies at the core of the progressive history of mankind'.[38] The Archbishop then broke with his predecessors' views and launched attacks on 'the awful, the horrible, the devil-devised barrier of war'. 'You and I', he told the congregation, 'have lived through the greatest war-cataclysm that the world has ever known'.[39] Davidson admitted the long-standing British tendency to romanticise warfare; 'we have long known something of what war meant, but our knowledge has been blurred and diverted by a sort of haze or glamour which has surrounded warfare when viewed from a distance, and by the memories of the heroism and the magnificent devotion to which it has given occasion.'[40]

The dilemmas increased in the 1930s as the hopes in the League of Nations collapsed following the Japanese expansion into Manchuria, its withdrawal from the League of Nations and the Nazi occupation of the Rhineland and Austria. The British policy of appeasing the aggressors was gradually revealed as unrealistic, yet it was one the Church had largely supported. In 1939 Sir Alfred Zimmern, the Montague Burton Professor of International Relations at Oxford, published a devastating critique of the Church's naivety based on a series of lectures he had given earlier in the year. He began by noting the Church's increasing involvement in political affairs and, after examining its activities, concluded:

[International relations] is a sphere where ignorance and inexperience are particularly dangerous and where amateurs, even gifted amateurs, can do untold harm. I am putting it mildly when I say that it is open to doubt whether the direct influence of the Churches on British foreign policy has done more good than harm.[41]

Zimmern recalled that a diplomat, who was working on the British draft of the League of Nations Covenant in 1918, warned Archbishop Davidson against putting too much faith in the organisation, a warning which, as we have seen, he ignored in the years immediately after the war. The core of Zimmern's message was that 'there is a technique of politics. Caesar has a business of his own, which requires knowledge, training, skill, a special quality of judgement. Politics – and more especially international politics – require more than goodwill and fine aspirations.'[42]

Despite such criticism, the Church did not abandon its new political activism and it would have been regarded by many of its members as failing in its duty if it had done so. Davidson's successor Archbishop Cosmo Lang and other bishops were determined to intervene in the national debates to a far greater extent than earlier bishops had done. In the epochal debate on 30 March 1933 begun by Lord Cecil on the persecution of the Jews in Germany, the Archbishop had made a brief but warm contribution associating the Christian community in Britain with the protests against German policy and encouraging the government to do everything possible to help the Jews. Because of his support for this campaign, the Archbishop became the subject of venomous attacks in the Nazi press.[43] In March 1939 Lang advised the government to build up its forces against the Nazi menace, to the horror of outright pacifists such as Lord Ponsonby, the former leader of the Labour party. When war broke out after Hitler's invasion of Poland in September 1939, Lang spoke in the Lords of the sympathy he felt for the Prime Minister Neville Chamberlain and the Foreign Secretary Lord Halifax for the failure of all their efforts to make peace, but no nation, he believed, could be allowed to trample on others: 'the primacy of this moral issue must be made plain, for it will enable us to enter upon that struggle with a good conscience'.[44] In saying so, of course, the Archbishop once again equated national interest in preserving the balance of power and the freedom of small states with moral rectitude.

The argument was now between those who believed that Britain should limit the methods it used in the conflict against the Axis and those who insisted that, once having taken the plunge to go to war, the priority was making sure of victory. The issue came to a head over bombing. For years airmen had argued that aircraft could be used most effectively in attacks on enemy cities and were inherently unsuited for defence since bombers could evade the fighters sent to intercept them.[45] However, when war broke out, both Germany and Britain had hesitated to attack each other's cities for fear of retaliation. It was only during the Battle of Britain in 1940 that mutual deterrence collapsed with British attacks on Berlin and the German blitz on London and Coventry. Now that the British army had been expelled ignominiously from Europe, the British had no way of bringing their power to bear on the Nazis except through naval blockade and air attack, and such attacks were too inaccurate in 1941 to target anything smaller than a city. Thus began the main British bomber offensive which was to turn German cities into smouldering ruins, to kill thousands and to 'unhouse' many more.[46]

If we believe the crude opinion polls available, opinion was initially evenly divided over the issue, but rallied to the government when Britain turned to strategic bombing. In November 1940, 46 per cent of those who responded to Gallup were in favour of a policy of indiscriminate retaliation against German cities following the start of the blitz on London, and 46 per cent against.[47] Those in favour argued that the offensive was the only way of restoring morale after successive defeats and of hitting a hated and feared enemy. George Bell voiced the opposition to this view. Throughout the 1930s the Bishop had struggled to find ways for the Church to encourage the democracies to resist the Axis while avoiding the blanket hatred of 'the enemy', which was so much a part of the total warfare of the 20th century, yet he insisted on facing ethical and political dilemmas squarely. He had a better sense of the horrors that Nazism portended than most in Britain. He had met Ribbentrop and other leading Nazis in the course of his abortive efforts to help German churchmen and to give them some modicum of independence.[48]

Bell's opposition to bombing German cities flowed from the distinction he made between government and the governed and his condemnation of the Darwinian idea that each nation was involved in an untrammelled struggle for survival with its neighbours. In November 1939, when the fighting had hardly begun, he told the readers of the *Fortnightly Review*:

> The Church must guard and maintain those moral principles in the war itself. It must not hesitate, if occasion arises, to condemn the infliction of reprisals, or the bombing of civilian populations, by

the military forces of its own nation. It should set itself against the propaganda of lies and hatred.[49]

In May 1941 he added:

One of the most barbarous features in the whole war is the night bombing of non-combatants. This is not only an added torment to the huge volume of suffering, but a degradation of the spirit for all who take part in it.[50]

We now know from the *US Strategic Bombing Survey* of German public opinion that Bell was partly right and that the night attacks were, indeed, as they were intended to be, one of the most demoralising features of the war for German civilians.[51] Whether they were a degradation of the spirit of the airmen is more questionable. The aircrews went about their highly dangerous tasks in a professional fashion with any doubts quietened by the code of discipline and by the general anger against Nazi Germany. Doubts, if any, only came later.

Bell continued his campaign despite the increasing hostility with which he had to contend. As pointed out earlier, debates are muted in warfare because each nation unites against the enemy and those who voice dissent can expect to be ostracised.[52] Nevertheless, Bell tried to involve Lang's successor, William Temple in July 1943, though the Archbishop refused to commit himself.[53] Temple's biographer F. A. Iremonger describes the 'kid glove' school of warfare as the 'most tiresome' of the Archbishop's correspondents and quotes from a letter Temple wrote on 24 May 1943 that once the decision to resist the Nazis had been taken, the allies must do,

what is required in order to defeat the enemy other than the infliction of useless suffering. I think there is no doubt that the bombing of the Ruhr dams was a perfectly legitimate act of war. There is a great deal to be said for refusing to fight, though I think myself that in this case it would be the shirking of duty. There is still more I think to be said for fighting in support of freedom and justice, but there is nothing whatever to be said for fighting ineffectively.[54]

Subtle as Temple's theological views may have been, this over simplified the moral and practical issue. In this case, and particularly as the war progressed, there were other ways of using airpower than attacking enemy cities. The RAF might, or might not, have been less effective, but it would not have been ineffective if it had used all its power in support of the army and Royal Navy, and interdicting enemy supplies. Bell was brave to raise the issue and to remind the government that intervention only had such widespread support if it continued to achieve a synthesis between morality and interest.

The views on international affairs expressed during the two World Wars by Davidson, Lang, Bell and others may have been right or wrong, naïve or wise, prescient or short-sighted but collectively their willingness to voice their opinions represented a major change. The Church now believed that it had a duty to comment on political issues and particularly on war. While it was more influential than the other religions, it was no longer so close to the government and aristocracy that it simply mimicked their views. While Britain became more secular, the Church was liberated to judge political actions by Christian standards. The problem was to bring these to bear on the exigencies of political life. Never was this truer than in the Cold War which froze East–West relations for 45 years. Lurking behind the tensions was the nuclear threat which the 1948 Lambeth conference saw:

> Lifts [war] into a new dimension, multiplying its destructive power a thousand fold and making civilians its chief victims... We are faced with a choice between the avoidance of war and race suicide. The issue before us is a matter of sheer survival. Peace is no longer merely desirable; it is an absolute necessity.[55]

The dilemma was increased by Western reliance on nuclear weapons to deter Soviet expansion and to balance the perceived Soviet superiority in conventional forces. The British government claimed in 1953 that the Soviets had some 4.6 million men under arms and over a million men in its allies' armies.[56] Accordingly, most of the Anglican hierarchy accepted that deterrence was, for the moment, the least bad alternative though, not surprisingly, some priests took the view that the threat to use nuclear weapons was so abhorrent that no Christian could support it.[57] No doubt, disillusionment with the failure of the League in the 1930s, fear of communism and suspicion of Soviet intentions played the major roles in encouraging Churchmen to remain quiescent.[58]

Because of the moral ambiguities of the Cold War and the prevalent guilt about past colonialism, religious idealism came to be channeled more and more into support for Oxfam and other humanitarian organizations. Indeed, if the Anglican Church was once described ironically as 'the Tory party at prayer', it now became 'Oxfam at prayer'. Churches were festooned with photographs of the Third World poverty and suffering. Embarrassment with the contrast between increasing Western prosperity and conditions elsewhere grew because of the feeling that one was the cause of the other. Private and official donations flourished and so, for a time after the end of the Cold War, did peacekeeping forces to try to abate the civil wars which plagued Africa. The number of troops from various nations involved in UN peacekeeping expanded from some 10,000 in the 1980s to 75,000 by 1994 and the annual cost grew to three billion dollars.[59] Again these were usually popular commitments inside the Churches and amongst the British public in general. Western countries had an interest in stability in the Third World since instability and violence led to tides of desperate refugees trying to enter Europe, to drug running and to disease, but, once more, it was moral passion rather than self-interest which was the prime motivator.

The Church of England had rediscovered the just war criteria for judging the rights and wrongs of a particular conflict during the Cold War. After the collapse of the Soviet Union, the West had, for a time, overwhelming conventional power against any combination of other countries, they provided standards by which the use of that power could be judged. The *jus ad bellum* criteria lay down that a war has to be authorised by the legitimate authority, the cause must be just, peaceful means of resolving the dispute must have been exhausted, there must be a reasonable expectation that more good than evil will come out of the war and there must be a probability of victory. Of course the re-emphasis on these principles has not necessarily brought greater agreement; whether a war is a last resort and whether it will bring more good than evil will always be questions of military and political judgement.[60] Does the last resort mean, for example, that all other ways of settling the dispute have been tried or that, if war is not made now, the opportunity of fighting with most chance of success will have been lost? The point is not theoretical; Britain and France had the best chance of defeating the Nazis in a limited war in March 1936 when Hitler's army re-occupied the Rhineland in breach of the Locarno Treaty which an earlier German government had negotiated. Waiting another three years in the hope that Hitler could be appeased meant that France was defeated in 1940 and Britain only escaped the same fate because Germany was unable to dominate the Channel.

Despite such difficulties, just war criteria do provide some of the best standards we have by which interventions can be judged and Catholics and Anglicans now employ the same terminology on these issues. In February 1991, for example, the Pope condemned the US-led war to liberate Kuwait, even though he had previously denounced the Iraqi invasion of the small Gulf state. He was concerned that more evil than good might come out of the war, stressing both the suffering involved and the dangers of it spreading to the rest of the Middle East. The Catholic Primate of All-Ireland, Dr Cahal Daly said that the power of modern weapons made it impossible to describe the Gulf War as 'just' and, like the Anglican Bishop of Manchester, he argued for the continuation of economic sanctions against Iraq as a lesser evil. Rowan Williams, who was to become archbishop of Canterbury in 2003, also argued that the war was unjust because the allies were only concerned about their own interests. He accused the United States and Britain of double standards for reacting with force in this case while failing to deal with the Turkish invasion of Cyprus, the Chinese invasion of Tibet and Israel's occupation of the West Bank.

Robert Runcie, the archbishop of Canterbury, and Richard Harries, the bishop of Oxford, who was the Church's leading expert on the ethics of warfare, rejected these criticisms. Harries denied that self-interested motives undermined the just cause or that the allies' failure to free Tibet or Palestine falsified the case for liberating Kuwait, not least, no doubt, because 'freeing' Tibet would have caused a world war, producing vastly more evil than good. Archbishop Runcie defended the allies' right to use force to expel Iraqi troops from Kuwait once other means were exhausted and denied that this would mean they had initiated the conflict, it was the Iraqis who had done this by seizing the small Gulf state. His general position was firmer than the one taken by his designated successor George Carey, who argued that the war might be justified while trying to avoid labeling it as just under the traditional criteria.[61] In the controversy over the Anglo-American attack on Iraq in 2003, Harries and Williams were in agreement this time that the war did not fulfil the just war criteria. To Harries it seemed likely that this war would unleash more evil than good. Williams, now archbishop of Canterbury, argued that it lacked 'right authority' because no government should simply decide on its own whether a war was justified and that the British and American governments had paid insufficient attention to the UN or to international law.[62]

Such arguments were useful because they integrated moral and political considerations. As pointed out before, British leaders tended to justify foreign intervention in moral terms even before the Churches participated in the debate because this fitted with British culture and was more likely to appeal to the population. Now priests, rabbis and mullahs operate as part of the conscience of the nation, reminding statesmen that they have to articulate their ends and to defend the violent means they choose to achieve them. During the First World War Asquith, Lloyd George and their colleagues wrestled with the terrible dilemmas presented by the military stalemate on the Western front; Randall Davidson forced them to defend the case in private for retaliating against German use of chemical weapons. Winston Churchill expressed Britain's objectives during the Second World War with a fervour and idealism to which people responded, Bishop Bell agreed with the objectives but made the elite aware of the moral dilemmas raised by Bomber Command's obliteration of German towns. The Archbishop of Canterbury and the Cardinal Archbishop of Westminster made common cause in 2003 in their protests against the government's decision to attack Iraq.[63] They forced the government to defend its belief that the Iraqis had chemical and biological weapons in breach of international agreements and that this justified their decisions.

The danger is always that religious arguments can be dismissed as unrealistic or irrelevant, but none of those quoted above could be simply rejected in this way. The Churches had widened the debate and performed a useful social role. Their arguments are appealing because Western society is suffused with Christian values. The Churches had also played a major part in the growth of the pressure groups which are the subject of the next chapter because they have had a major impact on debates about warfare.

3
Civil Society

Britain has been the starting place and home of many of the largest and most active humanitarian pressure groups and international Non-Governmental Organisations (NGOs). From the campaign against slavery in the 18th century, through the Anti-Corn Law League and the efforts to revive the Olympic Games in the 19th century[1] to the Peace Pledge Union in the 1930s, Oxford Committee for Famine Relief (Oxfam) in the Second World War, Amnesty International and dozens of other organisations subsequently, British culture spawns NGOs. Today, Oxfam and its kind offer aid to countries suffering from famine or civil war and try to encourage economic development, others try to prevent mistreatment of political prisoners, female circumcision, torture, damage to the environment and cruelty to animals. Benevolent as their intentions are intended to be, they involve interference in other cultures; Japanese resent being encouraged not to kill sharks and whales, Koreans not to eat dogs, Chinese not to use ivory as an aphrodisiac, Islamic states, such as Saudi Arabia, Iran and Pakistan, dislike being criticised for mutilating thieves and for their treatment of women, dictatorial governments everywhere object to being pressed to treat their citizens with more consideration. Very often the targets of such campaigns suspect ulterior motives and point to the deficiencies in the British or Western record. When at the start of the 21st century Western media were filled with stories about atrocities committed in the Darfur region of Sudan by militia supported by the government, the Islamic media and officials derided such reports as variously designed to damage the Islamic world, to enable the United States to gain control of Sudan's oil or to divert attention from Israeli mistreatment of the Palestinians and from US disasters in Iraq.[2]

NGO pressure is often motivated by some of the feelings which encouraged, or justified, imperialism and particularly the desire to 'improve' the behaviour of other nations. The sort of adventurous, idealistic young people who went out to govern parts of the Empire in the 19th century now join UN development agencies or NGOs working in the Third World. As communities in the West become more aware of what is happening in other continents, so the culturist urge to interfere becomes greater. Moreover this interference is often with age-old behaviour. As the philosopher T. E. Hulme once put it:

> There are certain doctrines which for a particular period seem not doctrines, but inevitable categories of the human mind. Men do not look on them merely as correct opinions, for they have become so much a part of the mind, and lie so far back, that they are not really conscious of them at all.[3]

The problem in a globalised world is that what seems self-evident in one country can be very different from what seems irrefutable somewhere else. In one part of the world many believe insults to the Prophet Mohammed should be punished by death, in another part many insist free speech means the right to criticise or satirise any doctrine or belief.[4] The Western NGOs believe that their views on freedom, torture, corruption, standards of imprisonment, women's rights, treatments of animals and the environment reflect absolute standards. But they are far from universal and they inevitably lead to friction.[5]

Thus, some humanitarian pressure groups have played a major part in sustaining the interventionist ethic over the last 200 years, while others have been the voice of those most opposed to war and to the exploitation of power by the Anglo-Saxon nations. The dilemma over the use of force is inescapable; oppose the use of force, as the free-trade movement did in the mid-19th century, and you ignore the slave trade; oppose the use of force in the 1930s and you close your eyes to the creeping spread of right-wing totalitarianism across Europe, North Africa and East Asia; oppose Britain's membership of NATO and you leave the world wide-open to the expansion of communism; oppose peacekeeping missions and you allow massacres in Rwanda or expose the Bosnians and Kosovans to ethnic cleansing by the Serbs. On the other hand, Western governments and peoples only have limited knowledge of areas outside Europe and their interventions are often supported by poor intelligence and have unintended consequences; it proved, for example, impossible during the Cold War to distinguish between the Third World nationalists and the anti-Western communists, while the removal of Saddam Hussein from control of Iraq in 2003 unleashed a violent civil war between Shiites and Sunnis. Some argue that the Western desire to encourage Third World states to develop economically leads to constant military intervention to stabilise and culturist efforts to 'improve' weak governments.

From the 1830s onwards wave after wave of anti-war movements broke over British governments in attempts to limit British interventionism in particular and war in general. Consciously, or more often unconsciously, they tried to emulate the success of the movement against slavery which led to the liberation of the slaves in Britain itself in 1772, to the banning of the slave trade in British ships in 1807, to the freeing of slaves in British Trans-Atlantic colonies in 1834 and finally to the ending of the open international trade in slaves. Slavery – the absolute possession of one human by another – was a human institution as old as war. Indeed it was a substitute for massacre after victory and, if it could be ended despite its longevity, it seemed that war could be abolished in the same sort of way. But Britain, as the leading power outside Europe, had used, or threatened to use, force against other states to stop the slave trade; ending war was not within British power and logically dependent on the willing cooperation of other states. Obviously such cooperation would not be given by Social Darwinist states, such as Japan and Germany in the 1930s. Nor would it be given by states or peoples who believe that war is the only way to achieve justice, as the Palestinians do today; nor would it be given by those who fear imminent attack. But, even if all these specific problems were overcome, war would still be the ultimate recourse of the state, just as rebellion or internal war is the ultimate resource of the persecuted subject. The United Nations has tried to make warfare illegal unless authorised by the Security Council or in defence, but there have been countless undeclared wars since 1945, while the United Nations itself had to decide between watching its peacekeepers humiliated, or turning to peace enforcement and the employment of lethal force.[6] In some ways, it must be said, the 'abolition' of slavery has followed the same course, for whilst it appeared to have been abolished more than a century ago, 'people trafficking' has actually increased in Europe since the collapse of communism, and women and children are still treated as virtual slaves in many poor countries.

Mass pressure groups began to emerge in the 18th century as the politically involved community, or civil society, expanded. The expansion was due to industrialisation, the spread of education and improvements in communications.[7] One campaign emulated another, though their methods were gradually refined and extended as experience accumulated. Those who believed passionately in the abolition of the slave trade or the establishment of free trade, and the widening of the franchise, had to mobilise the public if they were to have any impact on Parliament, not least because they were confronted with powerful vested interests. The slave owners and traders, and others who benefited from the prosperity of the East Indies, bitterly resented moves to abolish slavery; the great landowners generally opposed the repeal of the Corn Laws and Tories looked with dread on the widening of the franchise which they believed 'must accomplish the entire overthrow of the existing constitution'.[8] On the other hand, governments were willing, in the end, to cede ground to public opinion, hence the importance for the pressure groups of giving the impression that they were representative of a substantial minority; some historians have claimed, for example, that perhaps one in five British males signed anti-slavery petitions, an astonishing proportion given the primitive communications at the time, the predominantly rural population and the illiteracy of the vast majority.[9] Apart from the impact which such campaigns had on elections, governments had a very reasonable fear of civil unrest and their instinct was to compromise with the rising manufacturing interests and the ever-growing mass of urban workers. Home secretaries kept the ultimate resource of the state, the army, in the background as a last resort for maintaining order; they knew that the promiscuous use of force could provoke ever greater fury, an assessment reinforced by experience from the 'Peterloo Massacre' in Manchester in 1819, when several protesters were killed by soldiers.[10]

It has not been easy for historians to explain why the first great mass movement, the campaign against slavery, emerged in Britain at the end of the 18th century rather than in some other country at some other time. Even if it was attributed to the rise of the Evangelical movement and particularly the Clapham Sect and its leaders, this left unanswered the question why the Evangelicals became so involved when their main interest was in the general diffusion of Christianity at home and abroad and in the reform of the Anglican Church. Moreover, there were always commentators who loathed the Evangelical movement for its alleged self-righteousness and hypocrisy, and who disliked attributing any achievements to its actions. Prominent amongst these was the radical commentator William Cobbett, who argued that the Evangelicals ignored the sufferings of the British working class, a criticism also voiced by the slavers' leaders. After the end of the Second World War the Trinidadian Prime Minister and former Oxford student Eric Williams saw the anti-slavery movement as simply a reflection of the interests of the new capitalists. Others argued that African protest and revolt, together with popular opposition to slavery in Britain, did more to abolish the hated institution than the actions of a handful of Evangelicals. The most prominent abolitionist, the MP for Hull and Yorkshire, William Wilberforce was accused of monomania, racism and self-righteousness.[11]

Until the late 18th century most British people were hardly aware of the issue or simply accepted slavery as a fact of life though, ever since Britain began trading in slaves, there had been some educated people who did react with dismay. One such was Granville Sharp, who almost single-handedly forced the Chief Justice Baron Mansfield to reverse his view that slavery was legal in Britain and to announce in 1772 that 'the state of slavery . . . is so odious that nothing can be suffered to support it but positive law'. Sharp had been discouraged by his own legal advisers but had set out to teach himself the relevant laws and to disprove the conventional wisdom about the legality of slavery. As a result of his campaigns, several thousand slaves, who had been brought to Britain by their owners, were suddenly emancipated.

Anti-slavery sentiment was particularly prevalent amongst Methodists and Quakers. But their first instinct was to try to convert the slaves to Christianity; some even argued that the trade was beneficial because it made such conversions possible. Churchmen who attempted to convert slaves were generally better received in the American colonies than in the West Indies where planters tried to shut them out altogether.[12] But, after the American colonies broke from Britain, the British Churches could focus their attention on the remaining colonies. Recent scholarship has therefore stressed the vital importance of the War of Independence for the campaign against slavery.[13]

It was the Reverend James Ramsay's *Essay on the Treatment of African Slaves*, published in 1784, rather than Mansfield's verdict, which first drew the issue to the attention of the wider public. He was encouraged to write by the deeply religious Anglican group centred round the Kent village of Teston, including the authoress Hannah More, Bishop Porteus of Chester and Sir Charles Middleton, the comptroller of the Royal Navy and his wife. What made Ramsay's book so effective was that he could document the conditions which slaves endured because he had lived for many years in the West Indies and had actually owned slaves himself. He forced the slave owners and traders onto the defensive. Many retaliated by attacking Ramsay, others stressed the value of slavery and its importance to Britain.

The Evangelicals took up the subject for a variety of motives; they saw the evil of slavery, they wanted to waken the Anglican Church to its moral mission and to compete with the Nonconformists. They were profoundly culturist, they wanted to convert the slaves but they were stymied by the racism of the planters who did not want the slaves to be treated as men. Thus emancipation was the only hope and they struggled to end the slave trade through the French wars, when anything that could be represented as revolutionary was suspect and when any weakening of Britain's economic or naval power was bitterly resented. Thomas Clarkson, William Wilberforce and their colleagues spread information about slavery by articles in the press, pictures of Africans in chains and songs about the issue. And finally they were successful.[14] In January 1807 British ships were prohibited from carrying slaves and the decree was enforced on British ships by Royal Navy cruisers; in 1811, a further law sentenced any British subjects who broke this law to transportation to Australia and in 1824 slave trading became a capital offence. The abolitionists had been challenged to duels, they had been ridiculed inside and outside Parliament but they had persevered in their determination.[15] In 1834 overt slavery itself was abolished in the British Empire, the plantation owners were given £20 million, equivalent to 1 billion in modern terms, to ease the transition and the ex-slaves were asked to work as part-time 'apprentices' for the plantations for another 12 years.[16]

British anti-slavery patrols to stop foreign slave ships continued, despite intense domestic opposition. Mr Hutt, the MP for Gateshead, complained that by 1848 patrols had cost £21 million and worsened the slaves' conditions:

> In their solicitude for the welfare of the people of Africa, they had sacrificed in untold numbers the lives of their countrymen... [yet] the slave trade was more extensive now than before they undertook to suppress it.... The world never saw such horrors as were being perpetuated in these regions in consequence of their interference.[17]

Hutt claimed that the slaves often starved or were murdered if they became too weak to move because they were kept on the African coast until the British squadron departed and the slavers could make the Atlantic crossing. The French were unwilling to cooperate, while the Spanish and Portuguese authorities were deeply implicated in the trade, which was so lucrative that it turned paupers into grandees in a matter of months. MPs warned of the dangers that British merchant vessels would be accused by foreign officers of preparing to take slaves on board.

One such ship had been condemned by the Portuguese simply because it had more water on board than seemed justified by the size of the crew. In the later years the struggle against the slave trade was maintained by the bombastic Lord Palmerston, both as foreign minister and as prime minister, who insisted on keeping British cruisers off the African coast to catch British and foreign slave ships. Alongside those with an interest in the trade, the free traders and Quakers also opposed him because they objected to the use of force. It was indeed a perfect example of the perennial dilemma; do nothing and you may allow mass infringements of human rights and even murder; use force and you may initiate a prolonged war. In the February 1848 debate Palmerston disputed Hutt's claim that the conditions in the slaving ships were worse than they had been before the British began their efforts to interdict the trade and he denied that anti-slavery patrols were ineffective by pointing to the high cost of slaves in Brazil and the United States. If the cruisers were withdrawn, 'we should have the disgrace of being the authors of the crimes and barbarities which the people of this country would shudder to behold'.[18] Conversely, the leading free traders Richard Cobden and John Bright agreed with those who believed that the costly and 'futile' anti-slave patrols hindered the growth of normal trade, which they believed would lead to the demise of slavery, and threatened to involve Britain in wars. They also knew that the anti-slavery campaigners Thomas Clarkson and Granville Sharp had been behind the founding of the first British colony in Africa, Sierra Leone, where they landed slaves freed in Britain or escaped to Nova Scotia from the United States, and that they hankered after wider British intervention. Such activists believed that colonisation would develop the African continent and hamper the hated trade. In the meantime, the anti-slave patrols antagonised the slave-importing states led by Brazil and could, indeed, have led to war.[19] As one of Palmerston's critics put it:

> [The government] had set at nought justice and law – they had trampled upon the independence of sovereign states – they had endeavoured to fix the name and character of piracy upon acts which the law of nations recognised... They had scorned the warnings of the greatest modern judicial authorities... The consequence had been to disgust the nations with this philanthropic cant...[20]

One looks in vain in the index of John Morley's biography of Richard Cobden for references to slavery or the anti-slavery campaign.[21] The man who has gone down in history as the archetypal realist, Palmerston, took the moral high ground in this case against the liberal free traders.[22]

The free trader's pressure group, the Anti-Corn Law League was founded in 1839. It was dedicated to ending agricultural protection and thereby making food cheaper for the new urban working classes, thus helping industry at the expense of the landed interests. The League's methods owed much to the earlier anti-slavery movement and to the Chartists who campaigned for the widening of the franchise, but it was constantly developing new propaganda techniques or improving on old ones.[23] It sent tens of thousands of leaflets to local organisers who passed them on to potential supporters, it arranged lecture tours by its chosen speakers in all corners of the British Isles, had mugs and other presents made to publicise the League, and its supporters constantly lobbied Parliament to end agricultural protection.

The League's leaders had a semi-pacifist agenda – one reason for their opposition to the Royal Navy's anti-slavery patrols – and they insisted that increased trade would lead to peace between nations. They saw the Tories, the landowners, imperial interests and the armed forces as their enemies. Cobden told one of his colleagues in April 1842 that the economic isolation, produced by tariffs, had to be broken down by free trade so that war between economically dependent states would become more difficult; free trade would also erode colonial ties which in his view had been the chief source of war for the previous 150 years. In sum, 'free trade, by perfecting the intercourse, and securing the dependence of countries upon one another, must inevitably snatch the power from the governments to plunge their people into wars'.[24] In this Cobden and other free traders have been over-optimistic; Germany and Britain had very strong trading ties before the two World Wars and Japan's extensive trade with the British Empire increased antagonism between the two countries in the 1930s. Such trade was only too often seen as threatening and unfair rather than advantageous to all.[25] It may be, sometimes, that contact between financiers and businessmen does gradually reduce misconceptions and misunderstandings and pave the way to greater international harmony, but this depends upon general acceptance of the view that the trade is mutually beneficial.

Cobden and other free traders stoutly opposed the British decision to go to war against Russia to protect Turkey in 1854 and they were subjected to the same sort of obloquy which Bishop Bell received for his opposition to bombing in the Second World War. But humanitarian feelings were not entirely cast aside and a new sort of pressure group emerged to help wounded British soldiers. Protests over their poor treatment grew so loud that the Secretary for War Sidney Herbert tried to improve the situation by encouraging nurses to go to the front.[26] Amongst these was Florence Nightingale, then already known for her nursing abilities. At Scutari Nightingale and her 37 colleagues are said to have dramatically reduced the death rate amongst the wounded by buying the necessary medicines and improving the hygiene. Subsequently, Nightingale helped Herbert with the Royal Commission on Army Medical Conditions, which established an Army Medical School to train specialist military doctors and drew up sanitary rules for barracks.

Increased media coverage of warfare, even if the newspapers played down the sufferings involved, and the ease with which civilians could now journey to the battlefield and report on their observations internationalised pressure to improve the treatment of the wounded. The Red Cross was founded by the Swiss doctor Henri Dunant in 1864 in reaction to what he had seen of the battle of Solferino between the French and the Austrians in 1859, when many of the wounded received no treatment and no food or water.[27] Humanitarian pressure groups thus flourished in response to press reports and they, in turn, encouraged further public and media pressure to reduce the suffering involved. Thus the St John Ambulance Society and the Society for Aiding and Ameliorating the Condition of the Sick and Wounded in Time of War emerged from the Franco-Prussian War of 1870–1871. The British National Aid Society, which was also started in response to that war in August 1870, quickly raised over £294,000 under the patronage of Queen Victoria and her son, the future Edward V11.[28] Similarly, the Quakers set up a War Victims Relief Fund which provided food to civilians in Alsace and Lorraine, the provinces transferred from France to Germany.[29]

Each great war in Europe produced a corresponding increase in the activity and a number of humanitarian pressure groups, and the First World War heralded the emergence of societies popularising the 18th-century idea of preventing the outbreak of war by developing international organisations. Many radical intellectuals blamed the Liberal government's policy of balancing German power by aligning Britain with the French and Russians for the country's intervention in the First World War, if not for the war itself. This anti-war group included two future Labour leaders, Ramsay MacDonald and Arthur Ponsonby, who established the Union of Democratic Control to campaign for a 'new', more idealistic foreign policy. This policy was to be more open to public scrutiny and thus more democratic. The Union was critical of the aristocratic and secretive Foreign Office and of its failure to follow 'true' liberal principles which were anti-capitalist, anti-imperialist and anti-militaristic. Despite the hostility it evoked during the fighting, the UDC deeply influenced subsequent Labour party policy and contributed to the idealistic atmosphere in which foreign policy was debated during the inter-war period, the deeply felt support for the League of Nations and the opposition towards helping to preserve the European balance of power.[30]

Many UDC members worked during the war years for the League of Nations Society, which advocated establishing such an eponymous international body. They believed that the members of the League should agree to settle all their disputes either through judicial arbitration or through a Council of Inquiry; they should protect each other if attacked by a non-party and admit any 'civilized' state to membership.[31] The Society flourished after the United States entered the war in 1917 and President Wilson encouraged their activities. Members had long been in touch with parallel bodies in the United States, now they could exhort more people within the British elite, such as the Archbishop of Canterbury and General Smuts, to back their campaign. There is no doubt that their discussions and public meetings helped to create the general atmosphere in which the seminal idea of replacing the informal concert of Europe with a permanent international organisation to coordinate international affairs became acceptable to the British and other governments.

Meanwhile, the Women's International League for Peace and Freedom (WILPF) was founded at a conference in The Hague, which brought together some 1200 women from 12 countries in April 1915. The delegates wanted the neutral countries to mediate an end to the war. They also demanded the extension of the franchise to women and the representation of women at the post-war peace conference. In other words, just as some who opposed the extension of the franchise believed that it would empower the allegedly xenophobic working class, the League believed that enfranchising women would reduce governments' propensity to go to war and bring greater security to international relations. Public opinion polling has now confirmed that Western women are less interventionist than men. For example, in November 1940 Gallup apparently found over 56 per cent of US males, who responded to its polls, believed that the time had come for the United States to take strong measures against Japan, but only 42 per cent of women felt so.[32] On the other hand, once the war had begun, the gap between male and female opinion narrowed; Gallup found that 86 per cent of American men and 83 per cent of women supported the dropping of the atomic bombs in Japan in 1945.[33] The WILPF was right that women are generally less willing to accept the idea that war may be a lesser evil than doing nothing in some circumstances, though the gap between the two sexes is not always as wide as the organisation suggested.

In the inter-war years the WILPF added its voice to the UDC and others who denounced the Paris peace settlement for allowing the conquerors to expand their territories, allegedly denying the principle of self-determination and disarming only the defeated powers. They criticised the dominance of the League of Nations by the Great Powers and sent missions to areas of conflict to investigate conditions and seek out mediators. The League's members objected to British policy in Ireland, the US occupation of Haiti and the Franco-Belgian intervention in the Ruhr, and campaigned constantly for disarmament. In 1935 the WILPF condemned the persecution of the German Jews, and protested against the Japanese annexation of Manchuria and the Italian seizure of Abyssinia. However, when the democracies began belatedly to arm to meet Fascist aggression, WILPF campaigned against British and French preparations. Once war broke out, following the German attack on Poland, the League's members continued to call for mediation by the neutral nations, while its own headquarters was moved to the United States when Washington was still neutral.[34]

In 1934, as Hitler's control on Germany tightened, Dick Sheppard, the Canon of St Paul's, founded the Peace Pledge Union. The Union, whose members pledged to renounce war and never to sanction another, attracted the support of Arthur Ponsonby, the leader of the Labour opposition in the House of Lords from 1931 to 1934, George Lansbury, the leader of the Labour party from 1931 to 1935 and writers such as Aldous Huxley, John Middleton Murray, Bertrand Russell, Storm Jameson and Siegfried Sassoon.[35] The Union's ideas were spread through its journal, *Peace News*, as well as lectures and articles in the general press. The Union drew up a memorandum which was read by George Lansbury during the debate on the National Government's defence policy in March 1938. It argued that:

> Just as it is impossible to end war by war, so to-day it is morally and materially impossible to defend national democracy from fascism by war. Democracy itself must perish in that process.... Fascism flourishes because of the belief that in the world as it is violence is the only means by which the intolerable injustices under which nations suffer can be redressed. The ringed fence of arms which the democratic nations provide against fascism encourages it in its evil ways.[36]

In fact, unfortunately, the perennial moral dilemma about intervention could not be escaped so easily. The Nazis planned to dominate their neighbours by force and the Japanese to lord it over Asia. Only the massive armies deployed by the United States, Britain and Soviet Union could halt their tide of aggression. The pacifists focused on the horrors of war, not the horrors which would occur without it. When war did break out, the peace movements were temporarily stunned; as Christopher Driver pointed out in his sympathetic study of the Campaign for Nuclear Disarmament (CND), 'the opinion forming classes of Britain had lost their faith in political utopias'.[37]

Thus it was not until 1958 that a powerful new wave of anti-war feeling developed into the CND. Like the anti-slavery movement, this was essentially a moral crusade; 'if Britain could no longer rule by force then surely she might exert moral and cultural, and therefore, political, influence'.[38] Like the Peace Pledge Union, CND came to include large segments of the intellectual elite including artists and writers such as E. M. Forster and Henry Moore, historians such as A. J. P. Taylor, philosophers such as Bertrand Russell, clergymen such as Canon Collins, and journalists such as James Cameron. It is Cameron's memoirs which, perhaps, best capture the movement's urgency and passion. He ascribed his views to reporting on two US nuclear tests in the late 1940s, though, no doubt, his observation of subsequent crises increased his fear that they would 'escalate' out of control. He wrote afterwards, 'in those days there seemed to me nothing of comparable importance. Looking back, I see no reason to change my mind.'[39] While CND effectively captured the headlines by its marches on the nuclear weapons research centre at Aldersmaston, these tactics may also have alienated other people. Polling data suggests that many oppose demonstrations, even when they support the cause and thus CND polarised opinion by its methods.[40] CND failed to convert the Labour party to its views and split in 1960 over the best way of bringing pressure to bear on the government. A minority, including Bertrand Russell, set up the Committee of 100 leading figures who would employ passive resistance tactics, such as blocking the roads outside airbases.[41]

In retrospect, there was little disagreement between the campaigners and the successive governments in the 1950s about the threat to Britain's safety which the use of nuclear weapons represented. According to his doctor, Lord Moran, Winston Churchill worried constantly about mankind's chances of survival and the *White Papers* on defence were extremely blunt about the prospects: 'If global war were to break out it would...be a struggle for survival of the grimmest kind.... Whatever the preparations made, an attack on this country would involve loss of life and destruction on an unparalleled scale.'[42]

The CND's supporters simply disagreed with the government about means and risks; in their view there was no time to wait for agreement with the Soviets on disarmament or to rely on deterrence, Britain should reject continental interventionism and abandon its nuclear weapons forthwith in order to avoid becoming a target in the event of a war between NATO and the Warsaw Pact. This disagreement was often also a consequence of conflicting analyses of the Soviet Union; the government's supporters saw it as a totalitarian state similar to Nazi Germany, whereas many of CND's supporters saw it as much less threatening.[43] Again, a historian might say that they both were partly right; Stalin exercised tighter control and was more brutal to his people than Hitler was to the non-Jewish Germans, but Moscow's rulers were also more cautious in their foreign policy.[44]

Even after the end of the Cold War and the collapse of the Soviet Union, it is hard to assess the CND's impact on the course of events. On the one hand the movement never weakened government support for the maintenance of the British nuclear deterrent, on the other hand it encouraged the government to put its nuclear force 'off-shore' by deploying the weapons in submarines. James Cameron argued that CND played a significant role in bringing about the Nuclear Test Ban Treaty, prohibiting tests in the atmosphere, although this probably exaggerates the movement's influence in the United States.[45] The very fact that Western pressure groups were demonstrating in favour of unilateral disarmament may have generated a more benevolent or, at least, more divided image of the West. The Soviet leader Nikita Khrushchev, for example, appears to have seen Western society as profoundly split between warmongers and peaceful elements.[46] The peace movements emphasised Western idealism in the 1930s and the Axis took advantage of apparent Western weakness and divisions to push their aggression. In the nuclear age and confronted with the combined strength of the NATO allies, Stalin, Khrushchev and Brezhnev could only push the West so far without bringing NATO and the Warsaw Pact to the brink of a mutually disastrous war.

The richest pressure groups since 1945 have been those concerned not so much with ending wars as with feeding and generally assisting civilians afflicted by war, earthquake or famine. During the First World War the Commission for Relief in Belgium, encouraged by the American millionaire Herbert Hoover, helped to keep thousands of Belgian and French citizens alive under German rule despite the indifference of the occupation forces and the British naval blockade. Already by December 1914, 200,000 people in Brussels, one-third of the city's population, were receiving food in Hoover's free canteens.[47] In the Second World War Nazi rule bore even harder on the occupied peoples and the danger of starvation was particularly acute in Greece, which was still trying to incorporate refugees expelled by Turkey after the First World War.[48] During the winter of 1941–1942, 200,000 Greeks starved and, altogether, half a million may have died of starvation and resulting diseases during the war as a whole. Grass was boiled for its minimal food value, children scavenged in rubbish dumps, and the middle classes sold everything they possessed in an effort to survive.[49] Several famine-relief committees were established in response, encouraged by Bishop Bell and others, and on 5 October 1942 they were joined by Oxfam. The efficacy of such organisations was, however, limited by the British government's reluctance to take away the Nazis' legal responsibility for looking after the occupied peoples and the shortage of food in Britain itself.

Once the war ended, Oxfam joined the campaigns for famine relief in Germany and elsewhere to channel the funds they raised through the Friends' Relief Service. Despite the continued reluctance of the government, which was only too well aware how short rations were in Britain, such efforts helped offset some of the worst effects of the food shortages and cold devastating the continent. Rations in the British zone of Germany were set at 1000 calories a day against 2800 in Britain and this meant that many were poised on the brink of starvation.[50] One British army officer noted, 'I saw clearly the pallor, lassitude, listlessness and that apathetic resignation which accompanies early starvation...I was pestered by children for food. I saw women cry for bread in the streets. I saw numerous people collapse by the wayside.'[51] The economy recovered only very gradually and the threat of mass starvation slowly receded.

Oxfam made history when it established its first shop in the City of London in November 1947. This grew into the network of charity shops selling second-hand clothes, books and other items which are a familiar sight on the streets of British towns. The Committee advertised its objective as 'the relief of suffering arising as a result of wars or of other causes in any part of the world'. Over the years it helped to reduce famines in India and Africa, as well as the sufferings from the civil war in China, the Korean War and the Hungarian uprising. Oxfam also established the pattern for a whole series of humanitarian NGOs which have found fertile soil in Britain and elsewhere since 1945.[52] They act partly as pressure groups trying to persuade governments to give more help to poor countries and partly as relief organisations with their own funds and staff. They also moved from trying to bring relief to starving peoples to trying to help them develop economically so that famines would not occur and endemic poverty would be reduced or even disappear.

While anti-war pressure groups have become much less visible and less wealthy than those involved in helping the Third World, there are signs of a swing in the other direction. Some analysts have begun to criticise the whole idea of development, arguing that it produces 'unending' wars of intervention by the West and that it underplays or even destroys the self-reliance of the Third World. They suggest that during the Cold War 'NGOs expanded as petty sovereigns in the limited space between corrupt and inefficient Third World states on the one hand and complicit and bureaucratic Western governments on the other.'[53] This, in turn, encouraged Western (and UN) military intervention when, as in Iraq or Afghanistan, the Third World states deviated too obviously from Western hopes by, for example, harbouring terrorist groups or resorting to drug production. In other words NGOs were part of a new imperialism and limited sovereignty for the Third World states. The critics call instead for a greater acceptance of cultural differences between nations and thus much reduced Western intervention in the Third World. Despite their different political orientations, there is, in fact, agreement between such critics and Samuel Huntington's suggestions in his widely read and controversial analysis of *The Clash of Civilisations*, in which he also urged Western governments to recognise that all peoples do not want to become like the West and to accept that 'Western intervention in the affairs of other civilisations is probably the single most dangerous source of instability and potential global conflict in a multi-civilisational world'.[54]

The perennial dilemma for British governments is thus posed in new forms. Is it possible for Western governments and NGOs to help the Third World develop or should they confine their energies to assisting distressed people when summoned by the Third World governments after earthquakes or other natural disasters? Should they send peace-keepers to try to end civil wars or should they 'allow' civil wars to continue in the Third World even though they know the suffering these are causing? Even if humanitarian NGOs push for intervention, the choice remains with governments because the influence of such pressure groups has declined in recent years. The very increase in numbers of NGOs has ensured that no single group has the effect which the anti-slavery movement, the anti-Corn Law campaign or the Union of Democratic Control had when they were at their height. British political society is particularly receptive to moralistic pressure groups, which are often co-opted into the elite, but their numbers today mean that they can be marginalised if the government wishes to ignore them.[55] Secondly, the appearance of public opinion polls shows governments what the public think and polls have thus removed one of the most important functions of earlier pressure groups. The days have passed when MPs impressed the House of Commons and astonished foreign visitors by unrolling documents containing the names of hundreds of thousands of petitioners.[56] Mass demonstrations continue and, indeed, the protest against the March 2003 war with Iraq was said to have been larger than any in British history. Frustrated by their inability to make headway against the government's determination, marching seemed the only way to vent the activists' anger and fears. But, significantly, it did not force the government to change course.

In human affairs there are no panaceas. The prohibition of overt slavery has not abolished slavery in all its forms and the anti-slavers were unable to help the former slaves economically, the Caribbean islands and Sierra Leone remain poor and unstable 200 years later; the introduction of free trade by Britain did not avoid wars as Cobden and Bright had hoped it would; the establishment of the League of Nations after the First World War was certainly a step forward in international affairs, as the Union of Democratic Control had predicted it would be, but it did not prevent the outbreak of war and it discouraged support for the balance of power, which alone might have deterred Axis aggression in the 1930s; humanitarian NGOs have saved countless lives after floods, famines and earthquakes but they are increasingly accused of neo-imperialism; campaigns to protect animals or the environment are also attacked for being blind to the needs of the poor. All cultures and societies resent criticisms; the Australians were irritated by Norwegian and German threats to halt Australian lamb imports in 2008 because of the Australian farmers' alleged ill-treatment of sheep, but a poor and weak country would feel even more diminished.[57] Finally, many states accuse countries with a culture of interference as hypocritical; the Japanese have responded to Australian criticisms of their whale harvest by protesting against the Australian destruction of kangaroos. More seriously, Amnesty International's campaigns for political prisoners and parallel struggles against the use of torture in the Third World will, unfortunately, be similarly dismissed as patronising and hypocritical following the defence of the use of water torture by President George W. Bush during the 'war on terror' which followed the 9/11 attacks on New York and Washington.

4
The Media and War

The shadows of past wars, and particularly the most recent, hang over those conflicts which threaten to overtake us. Thus the shade of the First World War darkened the inter-war years, and the shadow of the Vietnam War, or the 'Vietnam syndrome', deeply influenced US' views until the Gulf War in 1990–1991. These shadows were shaped by war correspondents and ministerial speeches at the time and later by novels, memoirs and films. Much of their impact was unconscious and it interacted with other influences. We know, for example, from opinion polls that, since the Second World War, the US public have favoured the Air Force over the other services. On the other hand, the Europeans have been more sceptical and fearful of the impact of airpower on civilians. We can presume that this is because the US homeland has never been the victim of air attacks unlike every major European country, and reading or hearing reports of the blitz on London was not the same as being there. But it may also be that the US public wanted to fight wars which favour a country, like their own, with the most advanced technology.

European and American differences over airpower had a major impact on trans-Atlantic relations in the early 1990s. Even though massive US air attacks had failed to win the wars in Korea and Vietnam,[1] the Clinton administration believed that the war in Bosnia in the early 1990s could be ended by allowing the Bosnian Muslims to import arms and by bombing Bosnian Serb forces, whom they blamed for most of the killing. The administration also felt that the US people were unwilling to sacrifice their soldiers in battles on the ground. The European governments, led by Britain and France, were more doubtful about the utility of bombing the Serbs and preferred to try to abate the conflict with peacekeeping forces. The shadow of Vietnam and other guerrilla victories thus had one effect on the Americans and quite another on Europeans. In the event, peacekeeping did not stop the killing, NATO launched air attacks and the Bosnian Serbs eventually agreed to negotiate an end to the war, though whether this was due to such attacks on their forces, or to the fact that they had all the territory they wanted and had begun to lose the ground war to the Bosnian Muslims and Croats, remains uncertain.

In 1999, buoyed by success in Bosnia, the Clinton administration persuaded NATO to undertake a sustained bombing campaign against Serbia. The aim was to compel the Serb government to end their occupation of Kosovo and accept peacekeepers in the province. Once again Milosevic, the Serb leader, capitulated but whether this was because of Russian pressure, because NATO was beginning to talk of sending ground forces into Kosovo, or simply because of bombing remains unclear. What is certain is that NATO was running out of targets in Serbia which could be struck by aircraft without killing large numbers of civilians, and that it would have had to use its ground forces if Milosevic had not given way.

War correspondents played a very important part in creating the shadows which influenced such debates, yet it is not easy for them to shape these shadows so that they reflect a conflict. Those who serve in wars, and the journalists who cover them, are usually dissatisfied with media coverage because it seems to lack the 'feel' for the experiences which they have undergone, while historians rarely make use of journalists' accounts when they come to write about past campaigns. The question is, however, not whether media coverage has been comprehensive or invariably accurate, as it can never be either, but whether its general shape has been right, whether it has given people enough information to understand what was happening when British forces intervened overseas and to decide whether the campaign's continuation was justified. There are a number of inherent difficulties; the obscurity, complexity and pace of the battlefield; the prejudices and competence of the correspondents or of the editors whom they supply with information; the threat to the correspondent's life; censorship by the armed forces and influence by the government.

Wars are generally made up both of long periods of boredom when there is little for journalists to report, and very fast moving and complex battles which are extremely taxing to describe adequately, even for those who are familiar with such events. Police forces take months or years to decide who committed a murder and accumulate sufficient evidence to convince a jury. They interrogate those who witnessed the crime and all those who have relevant information. Yet still they make mistakes and innocent people are imprisoned. A battle, where conflicting groups try to achieve, and sometimes hide, their purposes and methods, and where noise, fear and confusion reign, is vastly more complicated than a murder. When a civil airliner or a train crashes, the subsequent enquiry takes months or years, while experts of all types give information to the investigators. On a battlefield hundreds of aircraft, tanks, trains and other equipment may be destroyed, the journalist has no time to await subsequent enquiries as to how they were destroyed. Even if he or she witnessed an event, their account might well differ substantially from the story told by another witness. They have only one advantage over subsequent and pains-taking enquirers, memory distorts and their instant reports leave no time for pride and absent-mindedness to obscure the truth.

Very often journalists have had no training to help them describe or analyse military affairs and this makes them more dependent on military briefings in their efforts to understand events.[2] On the other hand, they will still arrive on the battlefield with preconceived political ideas which will distort their descriptions of events. Journalists notoriously escape from the results of their mistakes and misinterpretations. Readers and viewers usually forget individual errors but, while they may enjoy journalism and probably admire war correspondents for their courage, they say that they despise the 'hacks' and their employers; Rudyard Kipling's description of the influence wielded by the owner of the *Daily Express* Lord Beaverbook as 'power without responsibility; the prerogative of the harlot throughout the ages' has stuck. Eighty-six per cent of Britons in one survey in 1992 professed to lack confidence in the 'press', though they discriminate between the different sections of the media.[3] In April 2003, 55 per cent said that they preferred television as a source of news on the war in Iraq to the newspapers, while only 8 per cent preferred newspapers. It was unclear whether this was because they read popular newspapers, which had less thoughtful coverage, or whether it was because they preferred to believe what they could see on the screen, even if it was carefully selected and edited.[4]

The problem of making sense of the battlefield, 'of telling the truth', has remained constant since William Howard Russell, arguably the first or one of the first war correspondents, tried to put together his own observations on the battles in the Crimean War with the fragmentary accounts he received from the officers and men involved.[5] After the battle of Alma he commented:

> How was I to describe what I had not seen? Where learn the facts for which they were waiting at home? My eyes swam as I tried to

make sense of what I had heard. I was worn out with excitement, fatigue and want of food.... I longed to get away from it – from the exultation of others in which thought for the dead was forgotten or unexpressed. It was now that the weight of the task I had accepted fell on my soul like lead.[6]

Russell's comment encapsulated the impossibility of adequately describing in a few words anything so multifarious and chaotic. Seen this way, the traditional war correspondent had a far more difficult task than the novelist who can, like Stendhal, simply say that battle is an incomprehensible mess and describe it in terms of haphazard and often inexplicable events, irrational passions, violence and confusion.[7] War correspondents often nowadays say that they can do no better, they look at war from the point of view of the soldier or civilian, not the general or the politician. As the television journalist Martin Bell put it, 'forget the strategic overview. All war is local. It is about the ditch in which the soldier crouches and the ground on which he fights and dies.'[8] Yet, as some media analysts have pointed out, such assertions may discourage attempts to make sense of what is happening.[9] Reporting or photographing a random series of incidents without any attempt to link them together or to explain them means that the primary purpose of the correspondent, giving the reader a general idea of what occurs, has been put to one side.

Before the First World War the viewpoint was very different. Many hard-bitten war correspondents were Social Darwinists who saw themselves as reporting the eternal struggle for survival and believed that peace made individuals and nations decadent, an attitude which led so many of the intellectuals to rejoice when war broke out in 1914.[10] The struggle for survival seemed particularly evident by the end of the century in East Asia where China and Korea appeared to be in terminal decay and where Japan secured an overwhelming victory against the Russians in the war of 1904–1905. Thus one of the war correspondents explained Russia's defeat by suggesting that 'the improvements, or the so-called improvements, of civilisation have a disastrous effect on the physique and stamina of a nation'.[11] Another protested at the end of the war:

After having tasted of the horror and sublimity of war I was to return to the contemplation of... that sordid, eternal squabble for pence which they call peace – a squabble in which there is no Red Cross, no quarter, no regard for sex or age, no dignity, not a single redeeming feature.[12]

He went on to write of the dead soldiers, 'better the death they died than the self-centred existence which seems the sum of our modern civilisation'.

The early war correspondents lavished praise on the officers' bravery in the face of danger, partly to encourage others to behave in the same way and partly because warfare had been described in these terms since the time of Homer. Casualties amongst civilians living in battle zones were not the centre of their attention nor the core of their reports because their readers expected them to concentrate on the fighting itself and the wars were often far away. In contrast, by the end of the 20th century the focus and the language had changed; correspondents did not normally use adjectives to allude to the bravery of the combatants, but to dilate on the sufferings of the civilians and of the military casualties. Paintings by war artists of the heroic battles waged by individuals were replaced by photographs either of tanks, ships and aircraft or of civilian casualties. The soldiers faded into the background. The explicit purpose remained the same, informing the public about the course of the war, but the journalists were looking at different aspects of war and interpreting events in different ways.

Histories of the media's coverage of military intervention suggest this change of perspective occurred during the Vietnam War. This was the first war to be observed so intensively by television, it was also the first prolonged, modern war in which many of the Western correspondents came to doubt both the desirability of Western intervention and the competence of a 'Command...that rode us into attrition traps on the back of fictional kill ratios, and an Administration that believed the Command, a cross-fertilisation of ignorance'.[13] But the coverage of warfare has been constantly altering; even at the beginning of the 20th century correspondents were beginning to pay more attention to the impact of war on civilians and, as pointed out in Chapter 3, the Red Cross was now an accepted feature of European battlefields.[14]

Thus, one of the correspondents covering the Russo-Japanese War in 1904–1905 recalled the Japanese bombardment of the Manchurian city of Liaoyang, when 'cries of pain and of mourning were heard in innumerable Chinese homes, mothers lamenting their shrapnel mangled babies, infants trying in vain to feed off breasts that would never suckle again'.[15] As war has succeeded war, correspondents tried ever harder to put such civilians into the picture. During the Second World War, the Australian journalist and historian Alan Moorehead typified the trend. Sent to cover the allied invasion of North Africa, he described the changes in Thibar, a tiny Tunisian village just over the border from Algeria. He recalled the confused rumours that swept the valley when the allied landing began and the overwhelming fear amongst the people that the fighting would spread to their village. Then the British troops came and German aircraft began to strafe the area so that moving vehicles were unsafe in the daytime. Thibar was, nevertheless, relatively lucky, Moorehead referred to the 'battered township' of El Aroussa, the 'depressing shambles' of Medjez-el-Bab and the 'blasted town of Sousse' where the Arab section had been badly hit by allied bombing.[16] During the final allied breakthrough to Tunis, Moorehead described how the beautiful Medjerda valley 'turned from green to dirty yellows and greys; the fields of wild flowers had withered entirely; the ripening wheat was flattened; the dust was appalling'. Tunis itself had escaped the worst damage except round the docks and the port of La Goulette where the wharves were badly cratered.[17]

Moorehead took an overtly pro-allied view but he was much more sparing in his use of adjectives than the 19th-century war correspondents. He described meeting one soldier John Anderson shortly after the action for which he had been awarded the VC, but his account of Anderson's own behaviour is nonchalant. Moorehead's assessment of the soldiers' attitudes is very different from his 19th-century predecessors:

> They have no high notions of glory. A great number of people at home who refer emotionally to 'Our Boys' would be shocked and horrified if they knew just how the boys were thinking and behaving. They would regard them as young hooligans. And this is because the real degrading nature of war is not understood by the public at home.[18]

All this has to be compared with the language Russell and others used to describe events in the Crimea and afterwards. Russell began his report on the battle of Balaklava, 'if the exhibition of the most brilliant valour, of the excess of courage, and of a daring which would have reflected luster on the best days of chivalry can afford full consolation for the disaster of today, we can have no reason to regret the melancholy loss which we have suffered in a contest with a savage and barbarian enemy'.[19] Russell's report is replete with adjectives and harks back to heroic ages; the flowery language, the historic references and the denigration of the Russians would be equally unacceptable today.

Of course, the bland language used by Moorehead and others could fail adequately to reflect what was happening quite as much as the focus on the courage of the troops in the 19th century. The effects even of nuclear weapons were, for example, hidden at the time behind the flat terminology used. *The Times'* headline on 8 August 1945 was simply 'Tokyo report on vast damage by new bomb', *The Daily Telegraph* headlined the story, 'Allies invent atomic bomb: first dropped on Japan'. *The Times'* report said that Japanese broadcasts indicated that 'enormous' damage had been done to Hiroshima and that they denounced the US attack as 'sufficient to brand the enemy for ages to come as the destroyer of mankind and as public enemy No. I of social justice'.[20] Unscathed by war themselves, the American people had to use considerable imagination to appreciate the effect of bombing on Hamburg and Dresden, Hiroshima and Nagasaki from the short reports published in the press.

Nevertheless, governments are aware of the potential impact of media reports on their own people and on foreigners. The balance of power between governments and media is unstable, and tension between them is both inevitable and, to some extent, desirable. The media are inundated with information by governments and the danger is that they will either accept it uncritically or slant their reports by selecting items which fit their preconceptions.[21] They are also subject to pressure from the armed forces and from governments to avoid certain issues altogether, not just because they believe coverage would threaten national security, but because it would inconvenience the government. On the other hand, ministers and serving officers know how much power journalists can wield. In wartime, as Russell showed in the Crimea, they can make or break reputations, and they can influence the attitude of the public to the campaign as a whole.

In the winter of 1854 Russell had to decide how much to report on the British army's lack of preparations for the freezing conditions in the Crimea and the effect which this had on their combat readiness. If he did not report, he would be conniving in the logistical failures and hiding the truth, if he reported fully then the Russians would realise that the British army had virtually no powers of resistance. In the end he decided to give at least some idea of the army's sufferings. The effect was a government crisis, a flood of donations for the troops and belated attempts to make good the deficiencies. In other words, Russell changed the perception of the war in London and the policy towards it. He cared about the outcome and behaved as much like a diplomat as a journalist; he could not be 'just' an objective reporter of events. The tension between reporting the truth and interfering in the progress of the war, between observing and acting is inescapable. In Bosnia during the early 1990s many journalists became so convinced of the case against the Serbs that they ceased to behave as objective reporters. The television presenter and writer Nick Gowing called this conscious abdication of any attempt at impartiality, the 'cancer' of modern journalism.[22] The journalists' campaign did not immediately push governments into action but it has left a lasting mark on the way that war has been viewed.

Lloyd George, the British prime minister, argued during and after the First World War that the media were unable to describe what the war was like because of the censorship his government imposed. He told the editor of *The Manchester Guardian*, C. P. Scott, 'if people really knew, the war would be stopped tomorrow. But of course they don't know and can't know. The correspondents don't write and the censorship would not pass the truth.' [23] This is patronising nonsense; people did have a general idea of the bloodshed and suffering involved. H. G. Wells' novel, *Mr Britling Sees it Through*, published in 1916, described the trenches, the barbed wire, the artillery fire, the mud and the casualties lying in no-man's land between the lines.[24] Despite the censorship, he could describe what the battlefield looked like from the press reports and personal accounts provided by friends. Similarly, a civilian diarist noted in January 1917:

> The mud at the front is unbelievable and men are sinking in it. Eugene Crombie has written a description of it to his mother.... Eugene says that ... there is the horrid sensation of treading on something soft and yielding which you know to be a corpse or part of one buried in the slush. Still, he adds, even this is nothing to seeing corpses half-gnawed by rats.[25]

The censorship prevented people knowing the details of battles but they knew what they cost because of the deaths of their relatives and their neighbours' children and the army's apparently insatiable demand for more recruits, leading for the first time to the introduction of conscription. Asquith's daughter wrote to one of her friends in October 1915, 'our poor generation – how its blossom has fallen – Rupert [Brooke] to me the greatest sorrow of the war – and one of the greatest of my life ... The living and the dead are curiously mixed in one's mind. Hell and heaven seem not much further than Gallipoli.' [26] All that was published after the war, all the criticisms and debates simply fleshed out the details. The conflict was much closer to home than the French Wars had been, the numbers serving in the armed forces were greater, the way in which industries had to convert from producing civilian goods to making munitions was unprecedented, the encouragement of women to serve in medical and paramilitary organisations was equally novel, the general interference with peacetime life was more extensive than it had been at least since the Civil War in the 17th century. Ordinary people may not have known how to put the conflict into historical perspective but they had an idea of the events unfolding across the Channel.

Today, with the ever-growing importance of the worldwide media and the ubiquity of the tiny camera, censorship of the details of a battle is increasingly difficult even for a dictatorship and counter-productive because of the importance of winning the journalists' sympathies. In March 2003 the Anglo-American forces tried to create a moral bond between the forces and the media by incorporating journalists in military units. This was by no means as unusual as it was presented at the time, war correspondents have been 'embedded' since Russell's period. It was no panacea, since the armed forces still depended upon the trustworthiness of the journalists and the journalists might become or seem to become the propagandists for the armed forces. The mistake the coalition made from its own point of view was that it failed to involve Arab reporters, and it was the sympathies of the Arabs and the wider Moslem world that it needed.[27]

War is so complex, dynamic and extraordinary that the principal group of people who try to describe it will inevitably be controversial to the governments involved, the armed forces and the public at large. Journalists see themselves, not without reason, as the Fourth Estate, a vital part of the governmental system. A clear distinction has to be made, however, between the various professions within that estate. Commentators and editors often urge governments to intervene in foreign countries and to go to war, but in the days or weeks before it breaks out war correspondents may have only a limited opportunity to voice their opinions. In the 19th century their Social Darwinist views would have led them to take a hawkish stance yet the general tone of their reports today is to encourage the public to want to avoid war if at all possible.

People are much better informed now about warfare than their ancestors were and, according to their political predispositions, they and the newspapers they read balance the military dangers of an impending conflict against the potential gains. Before the fighting began in and around the Falkland Islands in 1982 it was the liberal media which stressed the military dangers because they saw the looming conflict as irrational and imperialistic; as *The Guardian*'s editorial phrased it:

> We would not have sent the Fleet.... The separate logic of momen-
> tum and military action undermines peace at every step.... That is
> the curse of war, the irrationality that seems childish when we preach
> to the Turks and Greeks, the Pakistanis and Indians. Now we the
> British struggle with the same curse.[28]

The paper rightly emphasised the risks involved to the Fleet and gave space to writers who complained about the immorality, irrationality and ignorance of the campaign's supporters. According to the economic historian, Eric Hobsbawm, 'almost every single political correspondent in the country, and that goes from the Tory ones right down to the Left, thought the whole thing was loony.... The war demonstrated the strength and the political potential of patriotism in this case in its jingo form.'[29]

Before the campaign against Iraq began in 1991 there was proportionately less discussion of the rights and wrongs of the conflict, because the allied cause was generally taken as given, but very much greater emphasis was placed by all the media on the military dangers involved, although these were far less serious than they had been in the South Atlantic a decade before. Over Bosnia in the early 1990s there was extensive media pressure to follow US wishes and to bomb the Serbs to compel them to stop the massacres of the Muslims. *The Times'* and *The Guardian's* leading articles took this view and *The Independent* devoted its front page on two occasions to the signatures of those critical of government's policy for being insufficiently aggressive.[30] The dangers of becoming embroiled in a guerrilla war, which was stressed by government spokesmen, tended to be minimised by the commentators.

The weight given to the military dangers in these campaigns has, thus, depended on political viewpoints as well as military briefings. The riskiest conventional military operation was the Falklands War, although it was the liberal press, which was hostile to the campaign's objectives, which put most stress on these. British power depended upon the two aircraft carriers accompanying the fleet to the South Atlantic. If these had been sunk, and if the Harrier aircraft they carried had been unable to defeat the Argentine Skyhawks, then the war would have been lost. Britain might also have been defeated if one of the major troops carriers, such as the liner Queen Elizabeth, had been sunk on the way to the islands, because the public might have turned against the war. In any case, the task force commander, Admiral Woodward, pointed out afterwards that he lost nearly half the frigates and destroyers with which he started and that the casualty rate was ten times higher than anything the British had suffered in a similar period since the Second World War.[31]

The 1991 Gulf campaign against Iraq was very much less risky because Britain acted as part of a coalition, led by the United States, yet there were exaggerated warnings that the war might continue for years. In part these fears seem to have been spread by US military briefings, reflecting their determination not to be accused of minimising the risks as they had been during the Vietnam War. Some academic and political commentators also suggested that advanced Western equipment would not work, that the Iraqis were highly disciplined, battle-hardened veterans and that they would use chemical weapons effectively.[32] None of this proved accurate, US cruise missiles astonished the world by their accuracy, the Iraqis, however experienced, were quickly shattered by allied air strikes and tank columns, they were deterred from using their chemical weapons and sued for peace before inflicting casualties on the allies.[33] Fortunately, the tens of thousands of hospital beds set aside proved unnecessary.

The issue over former Yugoslavia was not the reliability of Western equipment but the concern in the British army that the campaign might become bogged down in guerrilla warfare. The army had been fighting against the IRA in Northern Ireland since the 1960s, the Yugoslav Partisans had fought courageously against the Germans during the Second World War and Tito was supposed to have prepared them for a similar struggle had the Soviets invaded during the Cold War.[34] But these misgivings were overlaid by media pressure from *The Times*, *The Guardian* and *The Independent* to intervene decisively. Of course, there were dissenting voices, including columnists such as Simon Jenkins in *The Times* and Edward Pierce in *The Guardian*, but they were a minority and the papers' editorial line was strongly interventionist.[35] In the event, military misgivings proved unfounded, neither in Bosnia nor later in Kosovo were the armed forces embroiled in guerrilla warfare, that was to wait for the 21st-century wars against Iraq and Afghanistan.

Over Afghanistan in 2001 the more radical journalists reverted to the critical tone which *The Guardian* and *New Statesman* had adopted during the Falklands War; one argued that 'the worst thing about Mr Blair's missions-pretty-impossible is that they have become coated with a patina of national pride. They seek to blend past glories with present imperatives.'[36] British commentators tended to exaggerate the initial military difficulties, as they had done over Iraq in 1991, not least because

British columns had been defeated in Afghanistan in the 19th century. They tended to forget that the British armies had quickly avenged these defeats and occupied Kabul, and the efficacy of US airpower against conventional armies. Jonathan Steele in *The Guardian* predicted that images of civilian dead would destroy support for the air campaign.[37] In the event, within a matter of weeks the anti-Taleban tribes allied in the Northern Alliance, together with US airpower, had driven the Taleban from most of Afghanistan. In the long run, however, journalistic caution was more than justified by the insurgency which gradually developed against Western forces. The Taleban came back from Pakistan, where they had taken sanctuary, and allied air attacks alienated many Afghan people and even evoked protests from the pro-Western government in Kabul.[38]

Plainly the participants in such pre-war debates were deeply influenced by the shadows of past wars, some long-gone and some more recent. They were touched by liberal hatred of nationalism and imperialism, by memories of Vietnam and of British defeats at Afghan hands in the 19th century, by experience of weapons which did not work, by the general tone of British culture and by their own political persuasions. Their responsibilities can hardly be exaggerated. They deeply influenced the public debates amongst the elite and sometimes governments themselves. If they encouraged conflict in an unwise campaign or if they opposed the use of force when it could have been constructive, they were indirectly responsible for the suffering and deaths involved. They have indeed dangerous power without responsibility and, generally, without the threat of being called to account.

5
War and Literature

Before the industrial revolution writers described imaginary societies as a way of criticising their own. The genre was named after the visionary polis conceived by the 16th-century statesman and writer, Thomas More. His Utopians loathed war and never fought except when they were attacked or their citizens and others were mistreated overseas. They tried to deter attack by forcing their defeated enemies to pay the entire costs of any war over a very long period so that they would be dependent and the Utopians better prepared for another conflict. They preferred deceit to battle and were happy to subsidise attempts to assassinate foreign leaders whom they held responsible for aggression. The Utopians concentrated in battle on attacking enemy commanders and they used mercenaries, whenever possible, because they valued their own citizens' lives so highly. It was not that More was necessarily advocating this unchivalrous behaviour but he was asking his countrymen to think about their own security policy and to consider whether other policies might be preferable.[1] Dean Swift turned to satire 150 years later to disparage international politics and warfare. To ridicule the causes for which rulers fought in the 18th century, he had his heroic traveller Gulliver discover the Lilliputians who fought with the inhabitants of Blefuscu over which end of a boiled egg should be opened. Later Gulliver was thrown out of the kingdom of the Houyhnhnms when he shocked their sensibilities by telling them how Europeans admired soldiers and successful wars.[2]

A new genre began when the pace of social and economic change increased with the industrial revolution. Commentators became more concerned about the way the society was developing and the future threats this posed than about existing failings. As far as warfare was concerned, they worried about the increasing destructiveness of weapons, a widespread concern reflected in the first modern arms control agreement, the St Petersburg Declaration which prohibited the use of exploding bullets in 1868 and in the two Hague Peace Conferences of 1899 and 1907. Fictional depictions of future wars are inevitably more visionary than those by armchair strategists, politicians or military officers; novelists and poets can look at the changes in military technology or society happening today and they can extrapolate these just as their imagination directs. Naturally, the vast majority of these extrapolations prove inaccurate but, at their best, they have been surprisingly prescient because of the authors' insights both into human nature and their own times. Moreover, novelists and film-makers can show how such imaginary wars effect ordinary families, and their work may be read or watched by millions, so their predictions can have far more impact on public opinion than the more cautious or less imaginative prognostications by armchair strategists, military officers or scientists. Fiction can thus drive the debate about policy and even influence policy itself.

After the beginning of the Industrial Revolution, there were four stages in the development of this fictional contribution to the debate on warfare; the first, which lasted until the 1880s, was characterised by attempt by poets and novelists to describe the industrial warfare waged in the Crimea or in the American Civil War and to predict how it would develop; during the second from 1880 to 1914, numerous novels and plays were published about the alleged threat to Britain from possible French and German 'plans' to invade Britain, and novelists began to dream up 'super weapons' which might either bring warfare to an end or destroy humanity; in the third, after the First World War writers struggled to describe trench warfare and to forecast how civil society would survive the effects of bomb destruction as aircraft grew ever more powerful. The fourth, during the Cold War, was characterised by gloomy depictions of the prospects for a world poised between the threat of an all-consuming nuclear war and a drab, murderous communist takeover. All were didactic; the participants in the first phase asked British people to think about industrialised warfare and how its destructive impact could be minimised; in the second, they were called upon to 'pull themselves together' to face the threat of invasion; in the third, they were warned about the prospects of another, even more destructive war; and in the fourth, they were torn between the two appalling evils of communist invasion or obliteration.

In the 1840s the romantic hero of Alfred Tennyson's poem 'Locksley Hall' foresaw the possibilities of extensive airborne trade, and aerial and chemical wars, in reaction to which a world federation would grow and become so strong that it could 'hold a fretful realm in awe and [let] the kindly earth slumber, lapt in universal law'.[3] Tennyson's path-breaking work was welcomed by the aged Duke of Wellington and it was widely read by Victorian school children; with its reference to the 'Central Blue' or sky it provided the title of the memoirs of the Chief of the Air Staff Sir John Slessor after the Second World War and it was used by President Truman to try to convince conservative Congressmen to support the embryonic United Nations.[4] The few stanzas devoted to the future formed, arguably, the most prescient short piece of poetry ever written in English on strategic and political issues.[5]

In 1865 the distinguished art critic John Ruskin examined the role of warfare in a famous lecture he gave at the Royal Military Academy in Woolwich when the brutality of the US Civil War was uppermost in men's minds. Ruskin first won the sympathy of his audience by asserting that 'all the pure and noble arts of peace are founded on war; no great art ever yet rose on earth, but among a nation of soldiers'. The critic claimed, equally tendentiously, that 'all healthy men like fighting, and like the sense of danger; all brave women like to hear of their fighting'. Just as the American philosopher William James was to do half a century later, he speculated on whether these instincts could be sublimated in competitive sports but, in the end, he found sporting events wanting because they lacked nobility and were not tests to the death. However, he then went on to circumscribe ever more closely what he meant by such a test, it should, for example, not be decided by 'which of the combatants has the longest gun... or which has the gunpowder made by the best chemists, or iron smelted with the best coal'. What Ruskin admired was a duel or joust between equally well-armed, professional volunteers who would confine their contest geographically and so not wreak havoc on the homes of the poor and vulnerable. The analogy with the Medieval joust was all the stronger because of the emphasis which Ruskin put on chivalry, and charity towards the weak and the vanquished.[6] Ruskin's was a reasonable but impractical protest against the mechanisation which had already become evident in the Crimea and which was to revolutionise warfare over the next half century.

The scaremongering literature on warfare published in the decades leading up the First World War has been dissected by I. F. Clarke in his classic study *Voices Prophesying War*.[7] Clarke dates this genre from 1871, when Sir George Chesney anonymously published *The Battle of Dorking* describing a German army suddenly landing and smashing the flimsy barrier of Volunteers the British had managed to mobilise against them. Chesney's story was followed by dozens of plays and novels on the same theme. He had succeeded in focusing the British defence debate for the next four decades on whether the Royal Navy was sufficiently strong to protect the country from invasion and whether, if not, Britain needed to follow the continental lead and build up an army numbering millions of men by introducing conscription.

This late 19th-century international rivalry provided the background to the works by the leading imperial poet Rudyard Kipling and by the pre-eminent British writer of science fiction H. G. Wells. Kipling defended the ordinary soldier against the prejudices common amongst civilians and lauded the courage which he and his Indian, African and Boer enemies showed on imperial battlefields from Kabul to Ladysmith.[8] He romanticised this type of war which he believed was necessary to 'veil the threat of terror and check the show of pride' amongst the conquered peoples. But the death of his only son in the trenches of Flanders in 1915 shook him out of the romantic view of war and transformed his image of the world. Both his stories and poetry became ever more pessimistic.[9] The distinguished American literary critic Edmund Wilson argued that the 1920s saw some of Kipling's finest stories but they were so 'full of inescapable illness' and gloom that they were 'the Kipling that nobody read'. As Wilson put it, 'the big talk of the world, of the mission to command of the British, even the hatefulness of fear and disappointment, have largely faded away for Kipling. He composes as a memorial to his son.'[10]

If Kipling's pre-1914 poems and stories epitomised the romantic view of the British Empire, Wells was closer to the fictional tradition emerging in the United States which envisaged Americans inventing weapons so destructive that Washington could impose peace on the rest of the world. Professor Bruce Franklin has pointed out that the future President Harry Truman not only remembered Tennyson's forecasts but also continued to read this type of literature up until the time that he became president. He also argued that it might have influenced the President's decision to use the atomic bombs in the hope that they would cause a revulsion against warfare and give him the power to change international politics, as the optimistic school of US science fiction writers had been arguing since the late 19th century.[11]

Wells' story about nuclear warfare, *A World Set Free*, envisaged the new weapons causing massive destruction and shocking rulers into cooperating together to form a world government with the right of onsite inspection to ensure that all nuclear forces were abolished. His other stories forecast the aerial wars of the future and the invention of 'tanks' more than a decade before they actually appeared.[12] 'The land ironclads', his story of tank warfare, was also a meditation on Social Darwinism, suggesting that the cleverer townsfolk would be able, in the end, to outwit the braver countrymen. Wells was associated with the group of Coefficients, founded by Sidney and Beatrice Webb, who saw Britain as an amateur nation threatened by the military and economic competition of the more professional Germans.[13] Like Kipling's, his mood was transformed by the carnage of trench warfare in the First World War. He tried in his wartime novel, *Mr Britling Sees it Through,* to show how the national mood was changing.[14] He devoted himself after the war to appealing for support for the League of Nations and warning against the threat which conflict presented to civilisation itself. Now he blamed nationalism for the world's ills though he continued to be deeply and overtly patriotic.

Roland Stromberg, who analysed the reaction of writers and intellectuals to the outbreak of war in 1914, noted how often they welcomed the break from bourgeois, commercial life and relished the unity which war appeared to bring to their divided communities. Even if their view of imperialism was very different, both Wells and Kipling briefly joined in this prevalent mood. It was the swansong of military romanticism amongst the Western literary community. Tennyson and Ruskin had felt attracted by the romanticism of war but, for them, there had always been a strong contrary pull which led Tennyson to advise his countrymen to pause before they went to war and to work towards 'a warless world, a single race, a single tongue'.[15] Wells and Kipling had been swept up by the international rivalry of the years before the outbreak of war in 1914; Stromberg does not argue that they and their contemporaries influenced the decisions statesmen took leading to war but it seems reasonable to believe that there would have been more hesitation amongst politicians in 1914 if Social Darwinism had not been so prevalent amongst the European elite.

It was the writers who had actually served in the First World War who subsequently dominated Western consciousness and shaped the vision of future wars. Contrary to the conventional wisdom, the military historian, Brian Bond has pointed out that the majority of them did not believe that their courage and sacrifice had been wasted. Middlebrow authors, such as Ernest Raymond and Frederic Manning, were both the most popular and the most supportive of British intervention in the conflict.[16] But the trenches and the massive artillery barrages were a far cry from Ruskin's chivalrous duel. Memoirs, poems and novels described the mud and squalor, the chance nature of the killing and maiming and the vast anonymous numbers involved in industrial warfare.[17] People now had a much clearer view of what war meant to soldiers than their ancestors had when they tried to understand the French Wars. All this tended to obscure Allied military achievements and the reasons for going to Belgium's defence and preserving the balance of power in 1914.[18]

It was hardly surprising then that intellectuals frequently followed Wells' lead and looked to the League of Nations to avoid another conflict. When this hope waned in the early 1930s, novelists speculated about the coming conflict and particularly about the impact which bombing would have. Wells' most original contribution came in his loose and baggy 'novel' *The Shape of Things To Come* published in 1933 and through the subsequent film version which was more disciplined and succinct than the book itself.[19] By 1933 Japan had already invaded Manchuria and Wells had the prescience to see that they would then go on to invade the rest of China, that the Chinese would use guerrilla tactics to resist them effectively, that the Western Powers would supply the Chinese with arms and that, eventually, the United States would be drawn into the war. At the same time, he correctly suggested that war would break out in Europe between Germany and Poland, though he was wrong to predict Anglo-French neutrality in that conflict and, above all, about his central prediction that economic dislocation and disease, together with the European and Asian wars, would bring about the collapse of the state.

Civilisation, Wells believed, would subsequently be restored by the aviation industry, which would sweep away the old divisions of nation and race.[20] This might seem wildly eccentric and it was satirised by *The Times'* film critic who commented, 'quite suddenly the airmen – presumably the same people who caused so much damage in the Second World War – emerge from the ruins endowed with such wisdom, detachment and nobility as would put Socrates to shame'.[21] But ideas about internationalising aircraft and air travel, as a way of preventing aerial aggression, were not unusual in the 1930s and were even proposed by the French government. Thus Wells' vision that cooperation would grow from economic necessity rather than be created from the top, as the League of Nations had attempted, was not so eccentric; he had stumbled across the functional theory of international integration more than a decade before it inspired the work of Jean Monnet and other statesmen who founded the European Economic Community.

Wells brought his considerable powers of imagination to bear on the threats to civilisation in the 1930s, Nevil Shute brought his experience of aircraft design and his considerable ability as a story-teller to analyse the effects of the most feared of the new weapons, the strategic bomber. In *What Happened to the Corbetts* he forecast in 1939 that German bombing could devastate a town like Southampton but that such attacks would be politically counter-productive for those who launched them. He has his French commentator say to his British friends after such a raid:

> You hold the seas. The aeroplanes, they can do nothing but destroy your homes, blindly. They have not been able to destroy your ships. They have not hit your arsenals or factories except by chance.... Only a nation of no understanding, who did not know the world psychology, would make such mistakes. Very nearly have they brought in America to fight beside England.... Every day the ships come from America, loaded with men, and money, and food.... England will now win the war.[22]

Shute was right about the inaccuracy of bombing and that bombing towns would increase US sympathy for the states under attack but wrong to assume that this anger would be enough on its own to bring Washington into the war.

When, during the Second World War, the bombing raids, the holocaust and other massacres confirmed the depth of the ideas, values and passions dividing mankind and the increasing destructiveness of technology, the prospects seemed ever bleaker. Western society was threatened after 1945 by the nightmarish horrors of a repressive communism graphically described in George Orwell's *Nineteen Eighty-Four*[23] and the nuclear destruction symbolised by Nevil Shute's pessimistic best-seller *On the Beach*. *Nineteen Eighty-Four* was published in 1949, the year before Orwell's death. He envisaged Britain renamed 'Airstrip One' with complete state control of all the media, with an omnipresent dictator, Big Brother who had total oversight of all lives through cameras located in their rooms and with the obliteration of history and suspect political words to prevent people even thinking of rebellion against the government. Airstrip One is part of the Oceania alliance and involved in interminable and futile warfare against Eurasia, which can never be brought to a conclusion because of deterrence, but which brutalises all involved who are taught to worship weaponry and gloat over films of the death of their adversaries. The wars had no objective except to use up the resources which would otherwise have made people richer and thus encouraged them to take power into their own hands.[24] Orwell was far too pessimistic. In contrast to his predictions, despite recurrent crises nuclear weapons were not used during the Cold War and, to the horror of those who doubted the efficacy of deterrence, they encouraged governments to reduce their military spending in the expectation that no Great Power would attack a state armed with such destructive power. But Orwell was correct to discern that, as people became wealthier, they would insist on exerting more power over governments and that society would become less deferential and hierarchical. Yet, we can see now that politicians had no alternative, failure to meet the material expectations of the people was ultimately fatal to the communist system, even if increasing wealth would have brought about its demise by another route.

In Shute's even more pessimistic nightmare a nuclear holocaust obliterating all life on the planet was triggered by an Egyptian attack on the United States, which Washington incorrectly assumed was a Soviet offensive against the West. When the West responded by attacking Moscow, the Chinese took the opportunity to bomb their communist colleagues with highly radioactive cobalt weapons to depopulate their cities and allow their own people to expand. Subsequently the inhabitants of Melbourne in Australia waited transfixed as the fatal radioactive tide gradually spread southwards across the planet. Some tried to drown their sorrows in alcohol, others coped with the looming catastrophe by continuing to speak as though they needed to plant for the coming Spring or to prepare for their children's wedding, and yet others turned to dangerous sports such as motor racing. *On the Beach* ends with the heroine watching the last surviving US submarine leave harbour to sink itself as the radiation intensified, while she herself committed suicide with poison.[25]

Although there were numerous novels and short stories about the aftermath of a nuclear catastrophe, there is no doubt about the impact on Western public opinion of Shute's novel and the popular film which followed. The American paperback edition carried claims by the reviewer in *The Philadelphia Inquirer* that it was 'the most talked-about bestseller in years! Explosive... shattering... Sensational – should be read by the world'. Senator Stuart Symington, a former secretary of the US Air Force, suggested that 'every American should read' the book, advice supported by the critic on *The Washington Post and Times Herald* which called it 'the most important and dramatic novel of the atomic age. If you read only one book a year, this should be the one.'[26] It was in vain that the

US nuclear physicist Edward Teller argued that Shute had his science wrong. As he wrote later:

> Nevil Shute's novel *On the Beach*, although it was based on a huge overestimate of the damage done by residual radioactivity from a nuclear war and dramatised the fate of the last human survivors, gained a wide readership, was converted into a movie, and had immense and far-reaching effects.[27]

Of course, by no means everyone shared in the gloom, expressed in different ways by Orwell and Shute. Indeed, from the very beginning of the nuclear age the majority hoped that the development of nuclear weapons would make a world war less likely; the percentage of the British and Americans believing that nuclear weapons had increased the likelihood of war was in the low teens in late 1945 against 50 per cent who believed the reverse.[28] However, fears undoubtedly grew when the Soviets developed their own nuclear forces and the Cold War intensified. Furthermore, while deterrence may have reduced the prospects for war, there was general awareness that it remained a possibility. Now that the archives are largely open on both sides, we can see that there were frequent misunderstandings and some could have led to conflict even though governments were only too well aware of the potential consequences.[29] What is remarkable is how, after living with the nuclear threat for some decades, the Europeans became more optimistic than the American public; through the 1980s half of all Americans believed that there was a 50 per cent chance of a world war breaking out over the next decade, compared with between 18 and 29 per cent of Britons and the same proportion of Germans.[30] The US media, armchair strategists and politicians put more emphasis on the dangers than their European counterparts, possibly, in part, because the United States had previously been so shielded from outside attack. Despite, or because of, Europe's devastating experiences in the 20th century, its inhabitants perhaps found it impossible to live with the idea that they might be the focus of a nuclear disaster even more horrific than the World Wars.

Novelists and film makers often influenced the general security debate, though they sometimes had a direct effect on government policy. Wells had contacts with government ministers but was frustrated by his inability to make the system more responsive to his ideas. Shute's account of the Corbett family's experiences simply added to the existing fears of air attack prevalent in Britain in the 1930s; fears which, admittedly, made sure that the government would provide the population with gas masks and encouraged it to evacuate women and children from the cities when war broke out. Truman may have been influenced by his reading of poetry and fiction, and Orwell's vision of totalitarianism certainly increased the general anxiety about Soviet tyranny because he appeared to show how it might destroy civil society and 'brainwash' the public. However, it was the Berlin blockade by Eastern forces which ensured that the Western allies would form an alliance and the Korean War from 1950 to 1953 which, in turn, led to substantial growth in Western defence spending.

Nor did Western governments abandon their nuclear weapons because of Shute's apocalyptic vision, though the nuclear threat lurked at the back of many minds, hence the rise of Campaign for Nuclear Disarmament (CND) and the general commitment to negotiating arms control measures. Igor Korchilov, the Soviet translator, who was present when the INF Treaty limiting European nuclear forces was signed in Washington on 8 December 1987, recalled afterwards:

> I looked round and saw tears glistening on the cheeks of some of the most famous faces in the room, but these faces were mainly American, not Soviet. Most of the Soviets I saw remained silent, as if trying to understand exactly what was taking place. It was all very moving.... For a moment it seemed the symbol of bright hopes for the future.[31]

If such emotions propelled arms control negotiations between Moscow and Washington, as Truman hoped would be the case, it seems possible that there was more than a coincidence between the publication of Shute's book in 1957 suggesting that an Egyptian nuclear attack could unleash a catastrophic nuclear war and the Irish government's decision the following year to launch the initiative at the UN which eventually resulted in the signature of the nuclear Non-Proliferation Treaty to stop the spread of nuclear weapons. In 1959 the Irish foreign minister warned the UN in words redolent with Shute's nightmare:

> No one can calculate in advance the interplay of forces if country after country, revolutionary group after revolutionary group became possessed, secretly or openly, of nuclear weapons.... The dangers involved in wider dissemination include... accidental atomic war, demagogic atomic war, and nuclear blackmail.... I greatly fear we are now on the edge of a slippery slope: that before long, if we do not

check this disastrous progress, the momentum acquired will be such that it will be beyond any human power to halt the increasingly rapid descent towards destruction.[32]

Admittedly Frank Aiken, the foreign minister, chose to quote a report on proliferation summarised in *Daedalus: The Journal of the American Academy of Arts and Sciences* rather than Shute's book in support of his initiative but one can be sure that Shute had done vastly more to create the general atmosphere prevailing at the UN on 13 November 1959, than Howard Simons' article in that prestigious journal.[33] Aiken's reference to the dangers of revolutionary groups acquiring nuclear weapons was his personal contribution to the debate; as a former member of the IRA, he was, no doubt, well aware of the fevered emotions which can determine such groups' behaviour.

What we can say is that deterrence between the Great Powers was more robust during the Cold War than Shute feared and that its strength was much aided by technology. Egypt could not have used ballistic missiles against the United States, or indeed any other states, without its responsibility for the attack becoming known. China could not have hoped to attack the Soviet Union without a devastating response from that state, and Beijing would have been most unlikely to drop nuclear weapons on the Russians so that it could colonise Soviet territory, given that this would poison the land it hoped to conquer. There was always a danger during the Cold War that some miscalculation could lead to utter disaster but much was done to minimise such mistakes – missiles were put underground or sent to sea, so that no nation could easily attack them. Communications between the nuclear weapon states were improved to prevent misjudgements, and constant efforts were made to stabilise the arms race through arms control negotiations.

Nevertheless, the nightmares outlined by Shute and Orwell formed part of the mental baggage of a whole generation. Theirs' was the fiction of total unremitting despair without the slightest chink of light or hope for humanity. The British literary elite had travelled very far from the idealism of Tennyson's Locksley Hall, through the catastrophe of the First World War to the nightmare of the Cold War years. The general view of human nature was far gloomier than it had been in the 19th century. William Golding, the first British novelist to win the Nobel Prize for Literature after the Second World War, epitomised this change. Most of his novels explored the causes of men's cruelty; in *Lord of the Flies*, he overturned the romantic 19th-century image of the honourable schoolboy and demonstrated how children were only held back from murdering each other by adult influence; similarly, in *The Spire* he showed how religious obsessions could lead to megalomania and in *Free Fall* and *Pincher Martin* the way in which sexual drives blinded people to their impact on others. It was not surprising that an age with such a pessimistic view of humanity should rely on the threat of mass destruction to preserve peace. Nevertheless, when the gloomy prognostications of nuclear war and communist success proved equally unfounded and the Soviet empire collapsed, the political pendulum swung again towards optimism.[34] And with this new optimism came the new wave of Western interventionism which we shall examine in Chapter 10.

6
The Rise of the Armchair Strategists

Professional civilian strategists began to influence the debate on intervention at the end of the 19th and in the early 20th century. Originally
these were solitary individuals, economists, lawyers, journalists or historians who became specialists on military affairs. Nowadays armchair
strategists are very often supported by universities and research insti-
tutes, and their numbers have dramatically increased. The debates to
which they contributed have been international with many of the most
distinguished contributors coming from Central and Eastern Europe
where the impact of conflict and totalitarianism was peculiarly devastating in the 20th century. Nevertheless, British writers from Norman
Angell and Julian Corbett before 1914, through Hector Bywater and
J. M. Spaight in the Inter-War period to P. M. S. Blackett and Robert
Thompson after 1945, have played a major part in the debate, even
if the largest concentration of armchair strategists has been located in
Washington since the Second World War.

The impact of the armchair strategists has, nevertheless, been limited
by the haphazard fashion in which the media pick up some of their
ideas and ignore others, and by the way in which politicians misinter-
pret their ideas. Some, such as Ivan Bloch, died before the outbreak of
the major conflict which they feared, others including Norman Angell
experienced two great wars and were able to assess the extent that the
conflicts vindicated their previous arguments. Their role is to puzzle out
from the ever more voluminous data available to the public what technical, economic and political developments may lead to violence and
what shape a new war might take. Looking back, we can see that naval
warfare was transformed by the development of the submarine which
threatened the survival of industrialised island states, such as Britain and
Japan, and warfare as a whole was revolutionised by the invention and

rapid evolution of aircraft which menaced all densely packed industrial cities. In recent years an equally important revolution has been brought about by precision-guided munitions and by the multiplication of television cameras on the battlefield. However obvious it seems in retrospect, it was by no means evident at earlier periods which of these particular technical innovations and economic changes would be the decisive ones rather than the others which were competing for attention at the time.

While, as we have seen, many of the most famous war correspondents before 1914 were Social Darwinists, armchair strategists, who studied the prospect of another great war in the late 19th and early 20th century, often became increasingly anxious about the impact of such a conflict on the world economy. It had been so long since a war convulsed the European continent, and industrialisation had proceeded so quickly in the intervening period, that it was difficult to imagine how financial institutions would adapt. The Polish railway magnate and banker Ivan Bloch was undoubtedly the most original of those who wrote on the issue. He has been described recently, and with some justice, as the 'father of civilian war studies'.[1] His analysis of the *War of the Future*, published in the 1890s, remains the outstanding example of what a civilian analyst can achieve by mastering the military literature and integrating it with expertise from another sphere. Unfortunately, it remains an equally outstanding example of the inability of politicians to respond appropriately to strategic warnings when war threatens and of military leaders to take civilian predictions about their profession seriously.

Bloch's contention was that wars between the Great Powers would no longer produce the results for which statesmen hoped. Because of the developments in weaponry, military operations would lead to a prolonged stalemate and the deadlock would only be broken by the economic collapse and ensuing revolution in the belligerent states.[2] The First World War justified many of Bloch's tactical predictions, producing a deadlock lasting for four years, despite all that military leaders and technologists could do to break their enemies through the introduction of tanks, poison gases, submarines, airships, bombers and a host of other technical and tactical innovations. But Bloch's economic predictions were, ironically, much less accurate than his military forecasts. The belligerents were able to pay for four years of war through taxes, by inflation and, above all, through mortgaging their future revenues. Moreover, Bloch expected Russia and Austria-Hungary to survive the war economically better than Britain and Germany with their more developed and, therefore, more fragile economies. In fact, it was Russia which collapsed first in 1917 and Austria-Hungary which followed a year later.[3]

Paradoxically, Bloch could envisage the field of battle, the trenches, barbed wire and the machine guns, what he could not imagine was that the financiers, amongst whom he had worked, would respond effectively in the short run to the challenge of war – experts are usually most pessimistic about their own area of expertise where they know just what can go wrong. Bloch ignored the work of the British economists from Adam Smith in the 18th century to Richard Cobden in the 19th. Smith had argued that the Great Powers' ability to borrow benefited the moneylenders in London and enabled people to 'enjoy, at their ease, the amusement of reading in the newspapers the exploits of their own fleets and armies'. Without the power to borrow, taxes would immediately have fallen more heavily on the population and intervention would have been avoided or brought to a speedy conclusion.[4] Similarly, in the mid-19th century, Richard Cobden attacked the City of London for lending to foreign combatants and thus, he thought, encouraging and prolonging their wars. He compared it to funding brothels.[5] Thus, the free traders pointed out that government borrowing made wars possible, while Ivan Bloch feared that the inability to borrow sufficiently would lead to national collapse. In the event, Britain borrowed $4600 million from the United States and loaned even more to Russia, France and Italy. It agreed to go on repaying the US debt, as well as the interest of $6500 million, until 1984; if war debts had not lapsed during the Great Depression, 17 years of peace would have been needed to pay for each year of war. Russia and Austria-Hungary liquidated their debts when they collapsed, and Germany achieved the same effect by massive inflation, which ruined the middle classes. While this experience may have discouraged the cost-conscious democracies from defending their interests in the 1930s, it did nothing to deter the Germans, Italians and Japanese who planned to pay for their future conquests through looting conquered states.

By no means all armchair strategists were as pessimistic as Bloch before the First World War. Indeed, some insisted that, despite the integration of the global economy and Britain's central place in it, technical innovations would actually strengthen the country's economic position in the event of war. Julian Corbett was making his name at the Royal Naval College in Greenwich before 1914 as Britain's leading naval strategist, lecturer and historian. Corbett's ambition and expertise were narrower than Bloch's. His objective was to show how naval strategy differed from military operations on land, what advantages Britain gained from being the greatest naval power, and what it lost by its total dependence on maritime trade. Like all naval analysts he was only too well aware how great this reliance had become for an industrial nation unable to feed its people. However, unlike the most famous naval historian of the day, Alfred Mahan who was a US naval officer, Corbett was by training a lawyer and he believed that British commerce was safer than it had been for centuries because of the legal prohibition on privateering which had previously been the main threat to merchant ships.

Britain was also favoured by the reduction in the range of enemy commerce raiders because they now depended on steam rather than sail. Warships could still threaten merchant ships but for much shorter periods because of their need for coal. Moreover, merchant ships also used steam and could, therefore, sometimes avoid the routes where commerce radars might lie in wait and their radio could give warning that they had been attacked.[6] All this was perfectly correct but took no account of what the world was later to learn was the most important development, the evolution of submarines. In the First World War these would sink merchant ships without warning and thus almost bring Britain to its knees in 1917. Like many British strategists, Corbett's methods were essentially historical; he tried to deduce the future from past experience but, in this case, his imagination, legal training and intuition failed him. When Britain imposed a tight maritime blockade on the Central Powers, the Germans could only retaliate by submarine warfare. The legal and moral restraints, which Corbett and others assumed would prevent such attacks on trade, gradually fell away in the heat of battle. By 1917 submarines had created what the First Sea Lord Admiral Jellicoe called 'the greatest crisis which ever threatened the population of this country'. Britain was on the brink of starvation.[7]

Corbett accepted Bloch's argument that maritime trade had knit the world together, while rejecting his conclusions. Another part of the argument was taken up by Norman Angell, a journalist with *The Daily Mail* whose pamphlet *The Great Illusion*, published in 1909, caught the imagination of the media in a way which Bloch and Corbett were unable to do.[8] Angell's writings were read by Edward V11, by the US industrialist and philanthropist, Andrew Carnegie, by politicians like Ramsay MacDonald, the Labour Party leader and George Lansbury, a later one, by Arthur Balfour, the former Conservative prime minister, by strategic analysts like Lord Esher and economists like Maynard Keynes. It was Esher who helped Angell set up a foundation, sponsored by Richard Garton, a wealthy industrialist, to spread his ideas and both Balfour and Esher became directors.[9] In some ways all this interest is surprising because Angell was much less original and well read than Bloch or Corbett. British Liberals had always emphasised the economic destructiveness of warfare.[10] Angell expanded their arguments by claiming that one developed state could not capture the trade and wealth of another. Ironically, the habit of making defeated nations pay for their own humiliation had been taken up by other states following Napoleon's example at the start of the 19th century. Bismarck had forced France to pay the full costs of the Franco-Prussian War in 1871 and the Japanese did the same thing in 1895 when they defeated China and compelled the Chinese to pay for their own defeat and for a major increase in the size of the Japanese armed forces.[11] Thus Tokyo showed that war could, in some circumstances, be made to pay handsomely, though its experience a decade later when the Russians determined to go on fighting, despite all their defeats at Japanese hands, rather than pay reparations, gave warning that the fear of paying such an indemnity might prolong and exacerbate conflicts.[12] When the nations ignored Angell's warnings and went to war in 1914, it seems likely that Germany, at least, hoped to pay for the conflict by imposing reparations on its enemies, just as it had forced the French to pay in 1871. War should always be seen as an expensive option, otherwise treasuries will fail to act as a necessary brake on intervention.

In the months leading up to the First World War, Angell was fully occupied attending student conferences and lecturing at universities and at other institutions to spread his views on international relations. He felt that the crisis immediately before the war was 'the result of an irrationalism which threatened somehow to engulf the world'. Consciously or unconsciously, Angell must have believed that economic arguments were unlikely to be convincing at such a moment; he seems from his own account to have spent less time warning of the financial costs and more arguing that Britain should remain neutral so that it could mediate between the belligerents to bring an end to the conflict. He also stressed the danger arising from a war, which would leave Russia the dominant force on the continent, since St Petersburg had long been the bête noire of Liberal commentators for its despotism.

Angell may have been wrong to play down the fears of economic chaos; at one stage Lloyd George, the Chancellor of the Exchequer, informed his cabinet colleagues:

That he had been consulting the Governor and Deputy Governor of the Bank of England, other men of light and leading in the city, also cotton men, and steel and coal men, etc., in the North of England, in Glasgow etc., and they were all aghast at the bare idea of plunging into a European conflict; how it would break down the whole system of credit with London at its centre, how it would cut up commerce and manufacture – they told him – how it would hit labour and wages and prices, and, when winter came, would inevitably produce violence and tumult.[13]

Economic experts were, thus, extremely anxious about the threat of war, but their fears had less impact on the government than political considerations. Moreover, economic collapse elsewhere could actually make the threat less horrific, if it brought war rapidly to an end. Sir Edward Grey wrote later:

Some of us thought that economic disaster would make itself felt more quickly after the outbreak of war; that it would rapidly become so acute as to bring the war to an end. In that we were wrong, but we were wrong only in our estimate of the time and manner in which the economic disaster would make itself felt. It might have been more merciful to Europe as a whole, if this disaster had made itself felt more quickly and imperatively and so had shortened the war.... Those who had the worst forebodings of what war would mean, did not over-estimate the human suffering or the economic distress that it has actually caused.[14]

In this passage, Grey showed himself familiar with the Bloch–Angell view of the likely economic impact of war and identified himself with it. Perhaps more than any other statesman he was torn then and later between fear of German domination of European politics and of the terrible suffering and social chaos which war would cause. But the effect of the Bloch–Angell view may have been the reverse of what they intended, for, from his account, Grey would seem to have comforted himself in August 1914 with the hope that war could not last long and thus that the deaths in combat would be restricted!

While Grey and his cabinet colleagues struggled with their consciences, Angell and his helpers sent hundreds of telegrams to influential people pointing out the dangers of Russian domination, if Germany were defeated, and the importance of British mediation. As we shall see in Chapter 8, the speeches by Liberal and Labour MPs in the crucial debates on the declaration of war suggest that Angell was not without influence.[15] However, it should be noticed that it was his colleague from the Garton Foundation, Arthur Balfour, who ended the debate in the

House of Commons by dismissing these speeches with contempt. Balfour and many others believed that the threat to the balance of power, Britain's commitments to France and the German invasion of Belgium overrode in importance the arguments which Angell and the Liberals were advancing. Late in life Angell admitted, 'where my work failed mainly was in giving a plain and simple answer to the question: "how shall a political truth once established, be translated into a workable policy?"'[16] Nowhere was this clearer than in Balfour's behaviour in August 1914.

Bloch and Angell were often misinterpreted then and later as suggesting that war had become impossible; what they actually argued, like Cobden and Bright before them, was that a great war would be economically devastating. Both Bloch and Angell believed that it might destroy the foundations of the Western economy and bring revolution in its wake. It is the fate of armchair strategists to be misunderstood or misinterpreted. After the First World War, strategists also had to try to influence debate when the elite consensus was profoundly anti-military and unsympathetic even to addressing strategic issues. However, in other ways, the general study of international affairs made rapid progress. Professorships were founded at Aberystwyth and the London School of Economics to turn the subject into an academic pursuit. The Royal Institute of International Affairs was also established to give more rigour to the debate and its annual *Survey of International Affairs*, edited for the most part by the polymath Arnold Toynbee, is still worth reading today for its insights into the politics of the inter-war years.[17] Foreign correspondents filled the newspapers with accounts of the troubles in South America, China or Europe, and frequently added to these brief stories by publishing books on their experiences.[18] Most newspapers had several correspondents in all the major capitals of the world and the large number of weekly and monthly periodicals gave extensive space to international topics. The Left Book Club claimed 60,000 members and the corresponding Right Book Club a further 25,000, each publishing informative accounts of foreign events and analyses of the international scene.[19]

The defect, as the British writer E. H. Carr pointed out, though with some exaggeration, in 1945, 'of nearly all [this] thinking, both academic and popular, about international politics in the English-speaking countries from 1919 to 1939 [was] the almost total neglect of the factor of power'.[20] Certainly, the well-known American and British journalists who published their accounts of European and Asian politics, Robert Bruce Lockhart, F. Yeats-Brown, Philip Gibbs, Douglas Reed, John

Gunther and Edgar Mowrer, tended to skirt round military issues.[21] Of course, they occasionally ventured judgements; the American journalist Edgar Mowrer unwisely concluded from the Spanish Civil War that tanks and aircraft were overrated, infantry were still dominant on the battlefield; similarly, in *Japan over Asia*, W. H. Chamberlain added to the widespread underestimation of Japanese warships and aircraft.[22] Generally, however, journalists left strategic judgements to specialised periodicals, such as the *Journal of the Royal United Service Institution*, and to the retired officers who acted as military and naval correspondents for the serious newspapers. The League of Nations itself published the *Armaments Year-Book* which collated reports from governments on their military organisation and the numbers in their armed forces.[23] For the tiny handful who took an interest, it provided at least the rudiments of knowledge about the numerical balance between military forces, even if the more unscrupulous governments bent the information they supplied to suit their interests.

The First World War had certainly accentuated the elite's general reluctance to face military issues squarely. In Britain the war had come increasingly to be represented as a fight against militarism, just as the Second World War was seen 20 years later as a struggle against Fascism.[24] The treaties imposed in 1919 on the defeated powers reduced the size of their armies and navies, and prohibited conscription, because Lloyd George and Woodrow Wilson considered this the best way of lessening the ability of their armed forces to spread their militaristic values across society. The war had been fought 'to end wars' and, exhausted by the costs of the war, the democracies were tempted to act as if the armed forces existed only because of the temporary imperfections of the League of Nations and the slow progress of its discussions on disarmament. As the writer and Cambridge lecturer Goldsworthy Lowes Dickinson put it in 1923, 'war and civilisation are henceforth incompatible... the very existence of mankind is incompatible with the further development of methods of destruction on which science is actually engaged'.[25] Of course, many Europeans took a more pessimistic view of the prospects for violence if Germany rearmed, but anti-militarism was pervasive amongst the elite in Britain and the United States. After Hitler had taken control of Germany, the children's writer A. A. Milne could still claim, 'it is unthinkable that one nation should break faith, and attack another nation. Even if that were not so, nations should take the risk [of espousing disarmament and pacifism] for a cause higher than any national cause, the cause of humanity.' [26] After the casualties in the First World War, it was hardly surprising that Milne should find such perfidy unimaginable, but, unfortunately, Hitler, Mussolini and Tojo were determined to prove him wrong.

There were, nevertheless, a number of original contributions to ideas on security during these years even if, as with Bloch and Angell in the pre-1914 period, their impact was sometimes not what the authors had hoped for. One of the leading British naval analysts of the inter-war period, Hector Bywater has been described by a recent biographer as 'the man who "invented" the Pacific war'.[27] Yet the books Bywater wrote in the 1920s were devoted to alerting Japan and the United States to the destructiveness of such a war. Moreover, the warning to Japan was the more strident because Bywater believed that the Japanese would be defeated if war came. Bywater may have invented the strategy which Japan pursued in 1941, he deplored the politics which led to the conflict. Like Angell, Bywater was a journalist and, therefore, adept at spreading his ideas and he engaged in an extended debate with Franklin Roosevelt in the 1920s, a debate from which, we can now see, he emerged as much the more prescient;[28] like Bloch, he had the sort of imagination which could, to some extent, envision how a great war would develop and tried to integrate military and economic developments.

In the 1920s, when many people in the West had forgotten Japan's devastating victories over Russia in 1904–1905, and were underestimating the Japanese armed forces' professionalism, Bywater pointed out that their warships sacrificed comfort to efficiency and so their submarines cruised for longer than those of other navies because of the toughness and endurance of the crews.[29] Bywater noted that Japan was totally dependent for its trade on the seas between its coasts, Korea and China. These were 'the vital arteries through which her life-blood flows. If they were severed she would perish.'[30] He foresaw that Japan would begin another war, as it had begun the war against Russia in February 1904, by a pre-emptive strike. This time it would attack the US navy and it would then go on to occupy an outer perimeter of islands to protect its empire. The ensuing war would be a 'terrible and protracted struggle' during which the US army would fight its way towards Japan by 'hopping' from island to island, as indeed it did between 1943 and 1945.

By the 1930s Bywater had seen that Britain would be unable to protect its base at Singapore from a Japanese attack, something which so many British politicians and senior officers failed to understand until the disaster occurred, despite their access to classified information. As late as 18 December 1941, L. S. Amery, the secretary of state for India, was still confiding in his diary that he did not expect Singapore to fall.[31]

Equally accurately, Bywater had warned the Japanese against 'provoking the lion' because Britain and the United States would eventually be victorious.[32] Not only was Bywater peculiarly prescient about the shape of a future war, but he had a better idea of the resentment felt in Japan against the West and thus of the threat it presented than some of the British writers who had lived there and of most politicians including Winston Churchill himself.[33]

If British armchair strategists often focused on maritime and financial affairs, Central Europeans, like Bloch, had good reason to meditate on the future of land warfare. British liberals continued to oppose rearmament into the second half of the 1930s, while continental realists understood that the dictatorships were arming for war. The argument was typified by the opposing views of the ageing British Liberal and former editor of *The Economist* Francis Hirst and the continental armchair strategist Max Werner. Hirst's analysis of the arms race appeared in 1937, when the armies raised by Nazi Germany and the Soviet Union were presenting a serious and growing threat to their British and French equivalents. Hirst's objective was to disparage warnings by Winston Churchill and others about the Nazi threat and to demonstrate that the dictatorships were undermining their economies by their military policy. Despite his economic expertise, Hirst proved much more mistaken about the relationship between armaments and war than Bloch had been three decades before.[34] Werner, the student of both armaments and economics, proved far more prophetic.

Born in Kharkov in 1901, Werner became an economist before emigrating to the West and making his living in Weimar Germany as a financial journalist. In 1933 he fled to France where he changed the focus of his interests to military affairs and spent his days in the Vincennes Library of Modern War.[35] He published *Towards the Second World War* in France the year after Hirst's book appeared and it was translated into English and published as the *Military Strength of the Powers* for the Left Book Club in March 1939. Werner not only saw that armoured warfare would dominate the next war but his assessment of the balance of power was also largely accurate. Germany and the Soviet Union now dominated Europe, Italy was a non-entity because of its industrial weakness and Mussolini's exaggerated idea of the importance of numbers of soldiers as opposed to equipment. Britain and France had failed to rearm quickly enough, while the United States was slowly but inexorably building up immense forces to challenge Japan.[36] Much of this now seems commonplace, but it was certainly not so at the start of the war when General Ismay, who was later to be Churchill's chief of staff, believed that, if Britain fell, the United States would follow suit.[37] It showed that an armchair strategist, working in his library and studying the mass of data published by the various armies, could produce estimates at least as accurate as many of those made within governments by those with access to secret intelligence.[38] Like Bywater, Werner foresaw the ultimate defeat of Japan, he also predicted the humiliation of Italian forces in the Mediterranean and the titanic struggle on the Eastern Front. It was that struggle which dominated Werner's next books, *Battle for the World*, published in 1941 and *The Great Offensive* which came out a year later.[39] In these he rightly pointed out that the Eastern Front was playing the pivotal role which the Western Front had taken in the First World War.

Werner agreed with the most famous British strategic writer during the inter-war years, Basil Liddell Hart, that the democracies' security policy had failed during the 1930s. Liddell Hart had served in the army during the First World War and became, along with J. F. C. Fuller, the foremost advocate of armoured warfare. In the 1920s he also developed a series of original ideas on grand strategy and wrote a number of major works on military history.[40] In the mid-1930s Liddell Hart believed Britain too weak to send an army to help France against a German attack and, though he moved somewhat from this position after the Munich agreement, his position was always ambiguous.[41] He knew many of the British political leaders and was for a time an adviser to Hore Belisha, the war minister. But he despaired of ever persuading politicians to take sufficient account of strategic factors, rather than public opinion or political advantage. In his memoirs he dwells on two of their decisions as evidence of strategic ignorance. In March 1939, when Hitler seized Czechoslovakia, the Prime Minister Neville Chamberlain suddenly reversed his policy of appeasement and guaranteed Polish territorial integrity. Liddell Hart believed that Chamberlain made these changes either because of 'the pressure of public indignation over "Prague", or his own indignation, or his humiliation at having been made to look a fool in the eyes of the British public'. Confidential diaries suggest that it was, in fact, a final attempt to deter the Nazis and a consequence of the feeling that at last 'something must be done' about Nazi aggression.[42] In any case, like many serving officers, Liddell Hart felt that it was absurd to give a guarantee that could not be fulfilled; more unusually, and probably rightly, he argued that it provoked Hitler to attack and thus to begin the war in September 1939.[43]

The second decision, which Liddell Hart deplored, was the sudden introduction of conscription on 28 March 1939. Again this was prompted by public anger with the government for its policies. But Liddell Hart believed it would cause confusion and slow the pace of mechanising the armed forces.[44] He also argued that it would increase Hitler's determination to attack before British preparations had reached their zenith. All this, together with what Liddell Hart saw as the vacuous boastfulness of Britain's political leaders, increased his alarm. He had already noted in his diary on 19 March:

> More vehement, and boastful talk, of our offensive strength, it is only too probable that the incompetence of the policy which has brought us towards a war will be exceeded by the incompetence of our policy in war – that we shall pay the maximum price for the minimum of effort. And we shall be lucky if we do not damage our strength irreparably before we learn by hard experience to fight in a way that conserves it.[45]

Given such mistakes, he seems to have become convinced that Britain would be defeated, cut off most of his military and journalistic contacts, and retired to Devon to recover from a heart attack he had had in June 1939.

Liddell Hart's worst fears were not to be realised thanks to the Channel separating Britain from the continent and the entry first of the Soviet Union and then the United States into the war. In the meantime, as pointed out earlier, once Britain had been expelled from Europe in June 1940, the only way it could attack Nazi Germany was by blockade or from the air. The leading British civilian expert on airpower in these years was J. M. Spaight, a lawyer who joined the civil service in 1901, and he made his reputation with the publication of his assessment of the legal position of *Aircraft in Peace and War* in 1919 and with the first of three editions of *Air Power and War Rights* in 1924. His 1919 book was one of the earliest to examine the legal problems posed by peacetime air travel, showing how rules about the sovereignty of airspace, the registration of aircraft, the certification of aircraft and pilots and responsibility for collisions were gradually being worked out.[46] Spaight rose to become Principal Assistant Secretary in the Air Ministry by 1934 and held that post until he retired three years later, collecting the conventional accolades of a CB and a CBE along the way.

Histories of airpower in the period tend to focus on the writings of the Italian commentator Giulio Douhet, who was regarded as the foremost exponent of the view that bombing attacks on civilians would decide future wars. Douhet published the first part of his major work, *The Command of the Air* in 1921, supplementing it in 1926, 1928, 1929 and 1930. The nub of his argument was that aircraft had great offensive power, but had very limited defensive capability. Anti-aircraft guns were useless and many fighters were needed to shoot down just one bomber. Auxiliary aircraft, that is planes employed by armies or navies, were also a diversion of effort from the real business of airpower which was to attack enemy airfields, factories and cities.[47] The terrible threat from the air would be beneficial because it would deter people from resorting to war since, wherever they lived, they would be as much at risk as the armed forces. The problem with this prognostication was that the Italian people might be deterred but Mussolini might ignore their feelings.

The contrast with Spaight's analysis of airpower is instructive. In 1938 Spaight published what was arguably his best book, *Air Power in the Next War*, in a series edited by Liddell Hart. Spaight wisely stressed the uncertainties about what would happen in a future great war, but he meticulously compared the total destruction which Douhet argued would overcome the civilian population with the actual destruction wrought by bombers in the Spanish Civil War and in the Japanese attacks on China. This had been bad enough, but it had not encompassed whole cities and it had not brought victory to the aggressors.[48] Spaight contended that air power theorists grossly magnified the number and effectiveness of the bombers under construction; 'the programmes are not colossal, and they will not give the number of machines required if the forecasts of universal destruction are to be realised'. The published estimates of the numbers of German aircraft varied widely but all the figures were an order of magnitude less than the 27,000 planes Britain had produced in 1918 and which alone could not have defeated Germany.[49] He went on to argue, again correcting Douhet, that so many were needed for training and maintenance that far more modest numbers could be kept on the front line and that large numbers would be employed in conjunction with the army and navy since 'a war without surface encounter is improbable in the extreme'.

Spaight did not deny that air raid precautions were necessary or that war would bring civilian casualties. He accepted the erroneous notion that totalitarian states were preparing to defeat their enemies through strategic bombing alone; 'we have the evidence of statements by Field-Marshal Göring and others...and also the record of what German airmen serving with General Franco have actually done. The signs and tokens of the wrath to come are clear.'[50] But Spaight was right to say that the threat was exaggerated; we can now see that the German air force was designed, in direct contrast to Douhet's proposals, to support its army and navy. The Luftwaffe's strategic attacks on cities during the battle of Britain in 1940 were not the outcome of long-term plans. Moreover, it was not until three years later that Bomber Command and the US Army Air Force were powerful enough to begin to devastate German cities in the way that Douhet had believed was already within the capacity of air forces in the 1920s.

Finally, and most importantly, as Spaight presciently noted, bombers had proved extremely vulnerable to enemy fighters in the First World War and they had to be escorted by fighters during the Spanish Civil War.[51] We now know that bombers unescorted by fighters could not then operate in daylight against a well-defended country. Had the British elite accepted Spaight's conclusion, their policy might have been less fearful in 1938 and 1939. His inability to convince national leaders to take a cool rational look at the 'bomber threat' shows that judicious assessments by armchair strategists are only too likely to be obscured by simplistic and alarmist phrases which make newspaper headlines, particularly if these phrases come from well-known politicians or commentators.[52] Armchair critics may have some influence in the long run, but in the 1930s the democracies were not to be given time before they were swept along by the tide of war.

Analyses by armchair strategists in the inter-war years thus appear to have had a limited impact on policy or opinion, and on the decision to declare war in 1939. If Bywater influenced policy at all, it was, allegedly, Japanese policy, and in the opposite direction to the one he intended. Liddell Hart's failure to persuade Hore Belisha and his colleagues to develop armoured forces as fast as he hoped led to his increasing disillusionment and to his exile in Devon. He was wholly opposed to the declaration of war in September 1939. Despite the prescience of his strategic views, Werner never achieved a wide readership in Britain until the war years when he became a journalist with *Reynolds News*. Finally, it might be supposed that, as a civil servant, Spaight was closer to the centre of power but he was unable to prevent the excessive fear of attacks from the air which helped to paralyse British policy up to 1939.

Once Europe had been overrun and as the United States gradually mobilised its industrial strength for war, it became the centre of the debate on war and peace. It was no accident that Werner made his home in New York and that Norman Angell came to spend much of his time in the United States. US armchair strategists sometimes appeared to have a considerable influence on administrations or at least foresaw what their strategy would be. It was in Washington in 1943 and 1944 that the distinguished US columnist Walter Lippmann sketched the outlines of the alliance systems which were to deter each other and help to prevent the outbreak of conflict after 1945. Lippmann led the move by his fellow countrymen away from the idealism of the Wilson years and the isolationism of the 1930s, to the interventionism of US policy after 1945.[53] He argued that all their previous policies had failed because they had relied on moralistic declarations rather than on realistic appraisals of international affairs. Such an appreciation should lead the United States to maintain forces within Britain and France after the fighting ended because it now recognised that their security was vital to its own. It would also be necessary 'to maintain combined staffs, intelligence services and military planning boards' – in other words much what NATO was to do.[54] Just as it is difficult to show how revolutionary the insights of Bloch, Werner and Bywater had been, so it is difficult to grasp the full extent of the revolution in security policy which Lippmann was proposing. No European country had *ever* previously based its armed forces in the territory of a group of sovereign states in peacetime.[55] There were no French forces in Russia or Russian forces in France in 1914 although their alliance had existed for two decades; the British government did not send forces to Poland in 1939, despite the guarantee London offered against attack. Not only were bases in foreign territory a major innovation after 1945 but so was the maintenance in peacetime of the sort of joint command and intelligence structure which had grown up in wartime.

In 1944 Lippmann predicted that three 'strategic systems' would emerge; the Atlantic Community, the Russian and the Chinese – a prediction which paralleled Orwell's but preceded it by half a decade. Contacts between them could be harmonious if they did not interfere in each other's sphere and if 'the foreign relations of every state [were] definitely fixed and not suddenly alterable...The evil...is a fluctuating, erratic foreign policy which causes uncertainty, tension, intrigue, insecurity.'[56] This was what NATO and the Warsaw Pact were to provide for four decades after the Second World War. Unaware of the development of nuclear weapons, Lippmann argued that the Soviet Union and the West had nothing to fear from each other. The elephant and the whale were each impervious to the other's strength. However, he forecast that US opinion could turn against the Soviet Union, particularly if Moscow repressed the Eastern European states. It needed to respect their independence while relying on them to provide a bulwark for its territory from outside attack. In the event, this proved impossible and the natural Western urge to 'play the Good Samaritan' would undermine

Lippmann's favoured policy of non-interference in the Soviet sphere of influence, just as Soviet ideology prevented it from abstaining from interference in the Western sphere.

Here, some years before the outbreak of the Cold War and long before NATO was a speck in the eye of Western policy makers, Lippmann had foreseen much of the future. The US analyst Robert Kagan argued in 2002 that 'no one would have spoken of a common grand strategy for the West before the Cold War'.[57] In fact Lippmann had produced just such an imaginative tour de force which did precisely that and achieved in grand strategy what Bloch had attained with his tactical vision at the end of the 19th century and Wells had achieved with his prophecies of tanks and nuclear weapons in the next decade. Moreover, Lippmann's proposed strategy helped to avoid war, while Bloch's gloomy vision was, as we have seen, either ignored or had the reverse effect in August 1914 to the one intended. Of course, Lippmann did not grasp the complete picture; the Western countries did sometimes use their forces unilaterally in ways which Lippmann hoped would disappear. On the other hand, Lippmann's predictions about the Third World were more prescient than Orwell's gloomy forecasts. Lippmann foresaw both the imminence of decolonisation and that it would unfortunately lead to 'prolonged and complicated civil and international strife' but 'eventually one or more constellations will probably form in the Hindu and in the Moslem Worlds'.[58] It has taken half a century for the Moslem states to create such a religious grouping and for India to emerge as a great power.

The US columnist's books can be compared with the writings of one of the leading British commentators in the period, E. H. Carr, a diplomat, assistant editor on *The Times*, professor at Aberystwyth and lecturer in Oxford and Cambridge. In *Conditions of Peace*, published in 1942, Carr reflected the demoralisation of the European elite. He argued that all the objectives which democracies had claimed to be fighting for had been discredited. Liberal democracy was outdated because it had failed to solve the problem of unemployment; capitalism would have to be replaced by state direction and small states were obsolete because they could not defend themselves and stood in the way of the need to develop ever larger economic units. Admittedly, Carr saw that the Europeans countries would collaborate together far more than they had ever done in the past and was, to that extent, a prophet of the European Union but his world vision was driven by feelings of pessimism and decline.[59] Fifty years later one can see that Carr's American colleague was a much better prophet; city states, such as Singapore, have flourished in a largely free-trading world, nationalisation and state direction of industry are discredited even in Russia and China, and democracy has been hailed by one US analyst as the only living political ideology.[60]

Lippmann's close contacts with the political establishment in Washington helped him foresee and influence US policy in the post-war years. And that establishment was entering into its own as the government of the world's strongest power. The problem for British and other commentators was that they were now so far removed from this centre that their ideas often seemed irrelevant or unrealistic. It was only in areas which did not interest US administrations and, in particular, guerrilla warfare that British commentators continued to exercise real influence. In the crucial area of nuclear strategy, on which the survival of the NATO and Warsaw Pact countries depended during the Cold War, US thinkers predominated.

The air of irrelevance pervading European contributions is illustrated by one of the most original and provocative works in the nuclear field, which was written by P. M. S. Blackett, a former naval officer and a distinguished scientist who had made a significant contribution to the British campaign against the U boats during the Battle of the Atlantic.[61] Blackett published *The Military and Political Implications of Atomic Energy* in 1948. It was a sustained polemic against Western policy in general and particularly against its reliance on nuclear weapons to deter a Soviet attack. Blackett argued that deterrence would not work because allied bombers could not penetrate Soviet defences and, therefore, they would be unable to restrain the Kremlin. Blackett drew his conclusions from what he saw as the failure of strategic bombing during the Second World War. Moreover, it was Blackett who popularised the idea that Washington had ruthlessly used nuclear weapons on Hiroshima and Nagasaki not to defeat the Japanese, who were already beaten, but to flaunt its nuclear power before the Kremlin.[62]

Blackett said nothing about the nature of the Soviet state. His criticisms were directed against the Western powers. Yet this was the height of the Cold War, when information about Stalin's mass murders in the Gulag Archipelago was trickling out into the West and when the Soviets were crushing the independence of the East European states. Blackett dismissed Lippmann's idea of a US commitment to defend Western Europe as unrealistic and undesirable, and argued in favour of British isolation. In other words his policy was the polar opposite of Lippmann's. It was at this time that Moscow was most vociferous both against Western nuclear policy and against its military coordination. This identity between Blackett's views and Moscow's, and Blackett's disparagement of Western policy in general, encouraged George Orwell, the Central European physicist Edward Teller and the US Intelligence services to consider him a Soviet agent. In his memoirs Teller recalled having a furious argument with Blackett, who maintained that the West should abandon Berlin to Soviet control, presumably to avoid provoking the Kremlin.[63]

Blackett knew that his views were unlikely to influence his countrymen. As he wrote in 1948: 'When the book was finished I found I had signally failed to write a recipe for action which would be likely at the present time to commend itself to the political taste of a majority of my fellow countrymen. But for this the state of the world, not I, must take the blame.'[64] This was typical of both his self-confidence and his feeling of alienation from the Anglo-American mainstream in 1948. The reviewer for the *Journal of the Royal Institute of International Affairs* referred to the author's 'odd tendency to view in a rosy light any Soviet attitudes and to be critical of the natural degree of caution showed by the United States in handling a situation for which that State feels so deep a responsibility'.[65] Similarly, the reviewer in the *Royal Engineers Journal* accused Blackett of justifying Soviet attitudes and increasing international suspicions.[66] Blackett's opposition to a coordinated Western policy and to reliance on nuclear deterrence put him so far outside mainstream thinking as to be irrelevant to the central debates.

Similarly, a decade later, Sir Stephen King-Hall, another former British naval officer, suggested an original but fundamentally unrealistic Western policy as a substitute for NATO and its nuclear weapons. King-Hall argued that 'defence had been revolutionized materially but remained mentally stagnant.... We must break through the thought-barrier in defence thinking and see what we find on the other side, a thought-barrier represented by the centuries old idea of most people that violence is the only practical means of defence against violence.'[67] Instead of relying on nuclear weapons or even on conventional forces, which he believed could not defeat a Soviet attack, King-Hall argued that Britain should prepare for mass non-violent resistance to a Warsaw Pact invasion. Such a policy would have to be agreed between the political parties, then taught in schools and in new colleges which would replace the conventional military establishments. King-Hall's strategy would have taken years to prepare but it would have avoided the risks of annihilation implicit in current policies. The trouble was that it lacked credibility; even India, where Gandhi's tactics of passive resistance weakened British colonialism in the 1930s, had maintained conventional armed forces when it became independent in 1947. Fear of nuclear weapons was widespread in 1958 but it did not inspire confidence in King-Hall's alternative.

Nuclear weapons and the two alliances froze the status quo in the Northern hemisphere during the Cold War. At the same time, the nationalist movements, which Lippmann had foreseen, were undermining the European colonies in the Third World. When the Europeans tried to resist, they found themselves confronting guerrilla armies which sapped their will in bloody, prolonged and debilitating conflicts. It was here that British writers made their greatest contribution to post-war thinking about war and overseas intervention. Where the British simply abandoned their colonies to competing groups of insurgents, as in Palestine, or where they rushed the final move to independence, as in South Asia, they left behind quarrels which continue to embitter international relations half a century later. As they sometimes offered a way in which Britain could hand power gradually to nationalists who were sympathetic to democracy and the rule of law, experts on counter-insurgency could play a major role in stabilising the post-colonial world.

Guerrilla warfare had always troubled the imperial powers and British military theory, whatever happened in practice, had stressed the importance of understanding why people supported the guerrillas and what could be done to persuade them that violent change was not in their interests; in other words, the theory saw the struggle against guerrillas as essentially a political battle for people's minds, with the military playing an ancillary role. In a classic study of *Imperial Policing*, published in 1934, Major General Charles Gwynn had argued that it was crucial for governments not to treat the mass of people as hostile:

> The admixture of rebels with a neutral or loyal element of the population adds to the difficulty of the task. Excessive severity may antagonize this element, add to the number of rebels, and leave a lasting feeling of bitterness.

Similarly, if the government and armed forces were faced with riots:

> Responsibility is often thrown on quite junior officers. Mistakes of judgement may have fear-reaching results. Military failure can be retrieved, but where a population is antagonized or the authority of government seriously upset, a long period may elapse before confidence is restored and normal stable conditions are reestablished.[68]

No doubt he was thinking of the massacre in Amritsar in northern India in April 1919, when General Dyer had ordered his troops to fire on Indian demonstrators killing several hundred and inadvertently giving a massive fillip to the Indian independence movement.[69] Gwynn argued that the civil government, not the military, should always control policy and that minimum force should invariably be applied to avoid antagonising the population.

Robert Thompson's writings on insurgency in the 1960s and 1970s fell into the same tradition. After a distinguished military record in Burma in the Second World War, Thompson spent 12 years in the Malayan civil service during the communist insurgency there and four years advising the South Vietnamese government on the same subject. He distilled his experience into a number of principles, which he believed governments should apply when dealing with guerrillas; first, that the government 'must have a clear political aim: to establish and maintain a free, independent and united country which is politically and economically stable and viable'. Secondly, the authorities would always have to function within the law and resist the temptation to go beyond it, which has so often overcome democracies leading them to torture and even murder those suspected of involvement in guerrilla operations.[70] Thirdly, they must have an overall plan of the way the guerrillas are to be defeated and government departments coordinated. Finally, the government should give priority to defeating political subversion, rather than to killing the insurgents.[71]

All this might seem either feeble or banal, but it is not the normal response to guerrilla warfare by politicians and armed forces who often lash out against those they think responsible and focus their attention on killing insurgents rather than winning the support of the mass of people. Although Thompson tried to advise the United States and its South Vietnamese allies in the 1960s, he was unable to convince them to reduce their reliance on conventional warfare and the expensive military equipment which accompanied it. To cope with US firepower the insurgents disappeared underground, digging out extensive subterranean villages and re-emerging, when least expected, to harry US forces. By 1973 the US public had had enough and the Nixon administration signed a humiliating peace treaty promising to withdraw.

Each generation apparently has to relearn these lessons. Very soon after the Anglo-American invasion of Iraq in 2003 the invading forces appeared to have lost Iraqi support and to be fighting a defensive war against ubiquitous guerrillas whose suicide bombers made them even more formidable in urban areas than previous generations of insurgents.

Much the same was true in Afghanistan where NATO forces found it very difficult to distinguish between innocent civilians and guerrillas, and where, because of their shortage of numbers, they needed air cover to protect them, although its use threatened the lives of the civilians and further alienated them from the foreign troops. Unless such troops can mingle amongst the people, help them and gather intelligence willingly offered to them, they simply become targets for guerrilla attack.

Politicians, led by Denis Healey, have accused some armchair strategists of being too belligerent, of enjoying the prerogative of the harlot, power without responsibility and of encouraging irresponsible interventionism. Yet, none of the armchair strategists discussed above could be described in this way. Bloch, Angell and Bywater intended their books as warnings of the destructive wars they believed were impending. Werner wanted to alert the democracies to the peril that faced them because of their tardy rearmament, and Spaight rightly feared that they were cowed by exaggerated fears of air attack into waiting until it was almost too late to resist Axis expansion. Blackett and King-Hall were searching for ways of avoiding reliance on nuclear weapons and the threats of mutual destruction they implied, while Robert Thompson was attempting to find a way the Western countries could both defeat guerrillas and help the Third World advance towards democracy.

Strategists recall that the outcome of military intervention is always uncertain. As the most famous Western strategist put it:

> From the very start there is an interplay of possibilities, probabilities, good luck and bad that weaves its way throughout the length and breadth of the tapestry. In the whole range of human activities, war most closely resembles a game of cards.[72]

The illusion harboured by statesmen that war may be short is one of the primary reasons for unwise interventions.[73] Many of the leading British armchair strategists today grew up during the Vietnam War. They know that elite public opinion and some elements in the media may encourage the government to undertake a war and then turn against the struggle if it is prolonged. They have generally been cautious about encouraging involvement in warfare and argued in favour of finding alternatives. While they have rarely been as imaginative and prescient as Tennyson, Wells or Orwell, they have destroyed the mythology that only professional military officers can comment knowledgably and sensitively about strategic affairs. Thus they have helped the process of widening the debate to take in the whole community. Bloch earned the sneers of many soldiers and journalists when he correctly predicted how warfare was developing. The atmosphere is very different today when academics and researchers from the International Institute for Strategic Studies and the Stockholm International Peace Research Institute crowd into the television studios to comment on war and the threat of warfare, and the shelves of the bookshops creak under the weight of their publications. But that places more responsibility on their shoulders to weigh their comments carefully, not to pretend that they have expertise beyond their chosen field and to avoid encouraging politicians to take hasty decisions.[74]

7
The Professional Military

On the evening of 31 March 1982 Prime Minister Thatcher was told by her Secretary of State for Defence John Nott that the Argentine fleet appeared to be on its way to attack the Falkland Islands, which were defended by a handful of Royal Marines, and that the islands could not, once fallen, be retaken. However, when the First Sea Lord Admiral Henry Leach finally reached the meeting, he informed the Prime Minister that a task force led by two aircraft carriers could be readied within 48 hours and that, if lost, the islands could be retaken, though at the cost of several ships. Apart from the failure of Intelligence and of coordination between departments before the Argentine attack,[1] the absence of the Chief of Defence Staff, who was in New Zealand, and the division of opinion between the Secretary of State and the First Sea Lord, the governmental system worked as most people would expect it to work. The Prime Minister wanted to recapture the islands, the senior military officer most directly involved informed her what was militarily practical and what the costs might be. The cabinet had then to decide whether to fight or whether the potential losses were too great, and Parliament confirmed the decision, though it could hardly be informed of the professional advice on the likely costs.[2] Many people would imagine this was how the governmental system normally worked.

But, in fact, the course of events in 1982 was unusual; there has rarely been a discussion of this sort between military leaders and ministers when war threatened over the last 200 years. British leaders have assumed that the country would eventually win and they have not wanted to hear the objections which military leaders might raise to the operations they have in mind. The editor of the *Westminster Gazette* J. A. Spender aptly described British diplomacy in the

19th century as 'an audacious game of bluff with a military force which was small, antiquated and quite unequal to the tasks proposed for it'. He described the consequences as 'splendidly reckless', citing the example of Palmerston's behaviour, as prime minister, during the Prussian attack on Denmark in 1864. The government admitted privately that Britain could only mobilise 20,000 ill-equipped men to face 200,000 or 300,000 well-armed Prussians, yet ministers boasted in the Parliament that the Danes would not fight alone against the Prussians and thereby implied that Britain would protect them. Palmerston appeared willing to act without considering the balance of military power and consequently faced the choice between public humiliation and military defeat when Bismarck called his bluff. Under pressure from wiser cabinet members, he chose humiliation.[3]

The memoirs by the Foreign Secretary Edward Grey, by the Lord President of the Council John Morley and other government ministers give the impression that in August 1914 senior officers were not asked for their assessment of the military implications of declaring war. One of the most influential officers at that time, General Henry Wilson claimed subsequently that he had to lobby hard to have the army's voice heard at all. Of course it might be said that the situation was different in 1914 from 1982 because plans had already been drawn up to send an expeditionary force to assist the French in the event of a German attack. The cabinet had only to decide whether to implement them. Argentine aggression against the Falklands was much less expected and, therefore, new plans had to be made and thus the government needed more extensive military advice. But this distinction between the two crises does not withstand examination. The majority of the cabinet were not aware of the detailed military plans in 1914 and their existence did not affect the nature of the discussion. In any case, the cabinet tried to change the plans fundamentally once war was declared. But British behaviour was not unusual in the Europe of 1914. According to the US historian Alfred Vagts:

It does not appear that to any leader was put that straight question which [the French Premier] Caillaux presented to [General] Joffre during the Agadir crisis of 1911: 'General, it is said that Napoleon only gave battle when he thought that he had at least a sixty percent chance of victory. Have we a seventy percent chance of victory if the situation drives us to war?' Joffre replied: 'No, I do not think we have it.' Caillaux: 'that's good. We shall then negotiate.'[4]

This lack of communication between civilian leaders and the responsible military officers was repeated in Britain in 1939. Many senior officers agreed with Liddell Hart that the guarantee given by the government to Poland in March 1939 made no strategic sense because it was impossible to send sufficient forces to protect Poland against a German attack or to deter such aggression by movements elsewhere. Critics included the former CIGS, Lord Milne, who wrote of the declaration of war:

> It was said of Mr Pitt that the statesman responsible for declaring war is apt to be a little vague as to the military means of prosecuting it. If Lord Kitchener was alarmed at the fact that the government had entered into the First War without any provision for carrying it on, what will posterity say of Ministers who gave to a foreign power a guarantee the fulfilment of which was beyond the wit of man?[5]

Odd as it may appear, British constitutional practice was at one with advice from the most influential strategic writer on how military and political leaders should interact over the decision to go to war. The Prussian strategist Carl von Clausewitz had argued that statesmen should decide policy, and policy had to guide the use of military force. Statesmen determined the objective and armed forces fulfilled their will. He admitted that 'a certain grasp of military affairs is vital for those [statesmen] in charge of general policy', but suggested that they 'can always get the necessary military information somehow or other'. What statesmen needed was intellect and strength of character.[6] In practice this advice was, and is, imprecise and dangerous. Politicians who had taken no interest in strategy were suddenly faced with the need to take decisions which might lead to the defeat and destruction of their country. At that moment, political judgement was insufficient. A realistic estimate of the chances of victory or defeat, and the likely human and financial costs, was vital and, to take an example from Clausewitz's own time, was not supplied to the British government during the Napoleonic Wars until the Duke of Wellington took control of the campaign in the Peninsula. Moreover, such an estimate has become increasingly difficult since that time.

Transformations in strategy and tactics have become more frequent, as the pace of change in technology and economics has grown. No one could have decided in a matter of hours or days how the evolution of railways, high explosives, submarines, aircraft, tanks, nuclear weapons or precision-guided munitions had affected strategy over the years in advance of the various crises. Given the magnitude of the issues at stake, before going to war, national leaders should ideally take the advice not only of professional military men but also of a variety of other experts including scientists, industrialists, lawyers, armchair strategists, doctors, logistics specialists, experts on the potential campaign theatre, opinion pollsters and economists. Obtaining advice 'somehow or other', in Clausewitz's words, is by no means straightforward and the memoirs of British politicians and senior officers on decision making before the two World Wars hardly suggest that it was either systematic or professional. This would not have been so bad if there was evidence that the decision makers had taken an acute interest in the debates on warfare before 1939. But cabinet ministers are always distracted by the multitude of economic and political issues looming before them in peacetime. Thus, in the 1920s and 1930s, politicians might claim that war was too serious a business to entrust to military men, but most politicians, even if they had themselves served in the First World War, concentrated on domestic and economic issues. In Britain, Winston Churchill was almost alone amongst senior politicians in his interest in military affairs and he was regarded as some sort of anachronism or dangerous and untrustworthy curiosity precisely because he bestrode the strategic debates in Britain for much of the 20th century.

Against this background, politicians and senior military officers found communication between them even more difficult than usual. Field Marshal Ironside, who was appointed Chief of the Imperial General Staff on the day the Second World War began, recorded in his diary in August 1940, 'I have been pondering over the last few weeks, and it astonishes me more and more that [the Prime Minister, Neville] Chamberlain had the courage to declare war on Germany. He certainly didn't want to do so'. One reason, of course, although Ironside did not mention this, was that Parliament pushed the Prime Minister into upholding the guarantee he had given to Poland. Chamberlain might have fought still harder against this pressure if he had realised the military difficulties ahead. Ironside believed that the Prime Minister had no idea of the military strength of the Germans and shared the widespread faith in the French army. He did not know how long it took to manufacture military equipment or that armies had to train for months with new equipment before they could use it effectively. 'I am sure that the Cabinet did not ask the War Office if they thought they were ready for war.... I am sure that the Cabinet did not ask any soldier's advice. *Mine certainly was never asked*' (italics added). Given that the very survival of the nation was at stake, it was an astounding recollection.[7]

Governments continued to avoid receiving candid military advice about pending operations after the Second World War. Before the Suez Operation in 1956 the chiefs of staff were asked to draw up various options for recapturing the Suez Canal, which had been nationalised by the Egyptians, and presented these to ministers.[8] The problem was that this made them complicit and apparently supportive of the government's plans, and the momentum of events and structure of government left them little opportunity to make fundamental criticisms of the enterprise. Yet, according to his account, the First Sea Lord Louis Mountbatten harboured the gravest reservations. Above all, he observed what anybody familiar with events in Palestine, Kenya and Indo-China ought to have known, that, even if the British and French succeeded in recapturing the canal, they would have to protect it against constant guerrilla attacks from infuriated Egyptians. He prepared two letters alerting Anthony Eden, the prime minister, of the dangers but was stopped by the First Lord, Lord Cilcennin, who argued that it would be improper for a First Sea Lord to address the Prime Minister directly. Mountbatten could make his points in the Chiefs of Staff Committee but they could be, and were, ignored by the prime minister.[9] The First Sea Lord was more successful at convincing the Minister of Defence Walter Monckton, who promised to protest against Eden's policy in the tightly knit Egypt Committee which Eden had established to deal with the Suez crisis, but Monckton's protests simply caused embarrassment rather than a change of course. Thus, one of Britain's most disastrous post-1945 military operations went ahead, thereby undermining the country's position in the Middle East and the wider world.

In Britain's next major action, the Falklands War, as we have seen, the system worked effectively, but Mrs Thatcher's memoirs do not give the impression that she consulted the chiefs of staff a decade later when she threw Britain's weight behind the US decision to expel Iraqi forces from Kuwait in 1990.[10] At the time she was in the United States meeting President Bush and encouraging him to take a very strong line with the Iraqis. No doubt, she rightly believed it was obvious that the United States would emerge victorious if it committed itself to driving the Iraqis from Kuwait, but a formal assessment of the military situation by the chiefs of staff would still have been appropriate, particularly if the two governments at any time contemplated overthrowing the Iraqi government as well as liberating Kuwait.

But, let us suppose that governments had asked the leaders of the armed forces for their opinion of the prospects before the two World Wars; if Grey and Asquith had asked the military leaders in August 1914 what the war would cost in terms of casualties, it is inconceivable that the man appointed to command the expeditionary force to France, Field Marshal Sir John French would have predicted that Britain would see 730,000 of its men killed and that the Empire as a whole would lose 1 million, that the investments made over the last century would be dispersed and the country burdened with colossal debts to the United States. Field Marshal Viscount Kitchener, who became war minister in 1914, might have had a better understanding, given his high view of German power and his belief that the war would last several years, but even he might have flinched before admitting to himself, or others, what the cost might be. Similarly, it seems unlikely that Ironside or Sir John Gort, who commanded the expeditionary force to France in 1939, could have calculated the losses Britain was to suffer over the six years of the Second World War.

The constitutional system worked well in 1982 because the Falklands War was limited and conventional, but committing a country to a world war is like fugitives jumping into a great river in full spate to escape their pursuers. If they are powerful swimmers they may hope to land lower down, and if they are familiar with the river, they may know where the currents and eddies are likely to be, but they will still be at the mercy of unknown and, as the comments by Joffe, Milne, Ironside and others suggest, this encourages a note of caution. Even if the military factors were calculable in wartime, which they are not because troops and weaponry are frequently untested in combat, political events are often crucial; Hitler's attack on the Soviet Union in June 1941 and Japan's attack on the Western powers six months later largely determined the outcome of the Second World War because they brought US and Soviet power into the equation, but they could not have been foreseen when Britain went to war in 1939, and forecasting them was not, in any case, something to which military expertise could contribute.

Not only is it impossible to forecast the course of a great war, but serving officers are unlikely to be able to predict when a successful conventional intervention will turn into a prolonged war against guerrillas, this is determined by the political balance, mood and culture of a 'defeated' state. What they can say is that, it if were to do so, a successful struggle against insurgents would last a decade, at the very least, would be bloody, and unpopular at home and abroad. In 1945 many believed, because of the indomitable courage they had shown, that the Germans and Japanese would go on fighting as guerrillas once their conventional armies had been defeated; yet, in the event, they made virtually no resistance. As we saw in Chapter 4, in the early 1990s

British military leaders hesitated to embroil themselves with the Serbs because of their reputation for resisting the Nazis in the Second World War. The British army had been struggling against the IRA for two decades in a tedious war, which took more than 3000 lives and in which their behaviour was under intense international media scrutiny.[11] Senior American army officers were equally reluctant to involve themselves in 'another Vietnam'. After 9/11 because of his experiences in Vietnam, Colin Powell led the 'doves' in George W. Bush's administration, while those who had evaded service in the war, led by Bush himself, apparently believed that US forces would be universally welcomed in Iraq in March 2003.[12]

But none of this means that senior officers should not be asked for their views, any more than an expert swimmer should be ignored when considering swimming in a dangerous river. Over the last 200 years society has come to rely ever more extensively on specialists, and the military are the specialists in warfare. There have been specialists for thousands of years, including priests, apothecaries, shepherds, cowherds and, indeed, soldiers, but now there are far more professions and their knowledge is ever more voluminous and esoteric. Non-specialists rely on specialists although they also resent this dependence. Despite what was said above about the inability of senior officers to foresee all the horrors of the two World Wars, by and large specialists will be more pessimistic than non-specialists because they know what can go amiss. Economists and businessmen know what can go wrong with the economy; environmentalists fear man's impact on the earth's biosphere; astronomers fear that an asteroid may hit the earth. The Marquis of Salisbury expressed the point famously in a letter written in June 1877 when many of the professions were becoming more securely established:

> No lesson seems to be so deeply inculcated by the experience of life as that you should never trust experts. If you believe the doctors, nothing is wholesome: if you believe the theologians, nothing is innocent: if you believe the soldiers, nothing is safe. They all require to have their strong wine diluted by a very large mixture of common sense.[13]

The financial demands of the professional soldier or sailor have to be 'diluted' in peacetime, because otherwise they would denude the national budget in order to insure against all military threats, but in preparing for war their caution is surely wise.[14] Their anxieties may sometimes be exaggerated but they know how easy it is to become involved in conflicts and how difficult it is to extricate armies from those which turn into disasters.[15] If Britain had a written constitution, there would be a good deal to be said for laying down that a government *has* to consult the chiefs of staff and listen to their estimates of the costs and likely outcome of an impending conflict before committing the country to war. The Ministry of Defence is now far better organised than the Admiralty and War Office were when J. A. Spender was writing, but the chiefs of staff do not have as much influence as they ought to do when the lives of troops and sometimes even the future of the country depend upon the government making the right decision about overseas intervention.

The First World War was the first total conflict fought when the armed forces had become a distinct professional group. A century beforehand, the Napoleonic Wars had broken out before the War Office and Admiralty had begun their very slow transformation into effective bureaucracies. For more than a decade, the Prime Minister, the younger Pitt dominated British strategy and dispersed forces across the globe in an ineffective effort to halt the expansion of French power. It was not until after Pitt's death in January 1806, and when Wellington came to command the British army in the Iberian Peninsula in 1809, that Britain acquired a strategy worthy of the name which, by supporting the Spanish guerrillas, began the process which led to Napoleon's defeat.[16] Wellington helped to protect the armed forces from public criticism in Britain because he stressed the importance of respecting the lives and property of the Portuguese and Spanish civilians amongst whom the war was fought, and winning them over in the struggle against the French. This was good military strategy but it was also highly attractive to the British elite. His published dispatches are full of warnings to his own and allied troops against looting. He was reluctant to take Spanish forces into France when he invaded enemy territory because he knew they would want revenge on the French people. When the allies placed him in charge of their occupation forces in France, he did his best to restrain the repression of the French people by the other allies and to end the occupation as quickly as possible. Furthermore, he took a thoroughly modern and instrumental attitude to warfare as a whole. He deplored casualties and regarded the romantic view, propagated by Napoleon, that wars are justified by the 'glory' they bring, as unmitigated nonsense.[17] In sum, Wellington was the ideal commander of coalition forces supported by a democracy. He brought victories after years of defeats under Pitt but not at excessive cost.[18]

On the outbreak of the First World War, the British Expeditionary Force was dispatched to assist the French and Belgians hold the line against the German advance in the crucial theatre of the war. As Bloch had forecast, the fighting bogged down into a vast siege, characterised by trenches, barbed wire, machine guns and heavy artillery. Most senior British officers believed that the only way to defeat the Germans was by concentrating the armies as they were raised in this decisive theatre and assisting the French to wear down their German counterparts. Politicians, worried about public opinion turning against the war and impatient with the explanations for delays put forward by senior officers, searched for some way of breaking the stalemate by attacking Germany via its Turkish or Balkan allies. They criticised professional military officers for what they saw as their conservatism and lack of imagination, and their waste of lives in frontal attacks on German trenches. We can now see that the professionals were right to oppose the frittering away of British forces in subsidiary theatres and to regard this as simply an attempt to repeat Pitt's failed strategy against France 100 years before. The politicians were correct to see that the officer corps were slow to grasp the revolutionary nature of the problem facing them, but they were not as conservative as they have often been painted. The First World War was technically highly innovative; at sea it saw the introduction of submarines and ships carrying aircraft; in the air it saw the first effective use of bombers, reconnaissance aircraft and fighters; and on the Western front, chemical weapons, tanks and flamethrowers were brought into service to try to break the stalemate. That these were not wholly effective simply demonstrated the overwhelming superiority of defensive over offensive technology at that period. A siege can only be ended successfully either by starving the besieged into surrender or by breaking through their defences.

After the war ended, the struggle to apportion blame for the losses on the Western Front was not just an argument about the past but a battle to influence the present and future between the armed forces and the politicians. Whoever coined the phrase, 'war is too serious a thing to be left to military men', it was from this period that the phrase became fashionable.[19] On the other side of the Channel, Lloyd George continued his wartime struggle against the military through his memoirs which contain an extensive, though deeply biased, analysis of the civil–military tensions during the war. Of course, his criticisms were sometimes justified; the former prime minister was, for example, rightly scathing about the Royal Navy's reluctance to introduce convoys to prevent submarine attacks on shipping. It was not until the country had been brought almost to its knees that the Admiralty finally agreed that convoys might solve the problem which, indeed, they very rapidly succeeded in doing.[20]

According to Lloyd George's account, the War Office also seemed 'ever to be... preparing, not for the next war... but for the last one or the last but one.... They only remembered the lessons that were better forgotten because they were inapplicable, and forgot all the experiences by which they ought to have profited because they were a foretaste of the methods of future warfare'.[21] Lloyd George claimed that the War Office and the commanders in the field like Douglas Haig dismissed the importance of machine guns and obstructed the development of tanks.[22] In sum, as he put it towards the end of his memoirs:

> They were not equipped with that superiority in brains or experience over an amateur steeped in the incidents and needs of war which would justify the attitude they struck and the note of assured past-mastership they adopted towards all criticism or suggestion from outside or below. The generals themselves were at least four-fifths amateur, hampered by the wrong training.... In the most crucial matters relating to their own profession our leading soldiers had to be helped out by the politician.[23]

Lloyd George went on to argue that the politicians were too cautious in asserting their authority over an army command which had never attracted men of talent and which had suffered 'a long course of mental subservience and suppression'. Finally, he denigrated senior officers who had shown a 'solicitude' to avoid 'personal jeopardy' during the conflict by avoiding the battlefield altogether.

It was a formidable attack reflecting the bitterness between the government and the senior officers, and the desire to place responsibility for losses on the shoulders of the military. Lloyd George's view became the conventional wisdom in the inter-war period and it is still the opinion of a minority of those who have written about the Great War.[24] But many of the leading modern historians of the First World War, including Brian Bond and John Terraine, have not subscribed to this picture. For example, Terraine dismissed that Lloyd George's claim that the War Office obstructed the production of machine guns. The Ministry ordered all the machine guns that the Vickers company could produce, and extra factories had to be built or converted before production could increase substantially; Field Marshal Haig had been an enthusiast for these weapons since 1898, he always encouraged officers to train with them and tried to obtain as many as possible for the army. By the end of the war, nearly 240,000 machine guns had been manufactured for the British army.[25] Terraine also disputed the criticisms by Lloyd George and others that the high command had wasted the advantages Britain should have gained from developing tanks before the Germans.[26] In fact, Haig and others wanted as many tanks as possible but production of such a wholly novel device was always slow, the first models were unreliable and they were vulnerable to armour piercing bullets, not just artillery. Useful as they were, they were not yet the war-winning weapons which Churchill and others hoped.

But, if Haig and some of his officers are now defended by historians, the attacks launched on them by Lloyd George and others in the 1920s were as effective politically as the politicians intended. They altered the terms of the political and strategic debates, reduced the influence of the armed forces in the 1920s and increased that of other institutions. The armed forces were deprived of funds very largely because of Britain's indebtedness after the war and the lack of immediate threats but, with scarce resources, their demands were hardly strengthened when they came to be regarded as incompetent and old fashioned.[27] It was not until the Second World War that the struggle for survival against the Nazis began to change the armed forces' public image.

In the inter-war years, there was a widespread, though erroneous, belief that soldiers were inherently belligerent. On the contrary, the man who was to control the British army as CIGS through most of the Second World War wrote in his diary, when it began, 'I find it impossible to realise. It is all too ghastly even to be a nightmare. The awful futility of it as proved by the last war! .... I suppose that conflicts between Right and Wrong are still necessary and that we have still got to be taught more fully the futility of war.'[28] In this case, the military were not more cautious than the generality, Allenbrooke's comment exactly summarised the horror and resignation with which Britain went to war in 1939.

The Second World War produced no Wellington but neither did it produce a public display of civil–military antagonism as the First World War had done. The friction between Churchill and his military counterparts was intense but hidden within the government. Even before Allenbrooke had become CIGS he had a long disagreement with Churchill who wanted to keep British forces in Western France after the withdrawal from Belgium and Eastern France via Dunkirk. The general had been sent to command the remnant of the British forces which had been left behind to work with the French army even though their allies were in a state of collapse. When Allenbrooke proposed falling back towards the Channel, Churchill told him by telephone:

> I had been sent to France to make the French feel that we were supporting them. I replied that it was impossible to make a corpse feel.... Our talk lasted for half an hour, and on many occasions his arguments were so formed as to give me the impression that he considered I was suffering from 'cold feet'.... This was so infuriating that I was repeatedly on the verge of losing my temper.[29]

Allenbrooke's diary entry illustrates perfectly the reasons for the civil–military clash. Politicians naturally emphasise political objectives rather than military means and in June 1940, if there were any ways of encouraging the French and keeping them in the war, this was obviously vitally important. But Allenbrooke had seen the demoralisation amongst the French soldiers and knew they would not go on fighting. He wanted to save the remainder of the British forces but he was in danger of being accused of cowardice or military incompetence by the prime minister who saw the larger picture, who had studied war but who was not aware of the latest developments in armoured warfare or of the actual situation on the battlefield.

Churchill's instinct was to behave as Pitt had done in the 1790s by launching attacks wherever opportunity appeared to offer except, in Churchill's case, directly across the Channel, where he foresaw that a premature attempt to invade might lead to a catastrophe similar to the landings in the Dardanelles during the First World War. The official naval historian Captain Stephen Roskill commented on the friction between Churchill and the admirals:

> The admirals [he regarded with suspicion] were perhaps too outspoken in their criticisms of some of his ideas, and too forthright in their replies to his signals and letters; for Churchill never took kindly to servicemen who opposed him on any score – which was, no doubt, the result of his experiences during, and study of, the first war.... His erroneous strategic concepts, such as his blindness to the threat from Japan and his share in the responsibility for the disasters in Greece and Crete in 1941, brought very serious consequences in their train.... His addiction to the capture of widely scattered islands led to the dissipation of valuable resources.[30]

As Roskill's quotation suggests, after the Second World War historical criticism often focused on Churchill and his strategic decisions and there was much less tendency to attack the British armed forces as a whole than there had been after the Armistice in 1918. The literature which emerged from the Second World War was very different from the war literature of the 1920s because the experience was so much more varied. The war fought by Fitzroy Maclean in support of Tito's partisans and the struggle for survival by Spencer Chapman and John Cross behind Japanese lines in Malaya were a world apart from the aerial combats in the Battle of Britain, which were just as great a contrast to the ground struggle in Burma.[31] It was only the extensive literature describing the sufferings in the Japanese prisoner of war camps which acquired the quality of sameness that characterised the accounts of the trenches in the First World War.[32] In both cases the reader comes to feel that he could write the story himself after he has read a dozen memoirs. In such circumstances the descriptions often have the identical air of bewildered, and furious, helplessness. But in the First World War the animus was against the officers and against war itself, in the Second World War it was against the enemy and sometimes also against the government which had contributed to their capture by failing to defend Singapore adequately.

Today, half a century later, the British army is now held in high esteem, higher indeed than any other major national institution and higher than any other West European army is held by its people.[33] Its reputation has survived decades of fighting in the most difficult circumstances against guerrillas in Palestine, Malaya, Kenya, Cyprus, Aden and Northern Ireland. As pointed out in the previous chapter, in such wars there is always the temptation to resort to the use of torture to extract information from suspects and to use excessive force against rioters and other civilians. No doubt, on many occasions army actions were open to criticism but there has not been such pervasive failure to maintain civilized standards as overcame French forces during the guerrilla wars in Indo-China and Algeria and United States' forces in Vietnam.[34]

This at least makes it more likely that governments will listen to the views of the armed forces before and during wars. But the struggle to ensure that this is the case is continual and the armed forces are caught in a bind; if they are accused of failing their profession, as they were after the First World War, then their advice will be disparaged; if, on the contrary, they are too successful, there is an increased danger that governments will be tempted to intervene abroad without sufficient thought. In 1982 Admiral Leach told Mrs Thatcher what it would cost to retake the Falkland Islands, subsequent successes in Bosnia and Kosovo encouraged the Blair government to ignore the defeats which guerrillas inflicted on conventional armies in Palestine, Indo-China, Afghanistan, Aden, Algeria and Vietnam; the consequences in Iraq and Afghanistan were all too evident.

Tensions between two very different professions – politician and soldier – are inevitable when they have to work closely together in particularly fraught and dangerous circumstances and over several years. Serving officers can appear as an obstacle to politicians' desire to go to war and an impediment to its rapid conclusion. Politicians are concerned with the ends to be achieved by warfare, serving officers are professionally involved with the means. Politicians want to finish the war as quickly as possible while public and foreign support lasts, officers have a better idea of the costs involved in pushing ahead too rapidly. Politicians have to judge whether senior officers' unwillingness to take a course of action is due to incompetence, conservatism, cowardice or prudent professional analysis. In the end, military commanders know that they and their fellow officers and men will pay the price for wrong strategic calculations.

8

Parliament and War

The right to commit the country to war is part of the royal prerogative in Britain which has passed in practice from the Crown to the government. However, over the last 200 years, whenever the country has become involved in a major war, Parliament has debated the issue as though power resided with the legislative as well as the executive, which, in the end, it does. Had the government been defeated on any of these occasions then it would probably have had to resign. This has never happened. Moreover, before April 1982 open Parliamentary debates were almost entirely confined to discussing the cause for which the country was being asked to fight, during the Falklands War, MPs also began to discuss the means to be employed and the interaction between the two.

This revolution occurred when Mrs Thatcher's government openly told Parliament which ships and aircraft were being mobilised to overturn the Argentine seizure of the Falkland Islands.[1] A government had never openly supplied such information before, though the revolution was unappreciated then and later. Indeed there were complaints in the House of Lords at the time that not enough information had been given to them and absolutely no recognition that, on the last occasion when an imminent war had been debated, the intervention against Egypt in 1956, not a scrap of military information had been offered by the government to the two Houses. During the crucial debate on 2 August 1956, the Prime Minister Anthony Eden merely told MPs that he had been compelled 'to take certain precautionary measures of a military nature', including the movement of 'certain' Royal Navy, Army and RAF units.[2]

Government control over all military information had, in fact, been the norm. On 3 August 1914, the Foreign Secretary Edward Grey told the House that the French Fleet was stationed in the Mediterranean leaving their Channel ports exposed, though the Germans had promised not to

116

attack the ports if Britain pledged neutrality. He made the ludicrously inaccurate forecast that, if Britain came to the aid of the French against the German attack, 'for us with a powerful Fleet, which we believe will be able to protect our commerce, to protect our shores, and to protect our interests, if we are engaged in war, we shall suffer but little more than we shall suffer even if we stand aside'. Furthermore, he assured the members that 'the readiness and efficiency of [the] forces were never at a higher mark than they are today'. Otherwise they were left in ignorance of the government's strategy and intentions.[3] Similarly on 29 August 1939, the Foreign Secretary Lord Halifax told the Lords only that, 'the air defence of the country is now in a state of instant readiness. The whole of our Fighting Fleet is ready at a moment's notice to take up the dispositions which would be necessary in war.' Preparations for the mobilisation of the Territorial and regular Army had been put in hand should this be necessary.[4]

Of course, there had been extensive debates over the previous years about naval and military policy in general, but such debates were confined to a minority of members and the final debates before war broke out were essentially political. Yet governments took daunting risks; in the French Wars British armies amounted to a small fraction of the great continental forces. London made up for this by subsidising its allies,[5] but, until Wellington's army was sent to aid the Spanish, the allies suffered a series of defeats. Similarly, at the start of the First World War, Britain had only a tiny army, the Royal Navy might dominate the seas but it was hardly going to have much impact on Germany in a short war, and most, like Grey, assumed that a long war was impossible for economic reasons. Some might argue that there should have been a debate on this central issue, alongside the legal implications of the German invasion of Belgium or the significance of British obligations to France. What is the use of declaring war if you are impotent to affect its outcome? But public discussion of Britain's weakness would have demoralised Britain's troops and its allies, and thus, even if the conventions had been more permissive about public debate, MPs would have had to evade the central issue in their open discussions.

It was not just government spokesmen but all those who followed them in the debates on the onset of war who eschewed military issues. The debates in 1793 and 1914 are symptomatic. On 12 February 1793 William Pitt argued that Britain was not responsible for the French decision to declare war, it had not interfered in French politics, despite the chaos, which the revolution had brought since 1789, that, nevertheless, the French had threatened to try to set up republics and overthrow existing governments everywhere. They had conquered Savoy, they had embargoed British merchants and they had started building up to 50 ships of the line. Thus 'secure and lasting peace' could only be achieved by war. For the Whigs, Charles James Fox replied that this was an ideological war, that it would involve the usual miseries inseparable from warfare, that it was being waged for the restoration of the French monarchy and that British diplomacy towards France had been inept and threatening. Edmund Burke then waded in to say that it was precisely because it was an ideological war that he supported it. The government were to be criticised not for going to war but for delaying too long so that the revolutionary menace had grown. There were a few asides on military affairs; Pitt referred to increases in French military expenditure, Fox to the sufferings of war and Burke emphasised the battle-hardened nature of Britain's enemies which would make the coming war one of the most dangerous on which Britain had embarked. But these *were* asides, the focus of debate was moral, legal and political.[6]

Anyone reading the debate of 3 August 1914 nearly 100 years later would think that it was moving strongly against the government as virtually all of the Liberal and Labour members, who spoke after Grey, disputed the wisdom of going to war. The MP for Burnley argued that there was no British obligation to France, that the Germans had agreed not to attack French ports and that Germany was not trying to annex Belgium, it only wanted to gain passage for its troops. Josiah Wedgwood took up Bloch's warning that thousands would be thrown out of work by the disruption to trade and this would bring about a revolution. Edmund Harvey advocated neutrality so that Britain could act as intermediary between the combatants; Keir Hardie doubted that the people were in favour of war and advocated compromise, while Arthur Ponsonby warned against war fever and against the horrors which war would bring. It was only then that Grey received some support when Sir A. Markham rose to throw doubt on the idea that Germany would evacuate Belgium at the end of the war. Markham admitted that the war was unpopular in the country but insisted that the House had to show that Britain could keep its word; Sir Albert Spicer called for more negotiations and Rowntree warned that Russia would prove a greater threat than Germany which had more in common with British civilisation; Molteno reverted to the frequent denials in the past by Asquith and other ministers that Britain was committed to sending an army to Europe. He deplored both the secret agreements, which Grey said made it a matter of honour to support France, and the notion that Britain was committed by open treaties to Belgium's defence. Llewelyn

Williams argued that no British interests were involved and no treaty obligations.[7]

And so the debate continued. It showed that many MPs did not share today's conventional wisdom that the war was popular. As we have seen in Chapter 6, the one-sided discussion was drawn to a close by Arthur Balfour speaking from the Conservative benches to warn that the interventions from the Liberal side might give foreign countries the wrong impression of the state of British feelings. 'What we have tonight are the very dregs and lees of the debate, in no sense representing the various views of the Members of the House.' This was, he said, 'an impotent and evil debate'. Colonel Seely rose to remonstrate with him, but the debate was effectively over. There had been references to the movement of the German army through Belgium, to the possibility of a German bombardment of the French coast, but, as in 1793, the military issues were peripheral.[8]

The 1793 and 1914 debates were not exceptional, on other occasions when Britain went to war in the past (in March 1854, February 1857, October 1899, September 1939, July 1950 and August 1956) there were extensive debates in Parliament about the political wisdom and morality of the course of action taken by the government.[9] There was always opposition from some members of the two Houses. But overt hostility did not appear to be based on the unlikelihood of military success; the Whigs in 1793, the Cobdenites in 1854 and 1857, the radical Labour and Liberal MPs in 1914, the pacifists in 1939 argued that war was wrong, not that it would be unsuccessful.[10] Some Whigs did indeed warn that it would be very difficult to defeat Napoleon before the Waterloo campaign in May 1815, but the emphasis they gave to this point was unusual.[11] It is also true that Churchill and his tiny band of followers had frequently called attention to the state of the armed forces in the 1930s and that there was a widespread public fear of bomber attacks.[12] But this was not the focus of debate in September 1939. All but a handful of MPs were by then determined that Britain should uphold its guarantee to Poland and, if necessary, go to war with Germany. The civil–military divide was complete, Parliament decided when to go to war, the armed forces had to weigh up how the battles were to be won.[13]

The widespread reluctance of MPs to demand more information from the government before war began and to discuss the impending campaign was, no doubt, based on reasonable fears of spreading anxiety about the military prospects, on confidence in Britain's ability ultimately to be victorious, on concern that military secrets might be revealed and enemies alerted to weakness, and on members' lack of faith in their own competence to second guess the decisions of the military commanders. Finally, it might be considered less unpatriotic to attack the government's poor political decisions than to suggest that the country was too weak to undertake the task in hand. Governments naturally encouraged Parliamentary reticence; Pitt told the Commons in July 1794 that they would, 'of course', not want a debate on whether allied troops had been deployed in the most effective theatres.[14] Moreover, a majority of the public accepted the need for caution about discussing military affairs; in October 1942, 46 per cent of the population said that they were against open discussion of the prospects for a second front to liberate Europe, while 37 per cent pronounced in favour of such a debate.[15] And a discussion would indeed have been barren because ministers could hardly describe the military calculations on which the timing of the decision to launch such a front had to be based.

After wartime reverses, the ensuing Parliamentary debates show how restraint operated. To take a classic example, in November 1915, there were extensive controversies after disasters suffered by British forces in the Balkans and the Dardanelles. But the comments by MPs reflected the inhibitions they felt about openly discussing military problems on the floor of the House. George Barnes, the Labour MP for Glasgow, expressed the prevalent view when he admitted, 'with respect to the conduct of the war, I shall say little.... I am not a soldier'.[16] Former officers elected to Parliament attacked the government for taking strictly military decisions, thus reinforcing the notion that, once war began, strategy was a matter for military men alone. In a veiled attack on the First Lord of the Admiralty, Winston Churchill, who was believed to be largely responsible for the Dardanelles campaign, Admiral Lord Charles Beresford claimed that 'politicians have been interfering with the Executive. Their business is to stick to the administrative and political situation. That interference was the cause of many disasters at the beginning of the war.' Other MPs immediately turned on him and argued that he was himself now interfering in strategy. As one put it, 'if private Members begin to discuss questions of high policy, it seems to me that it is extremely dangerous, and that no good can result'.[17] Thus MPs censored themselves over strategic questions. Most of those who intervened worried about the danger of giving comfort or providing secrets to the enemy and their views were reiterated in the Parliamentary debates of the Second World War, the Korean War and beyond.[18]

What had changed by April 1982 which broke down the civil–military divide and made governments supply more information and Parliament much more willing to debate military questions in open sessions?

On 2 August 1956 there were already a few complaints by MPs that the government was not supplying them with the information they needed on which to base a proper debate about the impending Suez operation. Major Legge-Bourke expatiated on the military difficulties and Desmond Donnelly complained, 'I understand that we are talking about commissioning aircraft carriers and putting troops on them, but how many troops? Where are they to go?.... At the very moment when the critical situation exists we have no information of any kind of this nature.'[19] Thus, it was coming to seem increasingly anomalous to ignore information on issues relating to security, including force levels, military equipment and training, which was openly available in peacetime, and that discussions on the subject were broadening amongst civilians only to shut down in Parliament at the crucial moment when the government was meditating going to war.

Continued controversy over nuclear strategy, which was far more important than a limited conflict over Suez, increased scepticism about the wisdom of governments' policies and thus reduced the general willingness to leave security policy in their hands.[20] If the United States supplied most of the intellectual leadership in the nuclear debate, it was in Britain that the issue first evoked a passionate response from a wider public, leading, as Chapter 3 showed, to the mass protests of the Campaign for Nuclear Disarmament (CND) in the late 1950s and early 1960s. Its supporters demanded the right to be heard when they saw that the issues concerned the very survival of the nation.[21] Strategic debate could no longer be confined either to government in particular or to the elite in general, as the bitter divisions over the Vietnam War demonstrated very clearly during the second half of the 1960s. Whether the media played any part in US political difficulties during that war is still a matter of debate, but what is certain is that the military campaign was watched and pondered in homes across the Western world and that US leaders were widely criticised for their tactics and for the effect of their decisions on the people of Vietnam.[22]

The widening of the defence debate may have been desirable or simply inevitable because of pressure from the media and public arising from nuclear issues and the Vietnam War, but successive British governments went with the tide by trying to inform the public and to convert it to their point of view. Until the election of the Blair government, annual *Defence White Papers* became ever longer, better presented and more detailed. While in the early 1950s such papers consisted of a handful of uninformative and uninviting pages, the *Statement on Defence Estimates* in 1983 ran to over 100 pages of well-illustrated and documented information.[23] Tony Blair's government made much greater use of websites which provided less information than the White Papers but gave copies of speeches by ministers and had the advantage of being free. The increase in the information provided by governments went in parallel with the growth in information on military questions published by the Rand Corporation, International Institute for Strategic Studies, Stockholm International Peace Research Institute and numerous other unofficial bodies in Britain and particularly in the United States. The public in general were given information if they chose to buy and read it, and an increasingly vocal community of armchair strategists took the opportunity to do so. The media in Britain and elsewhere demanded information, and foreign journalists had also to be kept sympathetic to Britain's cause. That meant feeding them with ever more information.

When, therefore, Mrs Thatcher and her colleagues listed the British ships and aircraft heading for the Falkland Islands in April 1982, they were responding to a demand which could not easily have been resisted. In the event, the demand dovetailed with the government's hope that revelation of the size of the task force would persuade the Argentines to withdraw from the islands without fighting. When this hope proved forlorn, it was of no great consequence that the Argentine government knew the types of ships and aircraft approaching them. The fact is that Britain's enemies have always been aware of the general make-up of the country's forces. As the former correspondent of the *Deutsche Allgemeine Zeitung* put it in 1939:

> We can count the warships and note the calibre of their guns. We can estimate the strategic value of Great Britain's naval bases. We know the number and kind of aeroplanes which make up her first-line strength. We know the equipment of her infantry battalions, and the arrangements she has made for anti-aircraft defence.[24]

This was a slight exaggeration, radar was secret, as were the numbers of front-line aircraft and even ministers were not always aware of the strength, or rather weakness, of key bases such as Singapore, but, as in 1982, it was generally the detail which was hidden, the strength of battleship armour, the elevation of the guns, the speed and manoeuvrability of aircraft. In the Falklands War the Argentines deployed British-designed Type-42 destroyers and an aircraft carrier built in Britain, although they would not have known the details of the computer programs in the Type-42s which Britain also employed in the conflict. Military handbooks showed the general performance of the

British Seas Harrier aircraft, although not the number or mark of their Sidewinder air-to-air missiles.

The armed forces complained in 1982 about the release of operational secrets, rather than information on equipment. They feared that the Argentines might monitor the public speculations of retired officers about where forces might land in the Falklands. Such officers were no longer privy to military plans but they might have revealed general British propensities and attitudes. The Liberal Leader in the Lords, Frank Byers complained:

> at the plethora of speculation in the press and the rest of the media on military tactics and operations available and in discussion of the minutest detail of the men and units of the task force, its equipment and its potential performance. I know that there is held a view that all this information is already in the hands of the Argentines. It may be, but I doubt it.[25]

He went on to argue that Hitler would have benefited from such discussion in the Second World War, particularly during the preparations for the D-Day landings in Normandy. However, younger retired officers, who participated in the media debates, could see no point in trying to hide statistics which had long been published in the *Defence Estimates* and elsewhere. There were graver reasons to complain, not least that the plans for the attack on Argentine positions at Goose Green had been given before the advance was completed and, potentially much more seriously, the Ministry of Defence revealed that Argentine bombs were wrongly fused and were, consequently, not exploding when they hit British warships.[26] These mistakes showed the difficulty of deciding what information would help an enemy who was carefully monitoring the press. Of course, the government could afford to be more open because the issues at stake were incomparably less momentous than they had been in the great wars of 1793, 1914 or 1939, but Britain's prestige was at issue quite as much as it had been in the Crimean, Boer or Korean Wars, and the likely outcome of those campaigns was not the subject of Parliamentary debate when the crucial decision to go to war was openly discussed beforehand.[27] The most important change was then not in the significance of the issues at stake, but in the assumptions and demands made by the media, MPs and the public at large.

When Iraq invaded Kuwait in 1990, Mrs Thatcher followed the precedent she had set in 1982 and again informed Parliament of the British weapons being sent to the Gulf including 'a squadron of Tornado F3 air defence aircraft, a squadron of Tornado ground attack aircraft, and a squadron of Jaguar aircraft for ground support....One Royal Navy destroyer and two frigates.... A second destroyer is on the way there, as are three mine clearance vessels.'[28] Two years later, following the collapse of Yugoslavia, the Foreign Secretary Douglas Hurd told Parliament that Britain would send 1800 troops to Bosnia to help with convoy protection.[29] Although the Blair government was generally more reticent about providing information than its predecessors, seven years later still, George Robertson, the secretary of state for Defence, gave some details to Parliament of the British equipment involved in the initial attacks on Serbia following its refusal to bow to international pressure over Kosovo. He reported that the submarine HMS Splendid had fired its cruise missiles in anger for the first time and that Harriers had carried out attacks on ammunition dumps and other targets.[30]

Following these revelations, on each occasion, the military strategy and tactics pursued have been extensively discussed by MPs, again in marked contrast to what had happened before 1982. During the Parliamentary debate in 1990, David Owen insisted that, in the event of war, 'there is little doubt that he [Saddam Hussein] will use gas'. Sir Peter Tapsell prophesied accurately that US air power would dominate the war and that the Iraqi tank force would then be powerless.[31] The Secretary of State for Defence Tom King told Parliament that the government believed the Iraqis had 150,000 men, 1500 tanks and 700 artillery pieces in Kuwait, and went on to describe in detail the military forces assembling from all over the world to liberate the country.[32]

In 1992, when Britain sent peacekeeping forces to try to stop massacres in Bosnia, Douglas Hurd introduced the Parliamentary debate by saying that the government rejected the idea of attacking the Serbs from the air, even though many believed that they were primarily responsible for the massacres. In contrast to his predecessors before 1982, Hurd focused on the military, not the moral issues, the difficulty of hitting Serb weapons, the way in which the combatants and civilians lived side by side and the likelihood that bombing would end the possibility of peacekeeping.[33] He was immediately put under pressure 'to do something about the situation', while backbenchers cautioned the government to make certain that the troops could be evacuated if necessary.[34] Altogether the debate showed considerable familiarity with the political *and* military problems and benefits of peacekeeping, as well as the anger aroused by the massacres shown on television, and the confidence of many members in the ability of the armed forces to improve the situation.

The debate over Kosovo seven years later echoed these considerations. Conservative speakers expressed anxiety that the air attacks being made on Serbia would have to be followed by ground action if Serb control of Kosovo was to be reduced and Alan Clark, who regarded himself as a military historian, suggested that half a million men would be necessary.[35] Tom Clarke, the MP for Coatbridge and Chryston, more presciently observed that it was 'ludicrous to suppose that all over Kosovo and Serbia, tanks are not being dispersed. They are hardly going to be left together in car parks for us to bomb. Of course the ideal place to park a tank is in the middle of a village in Kosovo.'[36] When the campaigns in Iraq and Afghanistan bogged down in civil war and insurgency, both Houses pressed the government not only for statements about their objectives but also for detailed responses to their criticisms about levels of equipment provided for the armed forces. In July 2006 Lord Garden urged the government to provide adequate transport helicopters and close air support aircraft.[37] In the Commons Liam Fox called for greater support in Afghanistan from Britain's NATO allies, and other MPs voiced anxiety about the pressure being put on the reserve forces.

No short description can begin to summarise adequately the breadth of debates on military operations from the Falklands to Afghanistan. They were characterised by reasoned arguments about the efficacy of military force, which were completely absent from the floor of the House before 1982. Given the uncertain outcome of any war, while many of the comments turned out to be prescient, others were completely erroneous. A modern MP would find 19th-century speeches verbose and flowery; a 19th-century MP would find the modern House noisy and abusive, and modern speakers lacking in good manners and verbal felicity. Modern debates lacked any tincture of the elegance of their predecessors in 1793 or 1854 and, most importantly, the focus on moral and political issues, but they are, consequently, far more comprehensive than any previous ones. Many MPs might be passionately committed to the liberation of Kuwait or the protection of the Bosnians and the inhabitants of Kosovo, but Parliament did not call on the government to launch into war without devoting attention to the military consequences.

Not only is the Parliamentary debate far more wide-ranging than in the past but the number of MPs who want to participate has grown in proportion. The speaker complained on 7 April 1982 that 80 MPs had indicated their wish to discuss the Falklands crisis including 14 Privy Councillors. In the great debate on the pivotal decision to go to war with revolutionary France in 1793, six MPs spoke after the prime minister, William Pitt had put the government's case. In the next debate

14 MPs spoke, while seven members of the House of Lords contributed. In the debate on the outbreak of the Crimean War on 31 March 1854, ten members of the House of Lords contributed and nine MPs spoke in the other Chamber. These were great rhetorical clashes between the parties' leading spokesmen Pitt, Fox, Burke and Sheridan in 1793, Bright, Russell, Palmerston and Disraeli in 1854. Speeches by government and opposition spokesmen do not appear from Hansard to have been widely interrupted. In contrast, Tony Blair was interrupted 20 times during the debate on Iraq on 18 March 2003.[38] In the 19th century and before, less prominent politicians kept quiet or intervened modestly and briefly, yet the summary of recent debates outlined above makes clear that, as in other areas of life, fame and wisdom are unrelated, unless inversely.

Whatever the quality of their speeches and interventions, MPs have rightly become increasingly sensitive to the way in which crucial debates now take place in radio and television studios rather than in the Houses of Parliament. Debates in Parliament were once reproduced verbatim in the broadsheets. Pitt could assert confidently in November 1800, 'with regard to the large and complicated question of peace and war, as on every other point of national interest, the eyes of the people are trained upon parliament'.[39] Now debates are hardly reported in the printed media and, although some are broadcast, they capture only a tiny audience. Governments have contributed to this indifference or, at least, tacitly, accepted it as a fact of life. As soon as Winston Churchill heard about the Japanese attack on Pearl Harbor in December 1941, he recalled Parliament because he felt that, 'it is indispensable to our system of government that Parliament should play its full part in the important acts of state and at all the crucial moments of the war'.[40] In August 1968, when the Soviets invaded Czechoslovakia, Harold Wilson recalled Parliament within a week, although there was nothing that MPs could do about the invasion except voice their anger.[41] It took Mrs Thatcher's government a month to recall Parliament in 1990 even though British forces were being sent to the Gulf. Tony Blair was bitterly attacked for treating Parliament with contempt over Kosovo by giving information to the media before it had been passed to Parliament.[42] Subsequently, Blair tried to avoid debates on prospects for an Anglo-American attack on Iraq for as long as possible from 2002 to 2007, not least, no doubt, because he feared attacks from his own backbenches.[43] The law officers of the Crown failed to attend the most extensive debate ever held in the House of Lords on the legality of the use of force, much to the anger of many present. As Lord Goodhart commented, 'we ... regret that the noble and learned Lord the Attorney-General has not given us the opportunity to ask questions and to hear the answers'.[44] There was a striking contrast to the extensive apologies offered by Pitt when his colleagues absented themselves from even the most unexpected debates.[45]

In the past the media were interested in Parliament, now Parliament is interested in the media.[46] Much of the debate takes place between the general public over the airwaves and MPs emphasise the importance of listening to their views. For example, one member warned during the debate on Kosovo in March 1999, 'on Radio Five this morning the airwaves were blocked with people of Serbian background and people of Albanian background phoning in. The hatred they felt for each other was so poisonous...that it would have given the most gung-ho supporter of the government's policy [of intervention in the war] second thoughts'.[47] In a discussion in Westminster Hall, Adam Price commented in October 2006, 'unfortunately, we learn more through leaks to the papers and odd, unscripted, off-the-cuff remarks from certain senior military figures than we ever do from the Government speaking on the floor of the House'.[48] In the same discussion Chris Bryant quoted John Humphry's comments on Radio Four, while Jeremy Corbyn and Paul Flynn quoted *The Lancet*. Plainly Parliament has been pushed to the margins by the debates going on elsewhere.[49]

When Parliament was eventually recalled after the Iraqi invasion of Kuwait in 1990, speaker after speaker rose to applaud the move and to warn that the House was threatened with relegation to the sidelines. 'Can anyone doubt', Tony Benn asked, 'that it was right to recall the House of Commons so that we could debate the matter outside the television and radio studios and without relying on the mass media?' From the Conservative benches Sir Rhodes Boyson argued:

> If the House does not meet, debate will be led by the media as if the House is redundant or even non-existent.... It was right to recall Parliament, because parliamentary democracy means that Ministers must be responsible to Parliament. The country would not understand if we did not debate the crisis here when it is debated outside.[50]

Most references to the media were defensive of Parliament's rights and critical of the journalists. But the government alone has the power to recall Parliament, the media are with it always and involved from the start of any crisis. Like other Western states, Britain has moved some way from a Parliamentary to a direct democracy; the 'voice of the people' reaches the government via public opinion polls and the media.

Just as complaints from MPs are natural and understandable, one might have expected that complaints from serving officers about the direct participation of so many people and institutions in strategic debates and their objections to the release of operational secrets during the Falklands War have already been quoted. But officers were unaware that strategic and tactical questions raised by a decision to go to war had previously been kept outside the public arena. Even if they had been aware of the change, they would generally have felt that it was no good protesting against the inevitable. In fact, the backlash often came from amongst the commentators themselves, a reflection of the guilt they felt about pontificating in the safety of studios, universities and assemblies on policies which consign young men and women to an early death. Older people have often felt guilty about sacrificing the young in war, but now the guilt was both more widespread and more frequently voiced.[51]

Thus 'armchair strategy' or 'armchair strategists' suddenly became a prevalent term of abuse amongst commentators and MPs in the 1980s and 1990s. The targets of these attacks were civilians, or those without responsibility and far from the battlefield, who pontificated on warfare. In the debate on 6 September 1990 about the Iraqi invasion of Kuwait, the Liberal Democrat leader Paddy Ashdown said he had 'heard talk about pre-emptive strikes and surgical wars. [But] I have learnt from bitter experience that when the armchair strategists and Whitehall generals start talking of a surgical war, it is time to start running for cover. A war is never surgical to those who have to fight it.' Denis Healey complimented Ashdown on his speech, adding 'nobody who has not fought in a war has much right to talk about what might happen if a war takes place'.[52] In the Kosovo debate on 25 March 1999, Menzies Campbell warned that, 'in the comfort of the television studio or the safety of the House of Commons, it is all too easy to underestimate the unmitigated horrors of modern warfare', while Tony Benn referred sardonically to 'the most valiant chairborne warriors' on both sides of the House.[53] Outside Parliament there were similar complaints. *The Times'* columnist Matthew Parris attacked 'the armchair bombardiers of the *Daily Telegraph*', while Jonathan Eyal, the East European expert at the Royal United Services Institution, dismissed the 'surgical strikes currently being weighed by every armchair strategist' and in December 2002 William Rees-Mogg, the former editor of *The Times*, grumbled, 'I have never had much sympathy for bellicose bishops or other armchair warriors'.[54]

Such comments hark back to those by Lord Charles Beresford during the Dardanelles campaign and are part of the attempt to stifle discussion or to ridicule opponents. Healey expressed the idea most succinctly; only ex-military personnel, like himself, should talk about war, thus confining debate to the favoured few. Ironically, Healey had contributed greatly to the broadening of the defence debate by assisting in the foundation of the International Institute for Strategic Studies and, when he was secretary of state for Defence, establishing defence lectureships at British Universities. Nevertheless, he subsequently claimed that civilians were too aggressive, too fond of proposing that solutions could be found through war, whose course was bloodstained and whose outcome was always uncertain. He never forgot the fury he felt at Oxford before the Second World War when elderly dons encouraged the young to fight for their country.[55]

In the 19th century and later former serving officers believed that they had to defend themselves in the House against the charge that it was they who were too aggressive and liked war for its own sake. When Captain Sir A. Acland-Hood supported the government's motion on the Boer War on 17 October 1899, he felt moved to add:

If there is a section of the House who most strongly oppose an unjust and unnecessary war, it is the military members, and especially those among us who have seen active service. Those of us who have seen what war really is...are the very last in this assembly to commit the country to war without very grave consideration.[56]

Fifty one years later, the former Foreign Secretary, Anthony Eden, complained during the debate on the Korean War on 5 July 1950:

I do get a little riled...when I hear those who, for the most excellent reasons of their own, have never taken part in any conflict, constantly calling others warmongers. That is not true. We who have seen war loathe it, and that applies to hon. Members on the Government side of the House as well as those on this side of the House who have experienced it.[57]

Today, as we have seen, former officers now serving as MPs are, if anything, even more vociferous at deploring the purported aggressiveness of their civilian colleagues. In reality, most people in Britain have become ever more sensitive to civilian and military casualties, not least because of the ubiquity of television cameras which can show the destructive effect of US and British weapons as much as they show the devastation wrought by the enemy.[58] There had been no cameras to relay round the world the burning of Hamburg, Dresden and Tokyo during the Second World War.[59] Even if there is a great difference between actually being present when the maimed survivors and the decomposing bodies of the dead are brought from flattened buildings and seeing their images on television screens, films give some idea of the event. Nobody can today plead ignorance about the effect of military conflict.

If the widening of the defence debate has caused problems, they have been particularly fierce within the government of the most powerful country in the world, the United States. The Vietnam War evoked bitter and lasting antagonism between political leaders and the armed forces, not least because senior officers believed that politicians advised by armchair strategists from the Rand and other think tanks were interfering in military affairs, whilst political leaders, including President John Kennedy, echoed Lloyd George's belief that the armed forces were professionally incompetent.[60] The war brought a certain type of armchair strategist, the operational analyst, into contempt, while the autobiography of Colin Powell showed that the wounds left by the arguments over the war were still open three decades later.[61]

British officers often deplore the absence of military experience amongst politicians but US debates do not suggest that such experience reduces civil–military antagonism – quite the contrary. In his memoirs Admiral Holloway, the former US Chief of Naval Operations dismissed President Carter with contempt because of the lowly rank to which he had risen in the service yet, in the nature of things, politicians are unlikely to rise much higher.[62] Civil–military antagonism had apparently died down by the early 1990s, only to revive again in 2002 over the debate on the threatened invasion of Iraq. Former military officers, led by Colin Powell, the secretary of state, were widely regarded as 'doves', while the President himself, who had evaded service in Vietnam, were seen as a 'hawk'. Powell complained that Bush's colleagues devoted so much time meditating on military scenarios, that they give little attention to international politics.[63] It was a very far cry indeed from General Ironside's belief that Chamberlain never focused on military issues at the outset of the Second World War. What the US debate showed was the need to balance military, political, legal and moral considerations and that, if any of these were given predominance, governmental policy would be undermined.

The benefits of taking military action cannot be decided on moral and political grounds alone. The chances of victory, the likely casualties and the economic costs of military action, have all to be weighed. This coincides, after all, with traditional idea of the just war under which the evil done by the conflict should be outweighed by the advantages. There must be omissions from the open debate, Mrs Thatcher did not tell Parliament in April 1982 that the First Sea Lord expected to lose warships when retaking the Falklands. The fear of demoralising the nation and armed forces or encouraging the enemy has to be balanced against the desire to keep the nation informed. There will be disadvantages; very occasionally military and political secrets will be revealed. But this price will have to be paid, just as we can no longer hide from our cameras, and thus from ourselves, the full impact on enemy peoples of our decision to intervene.

9
The Public Debate

Public opinion is the summation of all the influences previously described and polls suggest that, while British people are unfamiliar with the theories of armchair strategists or of military leaders, they usually take a balanced, commonsensical view of intervention because of the ways their ideas have been shaped by their own experiences and their history.[1] It is also clear that popular British attitudes have been far more cautious than intellectuals have allowed.

At the start of the 20th century, democracy was a novelty and the effects of the growth in the electorate were still unclear. The educated middle class was suspicious and contemptuous of the influence of ordinary citizens on foreign policy. Commentators imagined that the 'masses', unlike educated people, were rabid and xenophobic interventionists. Opinion polls, which began in the late 1930s, should have eradicated these prejudices but they persist out of ignorance, and because they flatter the chattering classes. Polls have shown, first, that the gap between the knowledge of international affairs amongst educated and less-educated people is nowadays less than many had supposed because everyone has to filter vast quantities of information and all tend only to memorise matters which consciously or unconsciously they believe are important to them.[2] Secondly, polls make clear that it is the most highly educated, broadsheet reading, non-specialists who are likely to be 'swept away' by the urge to intervene.

The Liberal economist and writer J. A. Hobson gave classic expression to middle class views in *The Psychology of Jingoism* published in 1901. His book was a reaction to the passions unleashed by the Boer War and his attack focused on the music-halls where:

> The artiste conveys by song or recitation crude notions upon morals and politics, appealing by coarse humour or exaggerated pathos to the animal lusts of an audience stimulated by alcohol into appreciative hilarity.[3]

The music-hall song, the popular art of the time, spread jingoism from the cities into the countryside. Minimal education had created 'a large population, singularly destitute of intellectual curiosity, and with a low valuation for things of the mind' who were capable of reading the popular press but without discriminating between the true and the false. While Hobson's worst fears were inspired by what he believed were working-class attitudes, he quoted examples from *The Standard* and other more serious newspapers to show the level of hatred excited even amongst the educated against the Afrikaners.[4]

The emotional crowds in London, Berlin, Vienna and other capitals rejoicing over the outbreak of the First World War in August 1914 confirmed Hobson's views, leading later analysts, such as Caroline Playne, to write of the neuroses sweeping West European people and impelling statesmen into the conflict.[5] However, as we saw in the last chapter, most of those who spoke in Parliament did not share that view of the popularity of war. Of course, it may be said that those claiming the public were opposed to Britain's entry into the conflict, were themselves of that view. But their appraisal of public opinion on the outbreak of war was not contested in Parliament, even if the young demonstrators in the capital were making themselves conspicuous. As Lloyd George wrote:

> The youth of the rival countries were howling for war. I shall never forget the warlike crowds that thronged Whitehall and poured into Downing Street, whilst the cabinet were deliberating on the alternative of peace or war. On Sunday there was a great crowd. Monday was a bank holiday and multitudes of young people concentrated in Westminster demonstrating for war against Germany.[6]

How do we reconcile the different manifestations of public opinion? Whatever may have been the situation in the large cities across Europe, there is plenty of evidence that rural people recoiled at the idea of conflict. One highly experienced British diplomat was in Normandy when war broke out. He wrote later:

> I shall never forget that sight. Sobbing and weeping women everywhere; the older men, who remembered 1870 and knew what this mobilisation meant, endeavouring to master their emotion and to keep up the appearance of calm; the younger men, who were to be thrust into the furnace, standing dazed and anxious-eyed at the prospect of the unknown tomorrow which they were to face.... I shall remember the weeping women ... and the two sharp strokes of the tocsin, sounding the knell of hope.[7]

When opinion polls were developed decades later, they would confirm the hypothesis that the older, more rural and less-educated people were more reluctant to be involved in war than the urban young. Amongst the elite, including the leading clergymen discussed earlier, many were deeply shocked by the invasion of Belgium and they would have regarded it as utterly disloyal to do anything which undermined the armed forces. Liberal party members were in the same position as Labour supporters after the attack on Iraq in 2003 or Democrats in the United States during the early years of the Vietnam War; while their instincts might have inclined them to oppose the war, they were influenced by loyalty to their party while it was in power as well as loyalty to the country.

As the demonstrations and the intellectuals' enthusiasm for war were so well publicised, this strengthened the conventional wisdom in the inter-war period that the onset of war had been popular across Europe in 1914 and, after 1917, in the United States. It was, no doubt, this feeling that helped to inspire Walter Lippmann to publish his classic study of *Public Opinion* in 1922. Although he expressed his fears in more academic and guarded language, Lippmann shared Hobson's concerns about democracy in general and the press in particular. He believed that government censorship and false newspaper accounts gave the mass of people bogus ideas about policy and distorted their views of foreign countries. The situation could be improved by the development of political science departments in universities and the establishment of intelligence services within government which should study and report on international affairs without their views being distorted by the administration.[8]

If it was the general view that crowds had pushed for war in 1914, it was equally widely assumed in the inter-war years that the British and American publics as a whole had swung round and would oppose war at almost any price, hence the policy of appeasement. Modern polls have shown that public opinion is far more stable than was believed at the time. Before the invention of such polls politicians relied on news-papers, chance encounters and demonstrations to assess opinion, but we now know how distorting these can be; newspaper editors, com-mentators and demonstrators want to influence opinion, they are not representative of it. Chance encounters can be equally misleading, one historian quoted the reaction of two navvies overheard at Waterloo sta-tion complaining that their newspaper was full of the resignation of the Foreign Secretary in February 1938 rather than of a football match, to prove that the working class was indifferent to politics.[9] It proved noth-ing of the sort, though no doubt it appealed to the lip curling prejudices of the elite.

If they can be believed, because their methods were very much cruder than their modern equivalents and left out those who expressed no opinion, the earliest opinion polls, organised by the British Institute of Pubic Opinion in 1937, tell a different story. The majority sto-ically accepted that the aggression of the Axis powers was making war inevitable.[10] Children recognise the playground bully and the ways of dealing with him. That experience remains with us for the rest of our lives, though it is overlaid amongst the educated by sophisticated (and unfortunately sometimes unrealistic) ideas of appeasement, arbitration and conflict management. International affairs were full of braggarts and bullies in the 1930s. Ordinary people, who spent part of Saturday night watching newsreels at the Gaumont or Odeon of the Nuremberg rallies, the Nazis' attacks on the Jews, Fascist bombing raids on Spanish cities and Japanese raids on Chinese ones, knew very well what such events portended, and how the bullies would have to be dealt with.

People still clutched at anything which offered the slimmest chance of peace, but they wanted the government to prepare for failure. Even in 1937, when Hitler had already swallowed the Rhineland and Austria and was making ready to take over Czechoslovakia, 52 per cent of those responding apparently told pollsters that they wanted a disarmament conference. However, the same polls seemed to show that respondents believed a European war would involve Britain (83 per cent), that Neville Chamberlain's appeasement policy was failing (58 per cent) and that Britain should increase its defence spending (75 per cent).[11] If this really was the public verdict, it was balanced and shrewd; but what is striking is that the general public would appear to have been more sensible than the government or many of the intellectuals. Britain's leaders were still hoping to follow a policy of limited liability in Europe and intellectuals were still to be found who argued that British rearmament would bring wars closer.[12] Of course, there were anomalies in popular opinion; despite their robust stance, many people were against conscription (75 per cent of those responding), a majority (62 per cent) said they would not volunteer to join the armed forces and 78 per cent of women said they would not urge their husbands to volunteer. People did not want to become warriors, they did not want to be involved or to involve their family members in a conflict, which would bring enemy bombers over British cities, but they believed war was coming and by July 1939, 76 per cent of those responding were in favour of Britain fighting to help the Poles if the Germans attacked Danzig, thus confirming the importance of moral commitments.[13]On one point alone were they wildly optimistic; when war broke out in September 1939, 82 per cent expected Britain to win, a supposition which proved in the end correct but which now appears panglossian, given the threats which Britain faced.[14]

Despite the historian's view quoted above of the indifference of the working class to politics, by March 1938, 72 per cent of those responding seemed to believe that the Foreign Secretary Anthony Eden was justified in resigning over Chamberlain's policy of appeasement. Yet, in all wars there is a tendency for the public to rally round the leader's policy and, after the war had begun, polls showed for a while that 64 per cent of the respondents supported Chamberlain's government and only 27 per cent opposed it. But this support was conditional; when the Nazis overran Norway in 1940 and the government appeared to be pursuing the war half-heartedly, support dropped to 33 per cent, and 57 per cent believed that the government had not done enough to save the Norwegians.[15] Chamberlain fell because he lost the backing of Parliament, but the public apparently agreed with his removal from office. Subsequently, Churchill's premiership seemed to have the backing of over 80 per cent of the population, even though approval of the government hovered around the 50 per cent level. Again this might seem anomalous since the government's strategic mistakes were very largely Churchill's, but, with the advantages of hindsight, we can see that the public were justified; they blamed the government for its collective mistakes while recognising that Churchill was by far the best leader available. Asked in March 1941 who should replace the Prime Minister, if anything happened to him, 37 per cent said Eden and 1 per cent said Clement Attlee. Later experience was to suggest that Attlee lacked the rhetorical powers necessary and Eden the balance and toughness of mind.[16]

And so the public came later to believe. In February 1951 some eight months after the Korean war broke out, despite the natural tendency for people to rally round the government, 47 per cent disapproved of Attlee as Prime Minister and only 44 per cent supported him. When Churchill replaced him, the percentage supporting the government rose immediately to 55 per cent; there was no longer the need to idolise him as they had in the Second World War, but he was regarded as a better war leader than his Labour counterpart. Gallup polls appeared to suggest that the public's attitude to the Korean War was cautiously interventionist; in October 1950, 63 per cent supported the Labour government's decision to send troops, but, after the defeat of the UN forces in the winter of 1950, only 28 per cent believed that the US commander of the UN forces General MacArthur was doing a good job and only 10 per cent were in favour of widening the war by attacking China as MacArthur suggested.[17]

Six years later, the Suez Crisis broke out with Colonel Nasser's nationalisation of the Suez Canal. Polls showed that the great majority (68 per cent to 14 per cent) believed that the Egyptians were not justified in taking this action, but only 33 per cent said that they were in favour of military measures to rectify the situation against 47 per cent who believed that political and economic pressure was all that should be tried. Asked retrospectively whether Britain and France should have acted as soon as Nasser moved to nationalise the vital waterway, only 22 per cent believed that this would have been justified, though 69 per cent thought it was reasonable to take military precautions.[18] Once again, these verdicts seem far from absurd; Nasser was in the wrong in the popular view, pressure should be brought to bear on him to reverse his policy and military precautions ought to be taken, but force was undesirable. Of course, we know from subsequent experience with Cuba, Iraq and elsewhere that economic pressure would have stiffened Nasser's resistance, rather than forced him to disgorge the canal, and Anglo-French criticism of the canal's nationalisation now seems an archaic throwback to the imperialist past. But, given this attitude and the information available at the time, it was not unreasonable to try economic pressure and this would have been less risky than the policy chosen by the government.

During the Falklands War there was a revival of the fears of popular jingoism expressed by Hobson and other Liberals in the early 20th century. The economic historian E. P. Thompson claimed that:

The Falklands War has shown us at least this – how close to the surface of our even-tempered life the atavistic moods of violence lie. We shall pay for it for a long time, in increases of muggings in our cities, in international ill will.... War in the Falklands will be a general license to disorder.[19]

Such fears seem exaggerated, and it is difficult to prove that either international ill will or muggings increased as a consequence. No doubt, there was general resentment about being pushed around by Latin American dictators and it is true that the public 'rallied round the flag'. Nearly two weeks after the Argentine invasion of the Falkland Islands, 34 per cent of the population supported Labour and 33 per cent backed the Tories, while 58 per cent expressed dissatisfaction with the way the government was running the country. This was hardly unreasonable since the economy was in the doldrums and the government had failed to deter the Argentine attack. Support for the government climbed steadily as the task force approached the islands and war began. By 21–23 June, it had risen to 51 per cent against 24 per cent for Labour and 23 per cent for the Liberals. By then 84 per cent expressed satisfaction with the way the government was handling the crisis.[20]

The public were not, however, in favour of extreme measures and did not share the jingoism of some of the popular media. Sixty-eight per cent objected to interning Argentine citizens in Britain, 93 per cent opposed the use of nuclear weapons, between 57 and 63 per cent opposed bombing Argentine bases and 73 per cent rejected an invasion of Argentina. Eighty-five per cent supported the deployment of the task force to the South Atlantic but the public were much more cautious about the loss of lives; at the beginning of May less than half believed that the lives of Falklands Islanders should be sacrificed, though the number who believed that the issue justified the sacrifice of servicemen's lives grew from 44 to 62 per cent. A bare majority 46 against 44 per cent believed that the decision to sink the Argentine cruiser General Belgrano with the loss of 368 Argentines was justified.[21] Some of these opinions were contradictory, it was inevitable that the servicemen's lives would be sacrificed if war began, yet some plainly supported the war while denying the corollary. But such contradictions reflected the hopes, rather than expectations, that humanity could be reconciled with defending British territory.

Much of the most extensive polling data we have about public attitudes towards warfare comes from the United States and some of the conclusions which can be drawn from this fit with what we know of

British opinion. John Mueller used this data in his study of war and public opinion to demonstrate that party supporters often back a war if it is their party which is in power. But these loyalties are cut across by age, education and sex. Support for war drops with age, which confirms what has been said above about events in 1914; 82 per cent of the Americans under 30 were in favour of involvement in the Korean war in July 1950 against 71 per cent of those over 49s; similarly, 61 per cent of the Americans under 30s were in favour of involvement in Vietnam in May 1965 against 43 per cent of those of 49; by May 1971 the corresponding figures were 34 and 23 per cent. In May 1965, 68 per cent of the college-educated were in favour of the war against 36 per cent of those who had only been to grade school; by May 1971 the figures had dropped to 31 and 21 per cent. Poll data shows that women tend to be more reluctant to use force than men. The figures would suggest that, contrary to widespread opinion, if one ignores the impact of party loyalty, the most hawkish are the young, college-educated males and the most dovish the least educated, elderly women.[22] Again, contrary to prejudice, attitudes amongst the elite are also the most volatile, while, paradoxically, 'ordinary citizens hold coherent attitude structures because they lack detailed knowledge about foreign policy'.[23]

Recent studies have focused less on the background of respondents to polls and more on the general international situation, the justification for war and the prospects of success.[24] However, the two approaches are complementary; younger people tend to be more idealistic, more incensed by perceived wrongs and more optimistic about the prospects for change. Older people will have lived through previous wars, seen hopes dashed and interventions bogged down until their original objectives were forgotten or discredited. Many will also have spent 20 years protecting their children from the lesser dangers of childhood, only to see them suddenly threatened with involvement in all the horrors of warfare. Similarly, highly educated people will be the most aware of the sufferings of foreign people, as in Bosnia in the 1990s or in Zimbabwe in 2008, thus they will tend to be more interventionist than those who are less interested in politics. They will also change their views more readily, turning against the war in Vietnam in the 1960s or against Iraq and Afghanistan more recently, when they learnt from the media of the suffering the wars unleashed.

Both national leaders and commentators simplify the issues involved in a threatened conflict and stress just one aspect of the complex political and strategic picture. Ministers also exaggerate the choice presented to foreign leaders and minimise their own.[25] In August 1914 the

Austro-Hungarian government emphasised the threat to its Empire from Serbian nationalism and, because of this threat, it was prepared to risk a European conflagration. For the German government and people the issue was wider; it was a matter of honour and strategic necessity to stand by Austria-Hungary, its only reliable ally. Berlin also feared the growing power of Russia and wanted to break out of the 'encirclement' of the Franco-Russian alliance. In the British public debate, Germany's breach of Belgium's neutrality predominated, but the political elite were also concerned with the commitment to France and the threat to the balance of power if the Entente were defeated. So it is with each impending conflict, each side stressing very different factors and issues. Before their attack on Iraq in March 2003, the US and British governments emphasised the menace to international security from Iraqi weapons of mass destruction and the horrors Saddam Hussain had perpetrated. The Iraqi government felt the need to convince its people and other Arab states that it would not bow to the 'imperialists' and maybe it hoped that they would draw back in the end from launching an attack. The chattering classes responded to the views of the columnists and to ministers' speeches, the wider public brought their previous experience and common sense to bear on the problem, the experts expanded the debates beyond the limits to which ministers and the more interventionist columnists wanted it confined; Bloch and Angell warned governments before 1914 that the greatest threat to their stability came from the economic impact of war itself, similarly some regional specialists alerted the US and British governments in 2003 to the dangers of exacerbating relations between the Islamic World and the West, and undermining the stability of those Arab governments which had supported the West in the past. After the Russian invasion of Georgia in August 2008, politicians on both sides of the Atlantic made belligerent speeches about Russian behaviour, while some of the experts on international relations warned of the dangers involved and explained the reasons for Russian policy.[26]

The wider public may not have read the warnings of the specialists, but they were not taken in by governmental arguments when they seemed to defy common sense. When the Conservative government continued to argue that Hitler could be appeased and relied upon to stand by agreements in 1938, the primitive polling methods of the time appeared to show that people thought it had lost touch with reality. When the Labour government joined with the United States in attacking the Taleban in Afghanistan in October 2001, the government had the support of 69 per cent of the British population, presumably because they were deeply moved by the film of helpless civilians caught in the Twin Towers on 9/11 and saw this as a just and defensive war. But they had no illusions; despite frequent government protestations, they were rightly convinced that these attacks would make terrorist incidents in Britain more likely. Fifty-nine per cent said this was the case and only 3 per cent accepted the claims by the British and US governments that it would have the reverse effect. Sixty-three per cent said they were either very or fairly worried about terrorist aggression, and only 19 per cent expressed 'great' confidence in the ability of the government to protect them.[27] That this public assessment was shrewder than the government's was demonstrated when British-born Islamists outraged by Western military actions placed bombs on the London underground in July 2005.

It seems fair to conclude that before a war breaks out the public are far more balanced and less gullible than commentators are given to suggesting and governments appear to believe. Indeed, before the Second World War, during the Suez Crisis in 1956, before the war in Afghanistan in 2001 and the attack on Iraq in 2003, they were, as suggested above, shrewder than those who made foreign policy. If this is the case, personal experience will have been most important for the less educated. But all will have been affected to some extent by education, films, novels, arguments between commentators, institutions and pressure groups, discussions in Parliament and in the media. Of course, some point out that the consistency of public opinion is not always a virtue; reconciliation with Germany was reasonable in the 1920s,[28] it was impossible when the Nazis came to power; similarly the international system changed completely after the collapse of the Soviet Union.[29] But the public were aware of these changes and their responses were reasonable enough.

The treatment of the electorate by politicians and the assessment by journalists fails to reflect the common sense of the majority as shown by the mass of polling data. The irony is that governments fear public opinion less than they did in the 1930s. They know that the general public will initially back them once war has broken out and thus they feel able to intervene in what they hope will be a short war.[30]

10
Iraq and Afghanistan

After the election of a Labour government under Tony Blair in 1997, Britain developed a more interventionist strategy than it had had since the Boer War. The previous government under John Major had sponsored the idea of establishing zones in Kurdistan and in the South of Iraq over which no Iraqi aircraft were allowed to fly and attack the Kurds and Shiites, but elsewhere it was cautious about involving British forces. In particular, it only slowly and reluctantly committed forces to participate in European peacekeeping operations during the collapse of Yugoslavia. Blair's approach to intervention there and elsewhere was much more enthusiastic; in his last tour in Africa in May 2007 he stressed that the basis of his policy was the conviction that 'it is better to intervene and try to make a difference than stay out and cope with the consequences at a later time... I believe in the power of political action to render the world better and the moral obligation to use it.'[1] It will be many years before the impact of this period of interventionism becomes clear, in the meantime the debate focuses on the short-term effects in Afghanistan and Iraq.

Because of the ferocious guerrilla attacks on coalition forces in these two countries and the failure to discover chemical and biological weapons in Iraq, there was more soul-searching in Britain between 2003 and 2008 than after any intervention since the First World War. In fact, to add to the other 'firsts' associated with the war in Iraq, it sparked the most fundamental re-examination of the efficiency of the governmental system for making decisions on war and peace since the Boer War at the start of the 20th century. The revisions then were designed to make the system more efficient for planning the defence of the Empire, the appraisals after 2003 were intended to assess the checks and balances, to see whether the executive could be restrained from unwise overseas interventions.[2] This was all the more ironic because few interventions by British forces have been preceded by such a long period of preparation, at least for the initial stage of the attack, as the operation against Iraq in March 2003. The gaps between the German invasion of Belgium in 1914 and of Poland in 1939 and the British declarations of war were only a matter of hours, the attack on Iraq was prepared over months.

The new interventionism and particularly the wars in Afghanistan and Iraq were made possible by long-term changes, or apparent changes, in the strategic balance. In the early 1990s, Britain's position in the international system was transformed when the Soviet Union collapsed and with it the balance between the Great Powers, creating a unipolar system and making Britain's closest ally the United States much more assertive. President George W. Bush expressed the new US approach most clearly in his speech to the US Military Academy at West Point in June 2002:

> We must take the battle to the enemy, disrupt his plans, and confront the worst threats before they emerge...America has, and intends to keep, military strengths beyond challenge – thereby making the destabilising arms races of past eras pointless.... The 20th Century ended with a single surviving model of human progress, based on non-negotiable demands of human dignity, the rule of law, limits on the power of the state, respect for women and private property...[3]

This was predicated on two fundamental misconceptions; first, that other cultures accepted Western views on human dignity and Bush's 'non-negotiable demands' and secondly that conventional power was the only sort of military power and thus that the United States had the capacity to intervene wherever it wished. But senior officers in the US armed forces knew their country did not have, and had never had, 'military strengths beyond challenge' because they had experienced defeat in Vietnam and setbacks in Somalia and elsewhere.[4] The area of the world in which even a superpower could intervene successfully had been steadily shrinking; China and India were no longer vulnerable to such interference because of their size and development, and in Southeast Asia guerrilla forces had rebuffed outside intervention by France between 1945 and 1954 and by the United States between 1964 and 1973.[5]

Appreciating the dangers inherent in Bush's misconceptions, many Europeans became increasingly uncomfortable with Washington's policies in the Middle East and elsewhere. However, so strong were the

British security links with the United States and so powerful was the Blair government's interventionism that these factors outweighed the centuries-old British determination to bolster the balance of power which would have led the government to move closer to Europe. Blair himself clearly shared many of the President's attitudes and particularly his belief in the possibility of spreading democracy by force. Both Bush and Blair were also convinced that the sort of terrorism displayed so graphically and horrifically on 9/11 was something that could be eradicated rather than simply a tactic employed by those who lacked conventional power and were infuriated by Western actions. The country's prosperity and the relative cheapness of the Falklands War and the Gulf War of 1990–1991, the second of which was largely paid for by the Saudis, Japanese and Kuwaitis, meant that financial interests were less of a constraint on British policy than they had been from 1919 to 1990. Similarly, the rapid military successes in these campaigns obscured the series of defeats the British suffered at the hands of insurgents in Palestine, Cyprus and Aden between the 1940s and the 1960s. The scene was thus set for the imbroglios in Afghanistan and Iraq.

As we saw in the previous chapter, when al Qaeda attacked the Twin Towers on 9/11 the majority of British (and indeed most European) people supported the US campaign against the Taleban government in Afghanistan which had given refuge to the terrorists. The British government realised the extent of the anger in the United States and thus the political importance of supporting its actions. The commitment also seemed relatively slight as US airpower together with the Afghan forces of the Northern Alliance quickly overcame the Taleban's conventional forces. Britain's contribution was initially confined to the provision of airborne tankers for US fighter-bombers and to Special Forces. But the long-term implications were not widely debated in the haste and heat of the moment; if the United States withdrew, the Taleban would probably return and the campaign would be seen as a failure, if they did not withdraw, they would become semi-colonial occupiers of a land peopled by a proud and ultra-conservative people with a long tradition of fighting invaders and an open frontier with the Northern provinces of Pakistan where the guerrillas could retire and refit.[6] In retrospect, it would have been better to follow the example set by the British rulers of India in the 19th century who periodically launched punitive expeditions against the Wazirs and Afridis on the Afghan frontier when their behaviour became too aggressive. Such expeditions might not have put an end to the Taleban but they would have been less expensive and temporarily effective.

As it was, the military and political difficulties were exacerbated by the Blair government's decision to become involved in a second campaign alongside US armed forces in Iraq in March 2003. This decision followed the pattern set in the French Wars and the two World Wars in which British leaders pushed for ever more interventions and were only restrained by the opposition of the armed forces. In 2003 the US and British armed forces either did not try or did not succeed, in insisting on finishing one campaign before starting another. The proclaimed objective was to destroy the chemical and biological weapons which the two governments believed Iraq was manufacturing and which it had been banned from producing after the 1991 Gulf War.[7] The erroneous claims were also spread by the US administration that the Iraqi ruler Saddam Hussein had, in some way, backed the terrorists who carried out the attack on the Twin Towers and that he had restarted his nuclear weapons programme.[8] Saddam Hussein had committed many crimes, ironically, in the end, he was attacked for some which he did not commit.

Once again the United States failed to plan for the long term and assumed that the Iraqis would adapt to Western ways as enthusiastically and easily as the Germans and Japanese had done after their defeat by the allies in 1945.[9] Initially the invaders were, indeed, welcomed by many of the Iraqi peoples, particularly Kurds and Shiites, and others who had been persecuted by Saddam Hussein. But the disbandment of the armed forces, the failure to restore water and electricity facilities and provide employment quickly enough, and the encouragement given to democracy, to the disadvantage of the minority Sunni who had previously run the country, meant that the invaders found themselves fighting a determined insurgency of the sort the British had encountered when they took over Iraq after the First World War.[10]

When the invading forces were unable to pacify Iraq, while the war in Afghanistan showed no signs of abating, there was growing anxiety amongst senior officers about the morale of the armed forces and the extent of British commitments. Although well-informed observers, including Richard Holmes, the military historian, who spent time with them in Iraq, were impressed by how well the young troops responded, press reports became increasingly pessimistic about the state of their morale.[11] This was partly because of the shortage of troops and the intensity of the fighting, but it was also because of the scepticism amongst the soldiers about the objectives of the two wars and the feeling that the British people were not giving them support.[12] During the Iraq War General Sir Michael Rose, who had commanded British forces in

Bosnia in the 1990s, commented on the motives which influence troops in any war:

> There can be no more debilitating effect on the morale of the members of the armed forces than for them to know that their country does not support the mission or that the case for war is based on doubtful moral or legal arguments. A proper justification should always be a sine qua non for engaging in conflict.[13]

The root cause of the problems was the determination of the United States and Britain to rebuild Afghan and Iraqi political institutions in the Western image. As Bush put it, 'Afghanistan and Iraq will lead the world to democracy. They are going to be the catalyst to change the Middle East and the world.'[14] But the United States needed the cooperation of neighbouring countries, and the governments of Iran, Saudi Arabia and Pakistan were hardly likely to support policies designed to subvert their power.[15] Furthermore, Afghans and Iraqis might tell Western representatives that they favoured democracy and, when offered the opportunity, they voted in elections, but their good intentions were undermined by feuds between the various groups in both countries, and the lack of the tradition of compromise which is the basis of democracy and of a stable legal system.[16] As we saw in Chapter 1, national culture is shaped over the centuries and, thus, democratic instincts cannot be created overnight by a foreign power. Western armed forces were left fighting against nationalists as well as Islamists and feuding tribes. Shortly after Tony Blair's resignation, the Chief of Defence Staff, Sir Jock Stirrup, commented:

> I think some people expected that, with the British presence on the ground, we could put Basra society, Basra infrastructure, Basra politics and Basra life back on its feet and make it look some sort of stable, secure, prosperous urban centre. That is the right aspiration to have, but we could never do that, only the Iraqis could do it.[17]

Resentment in the armed forces about being landed with an impossible task was increased by the widespread feeling amongst them that they were isolated from the rest of society because of the ending of conscription and the death of those who experienced the two World Wars. Everything that has been written in this book suggests that the perception is mistaken; they are held in very high esteem; whenever there is a problem from foot and mouth disease amongst animals to flooding in cities or to anti-terrorist measures at airports, the cry goes up to 'send for the army'.[18] Today, warfare and conflict are now all around us in a way that they have not been before because they come to us both directly and via the media. While the age of total warfare has apparently receded, at least for the time being, it has been replaced by ubiquitous insecurity. If the World Trade Centre and the Pentagon were vulnerable on 9/11, so, by definition, was every other building.[19] Britain had experienced similar events for three decades because of the IRA offensive; the City of London had been bombed, Downing Street had been the target of a mortar attack, members of the cabinet had been blown up in a Brighton hotel, MPs and senior civil servants had been bombed or shot in Britain and abroad. Other European countries including Spain, Italy and Germany have had similar experiences.

It is impossible to watch television or listen to radio news without being inundated with information about warfare in some distant country as well as about terrorist threats closer to home. During the last quarter of a century the British armed forces have been involved in half a dozen significant conflicts, in the Falklands, in the first and second Gulf Wars, in Bosnia, in Kosovo and Afghanistan, all of which have been extensively covered by the media. They have also been deployed in numerous smaller peacekeeping operations. As a result of the television coverage of these engagements, the mass of people know much more about weaponry and military operations than they have ever done, even possibly during the two World Wars; the media have made us all armchair strategists. The armed forces are far less isolated, because everyone knows what weapons and warfare looks like, however hard they might try to shut their mind to them. Nevertheless, because the armed forces believed that they were isolated, as well as involved in unpopular wars in Afghanistan and Iraq, their morale was affected.[20]

When this became clear, it increased the feeling that the British governmental system had failed or been circumvented by the Prime Minister and his immediate colleagues. The main cabinet committee responsible for intervention, the Defence and Overseas Policy Committee, apparently never met while preparations for the Iraq war were undertaken;[21] key papers were not circulated to the whole cabinet which, in the words of the official committee under Lord Butler's chairmanship investigating Intelligence on the war, meant that it was 'obviously much more difficult for members of the cabinet outside the small circle directly involved to bring their political judgement and experience to bear on the major decisions for which the cabinet as a whole must bear responsibility'.[22]

Above all, it was the first time in the last 200 years that Britain's casus belli had been shown to be false after a major war began. In March 2003 the Government laid down: 'Our primary objective remains to rid Iraq of its weapons of mass destruction and their associated programmes and means of delivery, including prohibited ballistic missiles.'[23] But it gradually became clear after the invasion that no such weapons existed. Other states had previously experienced similar dichotomies between claims and facts; the United States had attacked Spain in 1898 because it had erroneously believed that the US battleship Maine had been blown up by the Spanish, instead of by the spontaneous combustion of its own magazine[24]; similarly, the crew of the US destroyers Maddox and Turner Joy mistakenly believed that they had been attacked by North Vietnamese gunboats in the Tonkin Gulf on 4 August 1964, leading to the crucial Congressional resolution giving President Johnson authority to expand the Vietnam War. There had been no equivalent British error over a casus belli for a major conflict in the previous 200 years. It was rather as if the Liberal government had discovered in August 1914 that the Germans had not, in fact, invaded Belgium or the National government had found in September 1939 that the Nazis had not attacked Poland. The error in 2003 was vital because, although Tony Blair subsequently justified the war in terms of the repressive nature of the Iraqi regime, as the Butler report put it:

> Officials noted that regime change of itself had no basis in international law; and that any offensive military action against Iraq could only be justified if Iraq were held to be in breach of its disarmament obligations under Security Council resolution or some new resolution.[25]

It was perfectly true, as the government asserted, that Saddam Hussein had been a brutal dictator, but many believed his overthrow was illegal because he was not involved in genocide, which alone could justify the overthrow of a government by foreign troops.[26] Moreover, as the Iraqi civil war intensified after the invasion, it became clear that that unfortunate and fissiparous country could only be kept together by force.

There were criticisms of the Intelligence Services, the way the war was planned in the Cabinet, the legal advice tendered to the government and the Parliamentary response to those plans. Rightly or wrongly, there was a widespread feeling that the Attorney General's advice on the legality of the war had altered under government and US pressure. As one lawyer put it in a letter to *The Times*:

> The Government relied on the final opinion of a vacillatory Attorney General whose professional expertise was commercial, not public international law, in preference to the consensus stance of the legal staff of the Foreign and Commonwealth Office...whose view on the legality of the war without a second UN Security Council resolution was shared by almost every international lawyer of repute, as well as by Lord Goldsmith himself until his volte-face.[27]

As far as Intelligence was concerned, the Butler report concluded that more reliance had been placed on the information supplied by the half dozen Iraqi sources in contact with British Intelligence than was justified in the event:

> The fact that reporting from one of their important pre-war sources has been withdrawn, and that from the other two main sources is open to doubt, led us to question the standard procedures adopted by SIS to ensure that their sources are valid and that their reporting is subject to quality control.[28]

Such failings were brought to public notice by the attribution to the Intelligence Services of the document published in September 2002 claiming that Iraq had apparently not abandoned its banned weapons programmes and, of course, by the subsequent failure to discover any chemical or biological weapons. The fundamental problem was that it was most unusual, if not unique, for Britain to go to war on the basis of Intelligence reports alone. Given the tentative nature of human Intelligence (as opposed to signals Intelligence) and the impossibility of explaining the sort of sources, let alone the individual informants, on whose evidence it was based, this seems, in retrospect, to have been unwise.

While Intelligence had not been properly assessed or presented to the Cabinet and to the public, many blamed Parliamentary procedures for the failure to check the rush to war. In fact the House of Commons had held a very thorough and wide-ranging debate about Iraq on 18 March 2003, the problem was that some MPs, who harboured severe doubts, were not prepared either to trust their own judgement, to let down their party and the armed forces or to follow public opinion. Nearly 60 MPs spoke, not counting the numerous interruptions, and many of their speeches were both deeply felt and prescient. To take some of the most impressive examples, Ronnie Campbell, the Labour MP for Blyth Valley, warned:

> Moderate young Muslims will be told that that is what the West does to them: it invades a Muslim country and drops thousands of bombs on its people.... Such action will make it far easier for al Qaeda to recruit young people to become human bombs in this country..... That is the worst scenario if this war goes ahead.[29]

Sir Teddy Taylor, the Conservative MP for Rochford and Southend East, pointed out:

> There is a great feeling among us that we are going to intervene, improve matters and restore democracy, freedom and liberty, but where is the evidence that such intervention has been successful in the past? For example, a great deal has been said about Afghanistan, a country that I know a little about, but can we say that things are much better as a result of the intervention that took place? Rather, it is a pathetic country, run by a group of people who have no democratic responsibility whatever.[30]

Tony Worthington, the Labour MP for Clydebank and Milngavie, warned:

> We are going to invade a country of Balkanesque complexity where occupying forces will be unable easily to withdraw. We are rapidly in danger of becoming piggy in the middle for every discontented ethnic or religious group in the area. There seems little doubt of speedy initial victory but it is worth remembering that the Six Day War in the Middle East is still going strong after 35 years. This war has similar potential.[31]

Richard Page, the Conservative MP for South-West Hertfordshire, commented, 'I am greatly concerned that we have not spent enough time considering how to rebuild Iraq.... What exactly shall we put in place? I have heard about territorial protection and the maintenance of borders, but has anyone talked to the Kurds of northern Iraq about that?'[32]

There was also, and rightly as it turned out, a good deal of scepticism about the evidence that Iraq had chemical and biological weapons. Andrew Mackay, the Conservative MP for Bracknell, pointed out that the government's 'dodgy dossier' (which had been based on a student's thesis) and spurious claims of links between Iraq and al Qaeda had 'caused huge harm to the credibility of the government's case'. Similarly, John McDonnell, the Labour MP for Hayes and Harlington, argued, 'the great persuaders have failed to persuade. People have seen through the dodgy dossiers and the forged nuclear weapons evidence', while David Heath, Liberal Democrat MP for Somerton and Frome, talked of a 'superfluity of dubious evidence'.[33] On the other side, government and Conservative spokesmen and their supporters stressed the threat from weapons of mass destruction, the repressive nature of Saddam Hussein's regime, the way in which it had frustrated the United Nations, the blocking of the Security Council by the French and the need to support Britain's armed forces. In the event, the government won by 396–217 against a proposal to amend its motion and 412–149 on its motion that the United Kingdom 'should use all necessary means to ensure the disarmament of Iraq's weapons of mass destruction'. Invasion would lead to the installation of 'a representative government which upholds human rights and the rule of law for all Iraqis'.

Some of the government's critics argued later that a favourable Parliamentary vote should become mandatory before a government could again take the country to war, even though the House of Commons had failed to vote against the war on 18 March. One who made such a proposal was the former Development Secretary, Clare Short, who resigned over the war and explained that she believed that the system was 'outdated and undemocratic':

> I … remain stunned and worried by the way in which we saw our constitutional arrangements malfunction on the route to war and a trail of deceit, which I think helps to explain the failure to prepare for afterwards and the dreadful situation and the terrible loss of life.… The Defence and Overseas Policy Committee never met, so all the options were not properly scrutinised and the legal authorisation was concocted in a very disreputable way, which is now a matter of record.[34]

The former Conservative Chancellor of the Exchequer Kenneth Clarke argued that Parliamentary scrutiny had been similarly subverted as the government had waited until the last possible moment before allowing the House of Commons to vote 'because the Prime Minister seriously doubted he could get a majority for what he proposed to do. I think it is doubtful whether he would have got authority for what he did if he had tried to seek it two months earlier and been totally candid about where we were.'[35]

The war had precipitated such reflections but they were undoubtedly also the consequence of public attitudes. People now feel confident enough to reject dubious ministerial claims. At the same time, Parliament's position as the centre of the political nation had been usurped by direct democracy via the opinion poll and the television or radio station. Thus, as we saw in Chapter 8, the electorate has become ever more apathetic about Parliamentary debates; the 1918 election excepted, voting turnout fell to its lowest level ever in 2001, 59.4 per cent voted compared with over 70 per cent in every election from 1922 to 1997. Labour retained power in 2005 with the support of 21.6 per cent of the electorate or 9.56 million votes, fewer than any victorious party had polled since the 1920s, when the population was far smaller, and 4 million less than it had in 1997.[36] It is more accurate to say that, because of their unpopularity, the Conservatives lost three elections in a row, leaving Labour to win by default. Giving Parliament an overt veto on a government's right to declare war was an attempt to increase members' power, recoup their prestige and persuade voters that it was worth casting their ballots at elections.[37]

The House of Commons' Public Administration Select Committee published a report in 2004 agreeing with Clare Short that Parliament should have to approve a decision to engage in armed conflict either beforehand or as soon as possible afterwards. The Lords' Select Committee on the Constitution disagreed and recommended in July 2006 that a convention, rather than a law, should be established under which a Government should seek Parliamentary approval if it were proposing the deployment of British forces outside the United Kingdom into actual or potential conflict. If such prior application were impossible, the Government should provide retrospective information within seven days of the onset of hostilities or as soon as it was feasible. As a matter of course, it should keep Parliament informed of the progress of such deployments and, if their nature or objectives altered significantly, it should seek a renewal of the mandate.[38]

Some of the witnesses before the Lords Committee agreed with the Commons' Select Committee that the obligation to secure Parliamentary approval should become law rather than convention. However, even those in favour, sometimes recognised the difficulties. Some thought it might lead to wrangles in the courts and to impractical delays in military movements. A debate could warn a potential enemy of Britain's intentions precisely when the government wanted to move forces surreptitiously to a threatened area. As the former First Sea Lord, Admiral Lord Boyce, reminded the Lords Committee, this is particularly true of naval forces, which have the capacity to 'loiter' off a distant coast for a considerable time. Such was the situation in 1977, when Britain was involved in negotiations with the Argentine government over the Falklands, and to show its determination to resist an attack, 'one nuclear-powered submarine and two frigates were deployed to the area', though it was never necessary to tell Buenos Aires of the movement and the force was withdrawn once the threat receded.[39] It would have been both futile and provocative to announce such a deployment before it took place since it could have precipitated the very invasion of the islands it was designed to deter. Similarly, Lord Vincent reminded the Lords committee of the way in which British Forces had had to mount a secret and rapid rescue of peacekeepers captured by a group called the 'West Side Boys' in Sierra Leone.[40] In such cases, although forces have been moved into a potential combat zone, public debate can only take place afterwards, if at all. Servicemen involved in a deployment, which led to war and which had not received prior Parliamentary authorisation, would clearly worry about their legal standing if there were a statutory obligation on the government to receive prior approval.

Of course, even though it has not voted on the issues involved, before major wars there has, as we have seen, nearly always been time for Parliamentary debate. Since 1800 there has only been one significant occasion when debate was redundant because it was not a war of choice, following the Japanese attack on Hong Kong, Malaya and Singapore in December 1941, and even then Winston Churchill recalled Parliament. Before every other major war, as we have seen in Chapter 8, Parliament debated the issue as if the war was one of choice not just for the government, but for Parliament and for the people.[41] There was also time for such a debate even though preliminary military movements had already begun. Thus, for example, in 1914, before the crucial Parliamentary debate and the government's decision for war, the First Lord Winston Churchill had kept the Fleet mobilised following naval manoeuvres; in 1990 Tornado aircraft had been sent to the Gulf, nine days after the Iraqi conquest of Kuwait and some weeks before Parliament met, while a number of Royal Naval vessels were assembled in the region.[42] However, in both cases Parliament could have brought operations to a halt if a majority had been determined to do so.

Nevertheless, as the House of Lords committee suggested, it seems desirable to establish a convention that the government should seek Parliamentary approval, whenever possible, before it involves the country in a major armed conflict and while it is preparing the armed forces for this prospect. Where Parliament could be strengthened is by laying down that it should be reconvened immediately whenever substantial conflict threatened to involve British forces, or when a certain number of MPs believed such a conflict impended. This would not, of course, protect the country from a government, which has a clear majority and was determined to go to war despite the weakness of the casus belli.[43] As we have seen, the United States, the country with the oldest written constitution laying down that Congress must vote before the country goes to war, has done so three times under false pretences. On each occasion Congress simply accepted the executive's view of the situation. Nor would radical proposals to abolish the House of Lords or to make it entirely elective increase the constitutional safeguards against the rush to war, quite the contrary. The Lords have been a more effective brake than the Commons on government impetuosity in recent years.[44] The House of Lords has the potential to reflect the modern era by becoming entirely a house of professional experts made up of lawyers, trades unionists, retired diplomats and military officers, medical specialists, representatives of the NGOs, churchmen, academics, industrialists and financiers – something which Tony Blair appears to have recognised in his final appearance before the Commons Liaison Committee as Prime Minister where he claimed that he had never believed in an elected second assembly.[45]

People appointed for their expertise are not beholden to the government in the same way as Members of the Commons. A reformed and renamed House of Experts or Notables, chosen for a limited period by representative bodies, such as the Confederation of British Industry, Trades Union Congress, the universities, NGOs or the Royal Society, would command attention by its intellectual calibre. Its example would encourage MPs to be less obsequious to the government in power than they have been in recent years or than members of Congress showed themselves to be when they went along with the three administration's spurious arguments for war in 1898, 1964 and 2003. Professionalism confers greater legitimacy today than election; television and radio stations summon scientists, diplomats or doctors to give their views on their field of expertise, not MPs, when they need to inform the public. Indeed, despite the growing sophistication of the debates on war held today in the Commons, MPs are unfortunately held in disrepute, if not contempt; it is the House of Commons which must struggle to affirm its competence when we have direct democracy through the televisions studios, opinion polls and referenda.

Intervention in Iraq cannot be blamed primarily on the British 'people'. As we saw in the previous chapter, in the weeks leading up to the war polls suggested that the vast majority of British people had opposed such an attack without additional UN authority. In February 2003, 57 per cent did not believe the government had made a convincing case for war, 62 per cent were against an attack without a further UN resolution and more than twice as many, 24 per cent, were against an attack under any circumstances as supported an attack without another UN resolution.[46] A further poll, published on 15 March 2003, found 67 per cent of Britons, 90 per cent of French, 86 per cent of Germans and 93 per cent of Spanish opposed to the war.[47] Britain was taken to war in March 2003 against the wishes of its people and the majority of Europeans.[48]

The majority of people are, however, to blame in one respect; their tendency to rally round the government once war begins. This was less unsatisfactory before the age of opinion polls but it means that the public can no longer act as a deterrent to a government which wants to go to war. Many MPs who spoke on 18 March shared these public feelings: as John Burnett, the MP for Torridge and West Devon, put it, 'I cannot vote against a motion that offers support to Her Majesty's forces who are now on duty in the Middle East.' As a result he abstained on the government's motion but such attitudes, however well-intentioned, weakened the restraints on government policy and could endanger the armed forces and, indeed, the nation itself.

11
Do Debates on War Matter?

Some would argue that it is not so much that governments deliberately ignore public debates, as the previous chapter suggested, but that they are irrelevant because policy is determined by deeper factors and that all ideas are simply a reflection of these. Others would agree that debates matter but suggest that the British debates are too moralistic, that the Wilberforce or 'Good Samaritan' tradition has come to dominate discussion, rather than the more cautious traditions reflected in the work of Cobden, Bloch, Angell and Wells. This explains Britain's propensity to elect to become involved in wars, allowing its critics, including those quoted at the beginning of this book, to be able to accuse Britain of being the most belligerent of the Great Powers.

Determinists of all hues deny that debates matter. Biological determinists, Marxists and many members of the realist school of international relations would argue that the ideas analysed in this book are superficial and that there are underlying factors which mandate governments' decisions. Leo Tolstoy, Edmund Wilson and Karl Marx took this position, although they all found difficulty in sustaining it throughout their writings or acting as though they believed it. Similarly Communist governments, which purported to agree with Marx that economic factors controlled how men behave, spent vast sums propagating their views during the Cold War, persecuting their citizens for their heterodox ideas and jamming Western television and radio stations to prevent subversive alien notions creeping into their territories. Up to 70,000 censors allegedly watched over Soviet publications, while 15,000 people were employed jamming Western broadcasts at a cost of $150 million each year.[1] But they could not prevent Soviet citizens learning that their standard of living was falling ever further behind the West and the 'Asian tigers' and, by the end of the 1980s, this realisation had proved fatal to the communist cause.

Edmund Wilson's *Patriotic Gore* is one of the most comprehensive examinations of the intellectual ferment evoked by any war in history. Its dissection of the voluminous writings of poets, novelists, politicians, generals and ordinary citizens before, during and after the American Civil War would be difficult to better, yet the American critic claimed that none of their ideas was fundamental:

> The wars fought by human beings are stimulated as a rule primarily by the same instincts as the voracity of the sea slug.... It is, however, of course, very difficult for us to recognise that we, too, are devourers, and that we, too, are talking cant.[2]

Yet *Patriotic Gore* suggested that *Uncle Tom's Cabin*, the popular novel describing the sufferings of the slaves, published by Harriett Beecher Stowe in 1852, made war more likely by stiffening attitudes towards slavery on both sides of the North–South divide. At the same time, Sir Walter Scott's historical novels spread romantic ideas about warfare and Southern society amongst those living in the Confederacy and thus encouraged the Southern people to defend their values. Wilson also showed how Abraham Lincoln's ambitions and passionate belief in maintaining the Union clashed with the equally determined faith of Alexander Stephens, the vice-president of the Confederacy, that slavery was built into the US Constitution as, indeed, was the right of any part of that Union to secede.[3]

Marx and Tolstoy faced the same problems of consistency. However, much Marx might claim that economics rather than ideas shaped society he evidently thought it worthwhile to devote his life to propagating his ideas about economics and society, and appealing to the workers in the various countries to unite and support their interests.[4] Ironically, modern dermatologists have argued that Marx's own views were produced by the skin disease from which he suffered, covering him with boils and producing 'so much psychological distress... [which] explains his self-loathing and alienation, a response reflected by the alienation Marx developed in his writings'.[5] In the medical view, biological determinism caps economics.

War and Peace, Tolstoy's epic novel about Napoleon's invasion of Russia, published in 1869, purports to be deterministic; Napoleon thought he was making the key decisions but, in fact, like everyone else, he was being driven by deeper factors of which he was unaware. However,

Tolstoy became a Christian pacifist and he acted, wrote and spoke as though pacifists, acting together, would be able to stop governments driving their people to war. As he told the Swedish Peace Congress in 1909, governments 'have millions of money and millions of obedient soldiers; we have only one thing, but that is the most powerful thing in the world – Truth' and for Tolstoy the truth was that Christianity forbade murder and, therefore, condemned all wars. He called on the Congress to draw up an appeal pointing out that war 'is a criminal and shameful activity'.[6] The assumption that such a campaign could change governments' policies flatly contradicted the view expressed in *War and Peace* that 'it is altogether impossible to agree that intellectual activity has controlled the actions of mankind, for such phenomena as the brutal murders of the French revolution, which were the outcome of the doctrine of the equality of man, and the most wicked wars and executions resulting from the Gospel of Love belie this hypothesis'.[7] According to the novel, historians say ideas influence events because they deal in ideas and like to believe they are important, but they cannot prove that ideas have any effect.

Wilson, Tolstoy and Marx acted as though they had identified general tendencies rather than determinants. Such factors deeply influence but do not govern policy or the political debate – any more than Marx's boils determined the shape of his thought and writings. Most people accept that national culture, the balance of power, economic interests and social cohesion have very strong effects, while also believing that ideas and the debates they produce may rein in or exacerbate these tendencies. A balance of power has a major impact on politics, but that impact depends on the use which people choose to make of it and, in peacetime, on the estimates statesmen hold of it. In war the balance is put to one particular type of test. In peacetime statesmen are influenced by the impressions around them and the vague way in which countries are 'ranked' in the public mind. The figures, which economists produce of the domestic product and economic growth rate of a country, have become deeply influential since the Second World War. Thus, most people believe at the beginning of the 21st century that India has become much more powerful because of its rapid economic growth. This, in turn, affects politics; the United States has made a major effort to work with the Indian government and has tacitly decided to accept its nuclear weapons programme, which it had tried for years to prevent.[8] Similarly, the subsequent rise in oil and gas prices restored Russian morale, which had collapsed after the demise of the Soviet Union, and emboldened

Moscow to attack the Georgians in August 2008 to prove that they dominated the surrounding countries and that they were a power to be reckoned with.

The US propensity to use its military strength grew dramatically after the collapse of the Soviet Union undermined the balance of power. But this does not explain why Bush and Blair decided to attack Iraq rather than any other state in March 2003, or why they felt that they could replace the Iraqi government by another one more amenable to the West. As far as Iraqi reform was concerned, the memory of the overthrow of the Axis governments at the end of the Second World War and the successful democratisation of these countries seems to have played a part. Similarly, we can accept that economic considerations have an important effect on governmental policy without claiming that the lure of Iraqi oil was necessarily the only (or even the main) conscious or unconscious factor which persuaded George W. Bush to attack Iraq in March 2003, or Tony Blair to support him.

The so-called 'biological' factors, which impressed Edmund Wilson, are most influential after a government has taken the decision for war because it is then that many people behave in a herd-like fashion, abandon any reservations they had and support their government. As Wilfred Trotter pointed out at the beginning of the 20th century, man is a 'gregarious animal' and it is the tendencies which make it possible for him to associate with his immediate fellows that most endanger a foreign enemy in wartime:

> In a country at war all opinion is necessarily more or less subject to prejudice, and this liability to bias is a herd mechanism, and owes its vigour to that potent instinct.... A war apprehended as dangerous produces a more complete solution of the minor herds of society into the common body than does a war not so regarded.[9]

However, the fact that people 'apprehend' how great a threat the war is to their own country and that there have been domestic critics of every war Britain has waged show that men do not have to herd together in wartime, even if they feel both the need to do so themselves and strong pressure to conform from others. They are left with the power of choice.

If debates do matter, are British discussions too moralistic and indifferent to the country's interests? It was this tendency which the British military historian Correlli Barnett blamed for *The Collapse of British Power* at the start of the Second World War:

> It came to be more and more generally felt [in the 19th Century] by public opinion that moral principle and moral purpose rather than strategy or mere interest alone should be the inspiration of English policy.... It is indeed in the transformation of the British character and outlook by this moral revolution that lies the first cause, from which all else was to spring, of the British plight in 1940.[10]

It is certainly true that domestic critics have often been infuriated by what they have seen as the failure of British governments to live up to their moral responsibilities. There has frequently been more debate in Britain about those occasions when the country did not intervene to protect another state than about those occasions when it did. Thus its decision not to protect the Abyssinians in 1935 against Italian attack, its neutrality during the Spanish Civil War in 1936 and, above all, its decision to abandon the Czechs at the Munich conference in 1938 rankled for years afterwards. Indeed the Munich agreement profoundly influenced Anglo-American policy for the next half century, any initiative which could be represented as appeasement during the Cold War was instantly damned.[11] In more recent times the general failures to prevent genocide in Rwanda in 1994 or to attack Serbia in response to its policies in Croatia and Bosnia have caused similar controversy, as we saw in Chapter 4.[12]

The moral pressures to intervene have not abated in recent years. As Chapter 3 showed, the urge to interfere is particularly strong amongst Western commentators, leader writers and NGOs. When a vast area of Myanmar was flooded in May 2008, NGOs were horrified that the Myanmar government was reluctant to accept their assistance. The generals who held power in Rangoon did not want the Burmese people to see them dependent on foreigners and distrusted Western countries, which had tried to isolate and overthrow them. A member of a French NGO was quoted as saying, 'it's a crime against humanity. It should be against the law. It's like they are taking a gun and shooting their own people.'[13] Commentators claimed that the West had the right to intervene to force the Myanmar government to accept aid. The French Foreign Minister Bernard Kouchner argued that countries had the responsibility to intervene and so protect victims of genocide.[14] Menacing reports suggested that US naval vessels and 11,000 troops were approaching the region.

A few weeks later the intimidation of voters in Zimbabwe by President Mugabe's government led to further calls from commentators for intervention. On the other hand, retired officers stressed the practical military hurdles involved in an invasion while Britain was embroiled in the two continuing insurgencies in Afghanistan and Iraq, as well as the problems involved in flying into a land-locked country.[15] President Mugabe's career was also a standing warning of the difficulties Western peoples have in understanding the politics of the Third World and evaluating attitudes towards human rights; in 1981 Mugabe was short-listed for the Nobel Peace Prize, although the awarding committee eventually gave it to the Office of the UN High Commissioner for Refugees.[16] Mugabe was a hero amongst those who fought for independence in Zimbabwe, and his supporters ignored his subsequent decision to crush all opposition. Only if one argues that such repression was the sole way to maintain stability in the new country could one say that he ever did anything for 'peace'.

Attitudes to individual cases will differ but there remains a general consensus in Britain that the country could and should play an important part in the making of international security. It is not self-evident that it should do so. Much larger countries, including Brazil and Nigeria, or with stronger industrial bases like Germany and Japan, do not participate so actively. The English learnt from their history the importance of preventing the emergence of a dominant power in Europe which might build a great navy and launch an invasion across the Channel. Preserving the balance of power also protected small states such as the Netherlands against foreign attack. Thus the British came to see themselves as the guardians of such nations, Serbia, Belgium and Luxemburg in 1914, Poland in 1939. When they failed to defend weak states, such as Poland in the 18th century or Czechoslovakia in 1938, even if they had no military power to do anything else, they felt themselves morally weakened. As one of Neville Chamberlain's critics put it after the Munich agreement abandoning the Czechs:

> I doubt whether anyone can describe this as a peace based on negotiation, on reason, on justice. Will it figure in history as anything else than the greatest – and the cheapest – victory ever won by aggressive militarism?[17]

When they themselves were the conquerors in India and Africa, the British convinced themselves that the conquest was a minor matter and that they were the altruistic guardians of the peoples living there. As the 19th-century Cambridge historian, Sir John Seeley, put it:

> We are not really conquerors of India, and we cannot rule her as conquerors; if we undertook to do so, it is not necessary to inquire

whether we could succeed, for we should surely be ruined financially by the mere attempt.

The British could rule south of the Himalayas because, in his view, Indians had no sense of nationality at that time, were used to being ruled by foreigners and because they saw that British rule was beneficial.[18] Similarly, just before he became archbishop, Randall Davidson claimed that British power had 'not grown by the rude prowess of a conqueror's sword, but almost wholly by the spread of commerce and civilisation'. The Empire was not just for Britain's good but for the world's.[19] Seeley and Davidson would have deplored the conventional modern view that such colonialism was 'morally depraved' because it only benefited the British, and they would have thought it excessively pessimistic to accept that 'imperialism is a narcissistic enterprise, and narcissism is doomed to disillusion. Whatever other people want to be, they do not want to be forced to be us.'[20] Both would, however, have agreed that the British Raj would, and should, survive only if it benefited and was accepted by the Indians. When an aspect of imperial rule was clearly not beneficial, as slavery had been, then it had to be abolished; when the Indian National Congress began its campaign for independence then, as the historian had forecast, the only question was how soon and in what manner the British would leave. We now know from the 19th-century records that British ministers and civil servants in charge of the Empire had no overall plan, they simple responded day by day to events, although their 'judgements and actions in fact were heavily prejudiced by their beliefs about morals and politics, about the duties of government, the ordering of society and international relations'.[21]

Whether this supports the modern critics or the traditional supporters of imperialism, it is clear that, as Britain became more democratic so the need for its leaders to simplify the reasons for their decisions, to emphasise the country's benevolent ambitions and to demonise their opponents became more important. People will not, on the whole, risk their lives or their relatives' lives for grand strategic or general economic reasons. General David Barno, who commanded US forces in Afghanistan from 2003 to 2005, recalled a conversation with a former European defence minister who told him, 'I can't go back to my population and tell him that [the war in] Afghanistan is about the strategic importance of the region, that's not why they agreed to go to Afghanistan – they went there for humanitarian reasons.'[22] This could make politicians totally cynical: in the words of the long-time editor of the *Westminster Gazette*, 'whatever their personal beliefs may be,

Kings and statesmen must at least pretend to be on the side of right against wrong'.[23] But most ministers probably believed what they said much of the time. No doubt, they were inconsistent and confused even about their own motives; the same Lord Palmerston, who, as we saw in Chapter 3, strongly supported the interdiction of the slave trade, was also the minister who presided in 1840 over the Opium War against China, thereby protecting a commerce which reduced addicts to walking corpses and was rightly described by its critics at the time as 'unjust and iniquitous'.[24]

If consistency is rare, so are policies which contradict a country's interests abroad; rare but not unknown. Ever since the Suez crisis in 1956, the Washington elite has supported Israel in its confrontation with the Arabs, while US material interests lie almost wholly with Israel's enemies because of US dependence on Arab oil. The Arabs are also able to buy far more US weapons than the Israelis and make more investments in US companies and government stocks. The US political elite's support for Israel overrides national interest and the opinion of the public who rank Israel below Egypt, Mexico and Brazil, and equal with Philippines and Taiwan in terms of their general sympathies.[25] Empathy for a democracy surrounded by more autocratic states, religious sympathy for the Jews, the memory of the Holocaust and understanding for a people who have dispossessed the original inhabitants as the Americans have done themselves, all appear to play their part in deciding policy, alongside the influence of Jewish voters in US elections.

Human actions invariably have mixed motives and this will obviously be more so when an international coalition influences decisions. The United States and its allies went to war in 1991 to protect the oil-rich state of Kuwait from Iraqi attack. According to one well-informed account:

> Bush, the former Texas oil man seemed horrified that Saddam might get Saudi Arabia.... Would Saddam withhold Iraqi and Kuwaiti oil? Or would he try to flood the world market?.... Higher oil prices would fuel inflation, worsening the gloomy condition of the US economy.[26]

Greater oil resources would also have enabled Saddam Hussein to buy more weapons and possibly threaten other states, such as Iran or Israel. He had already shown indifference to international law by attacking Iran in September 1980 and using chemical weapons against the Iranian army and against rebellious Kurds in Iraq in breach of the Geneva

Protocol. If Iraq had absorbed Kuwait this would have been the first time since the foundation of the United Nations that one country had conquered an independent state and incorporated it into its own territories in breach of the Charter. Thus, in her memoirs, Lady Thatcher stressed the illegal nature of the Iraqi occupation and the dangers of appeasing aggressors. As she put it in a lecture at the time: 'Iraq's invasion of Kuwait defies every principle for which the United Nations stands. If we let it succeed, no small country can ever feel safe again. The law of the jungle would take over from the rule of law.'[27] There were, therefore, legal, economic, political, military and moral reasons for coming to Kuwait's assistance. To these were added press reports about Iraqi mistreatment of the Kuwaitis which made, or were intended to make, the UN operation against Iraq more popular.

Similar combinations of motives operated equally in other cases. As we have seen, Pitt in 1793, Clarendon in 1854, Grey in 1914, Chamberlain in 1939, Thatcher in 1982 and 1990 and Blair in 2003 did not separate Britain's interests from what they perceived to be the common good. Domination of the continent by the French revolutionaries, Russia or Germany, seizure of the Falkland Islands by Argentina or of Kuwait by Iraq, possession of chemical and biological weapons by Saddam Hussein seemed both undesirable in themselves because of the nature of the governments involved and the methods they used, and against British interests. The objectives might be expressed in moral terms although they incorporated all the different motives. What separated Tony Blair from most of his predecessors was the combination of his idealism and his confidence that the world could be changed for the better by force.

The general public are more cautious, they understand well enough the potential dangers arising from military intervention. They see war now not from the point of view of the generals and politicians but from that of the ordinary civilians and soldiers. They are aware how a well-meaning politician can lead the country into a guerrilla war from which withdrawal is extremely difficult. While the memory of British defeats in Palestine, Cyprus and Aden may be fading, people recall the US debacle in Vietnam and the Soviets' humiliation in Afghanistan. They see the effects of bombing from day to day on their television screens and watch the wounded rushed to makeshift hospitals, which gives war an immediacy that it could never have had for most of our ancestors. They know instinctively about the 'law of unintended effects' which means that leaders' actions have consequences beyond their imaginings.

But, as the previous chapter showed, it was still possible in March 2003 for a tiny group of people at the head of the government to commit the country to war despite the previous opposition of the vast majority of the public, as well as of many academics and diplomats who studied the Middle East, of the majority of British international lawyers and Churchmen, and without taking the cabinet into full confidence. The known propensity of the public to rally round a government drastically weakened their power and ability to act as a restraint. The public debate has widened over the last 200 years as the public have gained in confidence, but the governmental decision-making process has not improved to the same extent. The Committee of Imperial Defence was established by the government at the beginning of the 20th century to coordinate expertise on Britain's far-flung responsibilities, what is needed is an effort to utilise even more wide-ranging and varied expertise when crises threaten in the future. We now know how small groups of people, including governments, develop 'tunnel vision', the very opposite of the scientific approach in which general enquiry and argument advance the progress of knowledge. If the government is considering committing British forces to operations, and if time and military secrecy allows, all available information and expertise should be taken into account and as much of this as possible presented to Parliament and public. The country would be much safer from involvement in unwise conflicts, such as the Suez operation or the March 2003 attack, if the balance between government and people were changed, and the convention were established that, whether or not the leader writers and columnists are pressing for intervention, the armed forces would not be risked when the majority of people and military and civilian experts were opposed to the war.

Caution will be ever more necessary over the coming decades; the scope for Western intervention will be gradually reduced with the rise of Great Powers in Asia, and the increase in the ability of even the weakest of states to retaliate against Western targets through guerrilla warfare and terrorism. The emergence of new satellite television stations and websites increases the confidence of non-Western cultures and their determination to resist occidental influence. The violent opposition to Western intervention in Iraq and Afghanistan reaffirms the same lessons as the defeat of colonial forces in the two decades after the Second World War. Even if they make use of all the balanced theories that Robert Thompson and others deduced from colonial experiences, conventional forces have met their match in insurgency and no one who participates in debates about going to war in future should forget this.

Notes

Introduction

1. Reproduced in W. G. Knop, Compiler, *Beware of the English: German Propaganda Exposes England* (London, Hamish Hamilton, 1939), p. 147.
2. Lewis F. Richardson, *Statistics of Deadly Quarrels* (London, Stevens, 1960), pp. 173–175. Britain had participated in most wars, Germany in most battles, though Richardson warned his readers about the tentative nature of the statistics.
3. Ramsay Muir, *The Expansion of Europe* (London, Constable, 1935), p. 2. For a different formulation of the same pervasive thought, see Lord Acton, *Lectures on Modern History* (London, Fontana, 1960), p. 44 and Sir J. R. Sleeley, *The Expansion of England* (London, Macmillan, 1900), p. 212.
4. Philip Everts and Pierangelo Isernia (eds), *Public Opinion and the International Use of Force* (London, Routledge, 2001).
5. For a recent examination of the motives behind British and US foreign policy, see Walter Russell Mead, *God and Gold: Britain, America and the Making of the Modern World* (London, Atlantic Books, 2007).
6. *Statement on Defence Estimates 1996*, Cm 3223 (London, HMSO, 2006), p. 3.
7. *The Military Balance 2008* (London, International Institute for Strategic Studies/Routledge, 2008), p. 161. See also the speech by Tony Blair at the R.U.S.I. on 11 January 2007.
8. François Crouzet, 'The impact of the French Wars on the British Economy' in H. T. Dickinson (ed.), *Britain and French Revolution, 1789–1815* (Basingstoke, Macmillan, 1989), p. 195. For casualty statistics on the First World War, see David Stevenson, *1914–1918: The History of the First World War* (London, Allen Lane, 2004), p. 20.
9. Alex Mercer, *Disease, Mortality and Population in Transition* (Leicester, Leicester University Press, 1990).
10. Edmund Wilson, *Patriotic Gore: Studies in the Literature of the American Civil War* (New York, Galaxy/Oxford, 1966); Yuval Noah Harari, *Renaissance Military Memoirs: War, History and Identity* (Woodbridge, Suffolk, Boydell, 2004).
11. R. B. McCallum, *Public Opinion and the Last Peace* (London, Oxford University Press, 1944).
12. William Roger Louis, *Ends of British Imperialism: The Scramble for Empire, Suez and Decolonisation* (London, Tauris, 2006).
13. 'British Institute of Public Opinion', *Public Opinion Quarterly*, March 1940; Jean Owen, 'The polls and newspaper appraisal of the Suez Crisis', *Public Opinion Quarterly*, Fall 1957, pp. 350–354; Anthony King (ed.), *British Political Opinion 1937–2000* (London, Politicos, 2001); 'The war with Iraq: The ides of March Poll', MORI at http://www.mori.com/polls/2003/Iraq3 downloaded 11 August 2003.

14. David Dilks (ed.), *The Diaries of Sir Alexander Cadogan 1938–1945* (London, Cassell, 1971), p. 447, entry for 17 April 1942.
15. J. W. Fortescue, *British Statesmen of the Great War 1793–1814* (Oxford, Clarendon Press, 1911). For a defence of Pitt's strategy, see Piers Mackesy, 'Strategic problems of the British war effort', in Dickinson, *Britain and the French Revolution.*
16. David Lloyd George, *War Memoirs* (London, Odhams Press, 1938), preface; Stephen Roskill, *Churchill and the Admirals* (London, Collins, 1977); Alex Danchev and Daniel Todman (eds), *War Diaries 1939–1945: Field Marshal Lord Alanbrooke* (London, Weidenfeld and Nicolson, 2001).
17. For civil–military relations in Britain, see Hew Strachan, *The Politics of the British Army* (Oxford, Clarendon Press, 1997).
18. Jeremy Black, *The English Press* (Stroud, Sutton Publishers, 2001), Chapters 1 and 10.
19. *Parliamentary Debates, House of Commons* (*HoC*), July–October 1990, column 762.
20. J. A. Hobson, *The Psychology of Jingoism* (London, Grant Richards, 1901); C. E. Playne, *The Neurosis of the Nations* (London, George Allen and Unwin, 1925); Walter Lippmann, *Public Opinion* (New York, Free Press Paperbacks, 1997).
21. Lloyd George, *War Memoirs*, particularly the Foreword.
22. Sir Alfred Zimmern, *Spiritual Values and World Affairs* (Oxford, Oxford University Press, 1939).
23. 'Two nations: The curious role of social class in modern politics', *The Times*, 9 June 2004; John E. Mueller, *War, Presidents and Public Opinion* (New York, John Wiley, 1973), p. 272. Seventy-five per cent of college-educated were in favour of the Korean War in August 1951 against 49 per cent of grade-school-educated.
24. For a discussion of the debates about the First World War, see Brian Bond, *The Unquiet Western Front: Britain's Role in Literature and History* (Cambridge, Cambridge University Press, 2002).
25. A century beforehand, a British soldier serving in the Spanish Peninsula had complained, 'the duties of a besieging force are both harrowing and severe; and, I know not how it is, death in the trenches never carries with it the stamp of glory which seals the memory of those who perish in a well-fought field'. See Moyle Sherer, *Recollections of the Peninsula* (Staplehurst, Kent, Spellmount Library, 1996), p. 152.
26. *Parliamentary Debates, House of Lords* (*HoL*), 17 March 2003.
27. W. Trotter, *Instincts of the Herd in Peace and War* (London, Ernest Benn, 1930, first published 1916); Wilson, *Patriotic Gore*, p. xi.
28. *Public Opinion Quarterly* 1945–6, pp. 385 and 391.
29. For reactions to the end of the war with Japan, see H. G. Nicholas (ed.), *Washington Despatches 1941–1945: Weekly Political Reports from the British Embassy* (London, Weidenfeld and Nicolson, 1981), pp. 598 ff.; Hadley Cantril and Mildred Strunk, *Public Opinion 1935–1946* (Princeton, Princeton University Press, 1951), p. 20.
30. MORI, 'War with Iraq: Public view', 19 November 2002, www.mori.com/polls/2002/Iraq-approval.shtml. MORI, 'End of the Baghdad bounce', 8 June 2003, www.mori.com/polls/2003/t030526.shtml.

31. Linda L. Clark, *Social Darwinism in France* (Alabama, University of Alabama Press, 1984); Paul Crook, *Darwinism, War and History* (Cambridge, Cambridge University Press, 1994).
32. Ironically Charles Darwin himself had always seen that this was the case in warfare, see Charles Darwin, *The Descent of Man and Selection in Relation to Sex* (London, Penguin, 2004), p. 154.

1   Culture and Circumstance

1. A. H. Halsey, *Change in British Society* (Oxford, Oxford University Press, 1981), p. 2.
2. Viscount Grey of Fallodon, *Twenty-Five Years: 1892–1916* (London, Hodder and Stoughton, 1925), Volume 2, p. 1.
3. Francis Beer, *Peace Against War: The Ecology of International Violence* (San Francisco, Freeman, 1981), p. 16.
4. I use the term 'culture' rather than 'character' to emphasise its ability to change. On character, see Sir Ernest Barker, *National Character and the Factors in its Formation* (London, Methuen, fourth and revised edition 1948); Daniel Jenkins, *The British: Their Identity and the Churches* (SCM Press, London, 1975); Peter Mandler, *The English National Character: The History of an Idea from Edmund Burke to Tony Blair* (New Haven, Yale University Press, 2006).
5. For the way in which European romantic notions increased the gap between Japanese and Western culture, see Emiko Ohnuki-Tierney, *Kamikaze: Cherry Blossom and Nationalisms* (Chicago, University of Chicago Press, 2002).
6. Jonathan R. Adleman and Chih-yu Shi, *Symbolic War: The Chinese Use of Force 1840–1980* (Taipei, National Chengchi University, 1993).
7. M. A. Salahi, *Muhammad: Man and Prophet* (Shaftesbury, Element, 1995); Harfiyah, Abdel Haleem, Oliver Ramsbotham et al., *The Crescent and the Cross: Muslim and Christian Approaches to War and Peace* (London, Council of Christian Approaches to Defence and Disarmament, 1999); Bernard Lewis, *The Crisis of Islam: Holy War and Unholy Terror* (London, Weidenfeld and Nicolson, 2003).
8. John Proctor (ed.), *Village Schools: A History of Rural Elementary Education from the Eighteenth to the Twenty-First Century in Prose and Verse* (Oxford, Oxford University Press, 2005), introduction.
9. Harari, Y. N., *Renaissance Military Memoirs: War, History and Identity 1450–1600* (Woodbridge, Boydell, 2004), p. 21.
10. Peter Laslett, *The World We Have Lost* (London, Methuen, 1965), p. 68. For an individual view of mobility and immobility see Jack Ayres (ed.), *Paupers and Pig Killers: The Diary of William Holland a Somerset Parson 1799–1818* (Gloucester, Allan Sutton, 1984).
11. 'Review of the history of the ancient Barony of Castle Combe' by G. P. Scrope MP, *Quarterly Review*, March 1853.
12. Rowland Parker, *The Common Stream* (London, Paladin-Grafton, 1976), pp. 132–133.
13. Amiram Raviv et al., *How Children Understand Peace and War* (San Francisco, Jossey-Bass Publishers, 1999), p. 192.

14. See particularly the section from Joshua, Chapter 23 to Judges, Chapter 12. The nearest British equivalent is, perhaps, *The Ecclesiastic History of the English People*, written by 'the Venerable' Bede in about 731.

15. 'Banker "paid price" for being good citizen', *The Times*, 1 October 2008.

16. Quoted in W. O. Lester Smith, *Education* (Harmondsworth, Penguin, 1965), p. 9.

17. Kenneth Charlton, 'Mothers as educative agents in pre-industrial England', *History of Education*, 1994, Volume 23, No. 2.

18. For an analysis of the way modern children learn, see David Coulby and Crispin Jones, *Education and Warfare in Europe* (Aldershot, Ashgate, 2001), p. 69.

19. Oliver Morley Ainsworth (ed.), *Milton on Education: The Tractate of Education* (New Haven, Yale University Press, 1928), p. 55. See also W. O. Lester Smith, *Education* (Harmondsworth, Penguin, 1965), p. 9.

20. Knop, *Beware of the English*, p. 195.

21. F. H. Russell, *The Just War in the Middle Ages* (Cambridge, Cambridge University Press, 1975).

22. Snorri Sturluson, *King Harald's Saga: Harald Hardradi of Norway* (Penguin, Harmondsworth, 1966), pp. 102, 129 and 142.

23. Harari, *Military Memoirs*, p. 78 ff.

24. Blaise Pascal, *The Provincial Letters of Blaise Pascal* (London, Griffith Farran, Okeden and Welsh, undated), p. 109.

25. Eugenia Stanhope, *Letters Written by the Late Right Honourable Philip Dormer Stanhope Earl of Chesterfield to His Son* (London, Dodsley, 1792), Volume 2, p. 95.

26. E. de Vattel, *The Law of Nations and the Principles of Natural Law* (Washington, Carnegie Institution, 1916); Donald Read, *Cobden and Bright: A Victorian Political Partnership* (London, Edward Arnold, 1988), p. 128.

27. F. H. Hinsley, *Power and the Pursuit and the Pursuit of Peace: Theory and Practice in the History of Relations between States* (Cambridge, Cambridge University Press, 1981), part 1.

28. Marten Ultey (ed.), *Adapting to Conditions, War and Society in the Eighteenth Century* (Alabama, University of Alabama Press, 1986), p. 1.

29. Stanhope, *Letters Written by the Late Right Honourable Philip Dormer Stanhope Earl of Chesterfield to His Son* (London, Dodsley, 1792), Volume 2, p. 21.

30. William Hazlitt, 'Coffee house politicians', *Table Talk* (London, Humphrey Milford/Oxford University Press, 1925), p. 256.

31. Nicholas Shakespeare, *In Tasmania: Adventures at the End of the World* (London, Vintage, 2004), p. 97.

32. For US views, see Robert W. Oldendick and Barbara Ann Bardes, 'Mass and Elite Foreign Policy Opinion', *Public Opinion Quarterly*, 1982, p. 368 ff. For recent surveys, which show the pervasive nature of the interventionist ethic after the Cold War, see Everts and Isernia, *Public Opinion and the Use of Force*.

33. Proctor, *Village Schools*, p. 1.

34. Lester Smith, *Education*, pp. 194–195.

35. Barker, *National Character*, p. 212.

36. Review of David Hume's *History of England from the Invasion of Julius Caesar to the Revolution of 1688* in *The Quarterly Review*, June 1826, p. 252.

37. François Crouzet, 'The impact of the French wars on the British economy', in Dickinson (ed.), *Britain and French Revolution*, p. 195; Emma Vincent Macleod, *A War of Ideas* (Aldershot, Ashgate, 1998), p. 6 gives 315,000 casualties which would be a proportion of 1 in 38. The proportion would also be altered if Ireland were included thus bringing the population to just under 18 million in 1811 and 45 million 100 years later, Anthony Wood, *Nineteenth Century Britain:1815–1914* (London, Longmans, 1960), p. 449. For the war's impact on burials, see E. A. Wrigley and R. S. Schofield, *The Population History of England 1541–1871* (London, Edward Arnold, 1981), p. 128.
38. Macleod, *War of Ideas*, p. 6.
39. Richard Bonney (ed.), *Economic Systems and State Finance* (Oxford, Clarendon Press, 1995), pp. 377–390. Dickinson, *Britain and the French Revolution*, particularly Chapters 1 and 7.
40. Donald Read, *Cobden and Bright*, p. 121.
41. Crouzet, 'The impact of the French wars', p. 194. The primary reason for the high birth rate was the fall in the age of marriage from 26 to 23, though a subsidiary reason was the decline in the death rate, see E. A. Wringley, *People, Cities and Wealth: The Transformation of Traditional Society* (Oxford, Basil Blackwell, 1987), pp. 222–224. For casualty statistics on the First World War, see Robin Prior, *Churchill's World Crisis as History* (Beckenham, Croom Helm, 1983), Chapter 12.
42. Compare, for example, James Woodforde, *The Diary of a Country Parson 1758–1802* (London, Oxford University Press, 1949), Jack Ayres (ed.), *Paupers and Pig Killers: The Diary of William Holland A Somerset Parson 1799–1818* (Gloucester, Alan Sutton, 1984) and Peter Jupp, (ed.), *The Letter-Journal of George Canning 1793–1795* (London, Royal Historical Society, 1991) with Gavin Roydon (ed.), *Home Fires Burning: The Great War Diaries of Geogina Lee* (Stroud, Sutton, 2006); Mark Pottle (ed.), *Champion Redoubtable: The Diaries and Letters of Violent Bonham Carter 1914–1945* (London, Phoenix, 1999), part one. See also Parker, *Common Stream*, p. 202.
43. Arthur L. Bowley, *Some Economic Consequences of the Great War* (London, Thornton Butterworth, 1930), p. 101. For British borrowings from the United States, see Kathleen Burk, *Britain, America and the Sinews of War, 1914–1918* (London, George Allen and Unwin, 1985).
44. Gyorgy Ranki, *The Economics of the Second World War* (Vienna, Bohlau Verlag, 1995), pp. 285–290. For the initial efforts to raise income taxes, see Arthur Hope-Jones, *Income Tax in the Napoleonic Wars* (Cambridge, Cambridge University Press, 1939).
45. W. K. Hancock and M. M. Browning, *British War Economy* (London, HMSO, 1949), pp. 547–548. See also 'Sixty years on, we finally pay for the war', *The Times*, 27 December 2006 and Robert Skidelsky, *John Maynard Keynes: Fighting for Freedom, 1937–1946* (London, Penguin, 2002).
46. Alan T. Peacock and Jack Wiseman, *The Growth of Public Expenditure in the United Kingdom* (London, George Allen and Unwin, 1968), p. 170.
47. *The Military Balance 1974–1975* (London, International Institute for Strategic Studies, 1974), pp. 78 and 81.
48. *Statement on Defence Estimates 1956* (London, HMSO, 1956). Cmd 9691, para 103.

49. Walter Lippmann, *The Cold War: A Study in US Foreign Policy* (New York, Harper Torchbooks, 1972), p. 9.
50. For a defence of British strategy, see Piers Mackesy, 'Strategic problems of the British war effort' in Dickinson, *Britain and the French Revolution*, p. 147 ff.
51. 'The American crisis', *Encounter*, January 1970; Daniel Bell, 'Unstable America?' *Encounter*, June 1970.
52. For GDP levels, see Angus Maddison, *Dynamic Forces in Capitalist Development: A Long-run Comparative View* (Oxford, Oxford University Press, 1991), p. 7; Michael Shanks, 'The English sickness', *Encounter*, January 1972; Henry Fairlie and Peregrine Worsthorne, 'Suicide of a nation?' *Encounter*, January 1976.
53. David Caute, *The Fellow Travellers: Intellectual Friends of Communism* (New Haven, Yale University Press, 1988).
54. John Pollock, *Wilberforce* (London, Constable, 1977), pp. 132–136.
55. W. Trotter, *Instincts of the Herd in Peace and War.*
56. David Lloyd-George, *War Memoirs*, pp. 514–520, 1476.
57. General Baron von Schweppenburg, *The Critical Years* (London, Wingate, 1952), p. 19.

2 The Anglican Church and War

1. G. K. A. Bell, *Randall Davidson: Archbishop of Canterbury* (London, Geoffrey Cumberlege Oxford University Press, 1952). Davidson was Archbishop from 1903 to 1928 and was succeeded by Cosmo Lang who resigned in 1942 and was, in turn, succeeded by William Temple who died in 1944.
2. F. A. Iremonger, *William Temple: Archbishop of Canterbury, His Life and Letters* (London, Geoffrey Cumberlege Oxford University Press, 1948); Ronald Jasper, *George Bell: Bishop of Chichester* (London, Oxford University Press, 1967); J. G. Lockhart, *Cosmo Gordon Lang* (London, Hodder and Stoughton, 1949). *HoL*, 1 September 1939, columns 921–923. *HoL*, 11 February 1943, columns 1076–1082.
3. Though the meaning of secularism is elusive, see Owen Chadwick, *The Secularisation of the European Mind in the Nineteenth Century* (Cambridge, Cambridge University Press, 1990), p. 264.
4. Sheena Ashford and Noel Timms, *What Europe Thinks; A Study of Western European Values* (Aldershot, Dartmouth, 1992), p. 16.
5. *Social Trends 1995 Edition* (London, HMSO, 1995), p. 222.
6. See Barker, *National Character*, Chapter 5; Jenkins, *The British*, Chapter 4.
7. *Sermons or Homilies Appointed to be Read in Church* (London, Prayer Book and Homily Society, 1988), p. 72.
8. Ibid., p. 388.
9. Ibid., p. 410.
10. Hans Zinsser, *Rats, Lice and History* (New York, Bantam, 1965), particularly Chapter 8.
11. *Homilies*, p. 402.
12. J. A. Froude, *Life and Letters of Erasmus* (London, Longmans, Green, 1906), pp. 109,124 and 245. For a thoughtful discussion of Erasmus' views on war, see A. G. Dickens and Whitney R. D. Jones, *Erasmus The Reformer* (London, Methuen, 1994), pp. 65–78.

13. Clarendon quoted in Stephen Baskerville, *Not Peace but a Sword: The Political Theology of the English Revolution* (London, Routledge, 1993), p. 1.
14. Macleod, *War of Ideas*, Chapter 6; William Gibson, *The Church of England 1688–1832* (London, Routledge, 2001), p. 222.
15. Frederic W. Farrar, *The Fall of Man and Other Sermons* (London and Cambridge, Macmillan, 1868), p. 143.
16. J. B. Mozley DD, *Sermons Preached Before the University of Oxford on Special Occasions* (Oxford, Remingtons, 1886), p. 110.
17. Mozley, *Sermons*, p. 120. Mozley's view that civilian life was as sinful as warfare was widely shared amongst the laity. Tennyson's well-known poem, 'Maud A Monondrama' (1855), reflected the same values.
18. Grey, *Twenty-Five Years*, Volume 1, pp. 68–69.
19. *HoC Debates*, 11 February 1793, columns 345–346.
20. Ibid., 31 March 1854, column 141.
21. Ibid., 3 August 1914, column 1809.
22. Ibid., 31 March 1854, column 139.
23. Ibid., 14–28 June 1900. Alan Wilkinson, *The Church of England and the First World War* (London, SCM Press, 1996), p. 10. For a Boer view of British 'oppression', see Deneys Reitz, *Commando* (London, Faber, 1929).
24. John Morley, *The Life of Richard Cobden* (London, Fisher Unwin, 1895), p. 616 ff.; G. M. Trevelyan, *The Life of John Bright* (London, Constable, 1930), p. 215 ff.; *The Diaries of John Bright with a Foreword by Philip Bright* (London, Cassell, 1930), p. 155 ff.; Read, *Cobden and Bright*, p. 109 ff.
25. John T. Smith, 'Merely a growing dilemma of etiquette? The deepening gulf between the Victorian clergyman and Victorian schoolteacher', *History of Education*, March 2004.
26. William Irvine, *Apes, Angels and Victorians: A Joint Biography of Darwin and Huxley* (London, Weidenfeld and Nicolson, 1955); Cyril Aydon, *Charles Darwin* (London, Constable, 2002).
27. Charles Darwin, *The Voyage of the Beagle* (Ware, Wordsworth, 1997), pp. 99, 411–413, 424.
28. Hobson, *Jingoism*, p. 41.
29. For the new thinking in the Church, see William Leighton Grane, Vicar of Cobham in Surrey, *The Passing of War: A Study in Things which Make for Peace* (London, Macmillan, 1912).
30. William Temple, *The Life of Bishop Percival* (London, Macmillan, 1921), pp. 356 ff. Not all clergy agonised over the decision to go to war, see Arthur F. Winnington Ingram, *The Church in Time of War* (London, Wells Gardener, 1915); P. E. Matheson, *The Life of Hastings Rashdall DD* (London, Oxford University Press, 1928).
31. Bell, *Davidson*, p. 738. See also the observations on Davidson's behaviour by Wilkinson, *The Church of England*, p. 7. Wilkinson thought that Davidson was too sober and did not take sufficient part in debates about the war.
32. R. Geike and E. Montgomery, *The Dutch Barrier 1705–1719* (Cambridge, Cambridge University Press, 1930); Philip Towle, *Enforced Disarmament from the Napoleonic Campaigns to the Gulf War* (Oxford, Clarendon, 1997), Chapter 2.
33. Michael Hurst (ed.), *Key Treaties of the Great Powers* (Newton Abbot, David and Charles, 1972), Volumes 1 and 2, pp. 207, 213, 252, 449, 456 and 458.

34. Keith Robbins, 'Lord Bryce and the First World War', *Politicians, War and Diplomacy in British Foreign Policy* (London, Hambledon Press, 1994), Chapter 13.
35. *HoL*, 15 March 1915, column 756; *HoL*, 27 April 1915, column 870. James W. Gerard, *My Four Years in Germany* (London, Hodder and Stoughton, 1917), Chapter 10; Daniel J. McCarthy, *The Prisoner of War in Germany* (London, Skeffington, 1918); Matthew Stibbe, 'Prisoners of War during the First World War', *German Historical Institute Bulletin*, November 2006.
36. Bell, *Davidson*, p. 753. *HoL*, 26 January 1916, column 1038.
37. Bell, *Davidson*, pp. 757–760.
38. R. T. Davidson, *Occasions: Sermons and Addresses Delivered on Days of Interest* (London, Mowbray, 1925), p. 2.
39. Ibid., p. 18.
40. Ibid., p. 19.
41. Zimmern, *Spiritual Values*, p. 2.
42. Ibid., p. 7. Lang was well aware of these criticisms, see Barnes and Nicholson, *The Empire at Bay: The Leo Amery Diaries 1929–1945* (London, Hutchinson and London, 1988), p. 884.
43. *HoL Debates*, 30 March 1933, column 225. Knop, *Beware of the English*, p. 13.
44. *HoL Debates*, 1 September 1939, column 921 ff.
45. G. Douhet, *The Command of the Air*, translated by Dino Ferrari (Washington, Office of Air Force History, 1983).
46. Uri Bialer, *The Shadow of the Bomber: The Fear of Air Attack and British Politics 1932–1939* (London, Royal Historical Society, 1980); on the war itself, see R. J. Overy, *The Air War 1939–1945* (London, Europa Publications, 1980); John Terraine, *A Time for Courage: The Royal Air Force in the European War 1939–1945* (New York, Macmillan, 1985).
47. *Public Opinion Quarterly*, 1941, p. 157, survey by the British Institute of Public Opinion, 14 November 1940.
48. For a critical appraisal of Bell, see Angus Calder, *The People's War: Britain 1939–45* (London, Jonathan Cape, 1969), pp. 491–494. See also Jasper, *George Bell*, p. 202 ff.
49. G. K. A. Bell, *The Church and Humanity* (London, Longmans Green, 1930), p. 27.
50. Ibid., p. 49.
51. David Mac Isaac (ed.), *The United States Strategic Bombing Survey* (New York, Garland Publishing, 1976), particularly Volume 11, Chapter 1.
52. Trotter, *Instincts of the Herd*, p. 196.
53. Jasper, *George Bell*, p. 276.
54. Iremonger, *William Temple*, p. 545.
55. Quoted in Cyril Garbett, *In an Age of Revolution* (London, Hodder and Stoughton, 1952), p. 291.
56. *The Disarmament Question 1945–53* (London, Central Office of Information, 1953), p. 21. The figures were, no doubt, exaggerated and the quality of some of the troops dubious, but they were believed at the time.
57. Archbishop T. D. Roberts, 'Questions to the Vatican council: Contraception and war', in Michael de la Bedoyere (ed.), *Objections to Roman Catholicism* (London, Constable, 1964), p. 181. See also, *The Challenge of Peace: God's Promise and Our Response: The US Bishop's Pastoral Letter on War and Peace in*

the Nuclear Age (London, Incorporated Catholic Truth Society and Society for the Promotion of Christian Knowledge, 1983).

58. A. J. R. Groom, *British Thinking about Nuclear Weapons* (London, Francis Pinter, 1974), pp. 326 and 341. Garbett, *Revolution*, p. 288; *HoL Debates*, Volume 220, 7 December 1959 – 11 February 1960, columns 1137–1140; *HoL Debates*, Volume 236, 5 December 1961 – 1 February 1962, column 1070; Loc. cit., columns 1160–1164.

59. M. Goulding, *Peacemonger* (London, John Murray, 2001), p. 18.

60. Geoffrey Blainey, *The Causes of War* (Melbourne, Sun Books, 1973).

61. Richard Harries, 'The path to a just war', *The Independent*, 31 October 1990; Letter to *The Independent*, from the Bishop of Manchester, 'Where the church must stand in a "just war"', 1 November 1990; 'Respect Islam, Runcie Warns', *The Independent*, 16 January 1991; 'Catholic Primate warns of human cost of war', *The Independent*, 21 January 1991, Diana Hinds, 'When fighting becomes a question of faith', *The Independent*, 30 January 1991, Clifford Longley, 'Churches feel war strain', *The Independent*, 16 February 1991.

62. 'Attack on Iraq "cannot be defended as just war"', *The Times*, 15 October 2003. But for opposition to the Archbishop's general position, see Reverend Peter Mullen, 'The naivety of Rowan Williams', *The Times*, 7 September 2004 and Joseph Capizzi and Kim R. Holmes, *Just War and Endgame Objectives in Iraq* (Washington, Heritage Foundation, 12 May 2008).

63. 'Bishops protest over Camp X-Ray', *The Times*, 21 January 2002; 'Church protest on war strongest since Suez', *The Times*, 6 August 2002; 'Bishops want to apologise for Iraq war', *The Times*, 19 September 2005.

3 Civil Society

1. Dr William Penny Brookes revived the games in 1850 in the little Shropshire village of Much Wenlock; he, in turn, influenced Baron de Coubertain, who was instrumental in creating the first modern Olympic Games in Athens in 1896.

2. Steven Stalinsky, 'Darfur and the Middle East media: The anatomy of another conspiracy', Middle East Media Research Institute, 15 February 2008.

3. T. E. Hulme, *Essays on Humanism and the Philosophy of Art* (London, Kegan Paul, Trench, Trubner, 1931), edited by Herbert Read, pp. 50–51. Quoted in E. H. Carr, *Conditions of Peace* (London, Macmillan, 1942), p.107.

4. 'Send Rushdie to hell, says the Ayatollah', *The Times*, 23 February 1989; 'Ayatollah revives death fatwa on Rushdie', *The Times*, 20 January 2005; 'Newsweek sparks global riots with one paragraph on Koran', *The Times*, 14 May 2005; 'Terror suspect in Dutch murder link', *The Times*, 24 June 2005; 'Islamist accused of killing director offers no defence', *The Times*, 12 July 2005; 'Newspapers defy Muslim fanatics to support death-threat cartoonist', *The Times*, 13 February 2008.

5. 'Scorched lives', *Friday Times*, Lahore, 3–9 December 2004; 'Hypocrisy and moral chaos over karo-kari', *Friday Times*, Lahore, 4–10 March 2005; 'Smuggled film shows Iran public hangings', *The Times*, 2 June 2005; 'Pakistan's moderates are beaten in public', *International Herald Tribune*, 15 June 2005; 'Oppression of women by religion', *Friday Times*, Lahore, 8–14 July 2005;

'Christians face jail for offering treats to Muslims', *The Times*, 25 July 2005; 'Oppression of women by religion', *Friday Times*, Lahore, 8–14 July 2005.

6. For a first hand account of the difficulties involved in UN peacekeeping, see Marrack Goulding, *Peacemonger*.

7. For the importance of communication in civil action, see Todd Sandler, *Collective Action: Theory and Applications* (New York, Harvester Wheatsheaf, 1992), p. xiii.

8. 'The reform ministry and the reformed parliament', *Quarterly Review*, October 1833, p. 219.

9. Seymour Drescher, 'Public opinion and the destruction of British colonial slavery' in James Walvin (ed.), *Slavery and British Society 1776–1846* (London, Macmillan, 1982). See also Joel Quirk, 'The anti-slavery project: Linking the historical and the contemporary', *Human Rights Quarterly*, 28 (2006), p. 582. For the importance of the numbers backing a pressure group, see Graeme C. Moodie and Gerald Studdert-Kennedy, *Opinions, Publics and Pressure Groups* (London, Allen and Unwin, 1970), p. 67.

10. Successive governments had, however, to rely on the army to deal with large-scale disturbances and to fight groups of smugglers, see, for example, Allan Jobson, *Suffolk Remembered* (London, Robert Hale, 1969).

11. Marika Sherwood, *After Abolition: Britain and the Slave Trade since 1807* (Tauris, London, 2007), p. 10.

12. Christopher Leslie Brown, *Moral Capital: Foundations of British Abolitionism* (University of North Carolina Press, Chapel Hill, 2006), p. 55 ff.

13. Ibid., p. 451 ff.

14. Pollock, *Wilberforce*.

15. For a typical contemporary defence of slavery, see *Journal of a West India Planter* and *Domestic Manners in the West Indies*, reviewed in the *Quarterly Review*, January 1834, p. 374 ff.

16. Sir Regional Coupland, *The British Anti-Slavery Movement* (London, Frank Cass, 1964). See also William Roger Louis, *Ends of British Imperialism* (London, Tauris, 2006), p. 979; Sherwood, *After Abolition*, p. 2.

17. *HoC Debates*, 22 February 1848, column 1091 ff.

18. Loc. cit., column 1124.

19. Coupland, *Anti-Slavery Movement*, p. 181.

20. *HoC Debates*, Loc. cit., column 987.

21. John Morley, *The Life of Richard Cobden* (London, T. Fisher Unwin, 1906).

22. Jasper Ridley, *Lord Palmerston* (London, Constable, 1970), p. 297.

23. Asa Briggs, *The Age of Improvement 1783–1867* (London, Longmans, 1959), p. 316.

24. Morley, *Richard Cobden*, p. 231.

25. For antagonism towards German and US trade before the First World War, see Bernard Semmel, *Imperialism and Social Reform* (London, George Allen and Unwin, 1960), p. 88. For the 1930s, see Naoto Kagotani, 'Japan's commercial penetration into British India', in Philip Towle and Nobuko Margaret Kosuge (eds), *Britain and Japan in the Twentieth Century: One Hundred Years of Trade and Prejudice* (London, I B Tauris, 2007).

26. A. W. Kinglake, *The Invasion of the Crimea* (Edinburgh, William Blackwood, 1878), Volume V11, Chapter 11.

27. Ellen Hart, *Man Born to Live: Life and Work of Henry Dunant Founder of the Red Cross* (London, Victor Gollanz, 1953), p. 79. James Avery Joyce, *Red Cross International and the Strategy of Peace* (London, Hodder and Stoughton, 1959).

28. Peter Morris (ed.), *First Aid to the Battlefront: Life and Letters of Sir Vincent Kennett-Barrington* (Gloucester, Alan Sutton, 1992), p. 6.

29. Grigor McClelland, *Embers of War: Letters from a Quaker Relief Worker in War-torn Germany* (London, Tauris, 1997), p. 1.

30. Marvin Swartz, *The Union of Democratic Control in British Politics during the First World War* (Oxford, Clarendon Press, 1971); Sally Harris, *Out of Control: British Foreign Policy and the Union of Democratic Control* (Hull, University of Hull Press, 1996).

31. Henry R. Winkler, *The League of Nations Movement in Great Britain 1914–1919* (Metuchen, New Jersey, Scarecrow Reprint Corporation, 1967), p. 51.

32. Hadley Cantril and Mildred Strunk, *Public Opinion*, p. 1076. See also Hadley Cantril, *Public Opinion Quarterly*, 1940, Volume 4, p. 400.

33. Loc. cit., p. 20.

34. This summary of the League's history is based on Gertrude Bussey and Margaret Tims, *Women's International League for Peace and Freedom 1915–1965* (London, George Allen and Unwin, 1965).

35. S. Morrison, *I Renounce War: The Story of the Peace Pledge Union* (London, Sheppard Press, 1962), p. 11.

36. Ibid., p. 28.

37. Christopher Driver, *The Disarmers: A Study in Protest* (London, Hodder and Stoughton, 1964), p. 16. Nevertheless, the war did persuade some to become Quaker pacifists, see Kathleen Lonsdale, *Is Peace Possible?* (Harmondsworth, Penguin, 1957).

38. Richard Taylor and Colin Pritchard, *The Protest Makers: The British Nuclear Disarmament Movement of 1958–1965, Twenty Years on* (Oxford, Pergamon Press, 1980), p. 55.

39. James Cameron, *Point of Departure: Experiment in Autobiography* (London, Grafton, 1986), p. 188.

40. Etzioni, *Demonstration Democracy*, p. 10.

41. Groom, *British Thinking about Nuclear Weapons*, pp. 384–385.

42. *Statement on Defence 1956*, CMD 9691 (London, HMSO, 1956). Reference Section, Introduction, paras 7, 102 and 119. Lord Moran, *Winston Churchill: The Struggle for Survival* (London, Constable, 1960), p. 420.

43. See Cameron, *Point of Departure*, pp. 54 and 305 for his views of the USA.

44. Compare the relative freedom described in Ursula von Kardoff, *Diary of a Nightmare: Berlin 1942–1945* (London, Rupert Hart-Davis, 1965) and Lali Horstmann, *Nothing for Tears* (London, Weidenfeld and Nicolson, 1999), p. 43 with Robert Conquest, *The Great Terror: Stalin's Purge of the 1930s* (Harmondsworth, Penguin, 1971) and Alexander Solzhenitsyn, *The Gulag Archipelago* (London,Collins-Harvill-Fontana, 1974).

45. Cameron, *Point of Departure*, p. 295.

46. Aleksander Fursenko and Timothy Naftali, *Khrushchev's Cold War* (New York, Norton, 2006), p. 530.

47. Helen McPhail, *The Long Silence: Civilian Life under the German Occupation of Northern France 1914–1918* (London, Tauris, 2001), p. 64.

48. Henry Morgenthau, *I Was Sent to Athens* (New York, Doubleday, 1929).

49. Mark Mazower, *Inside Hitler's Greece: The Experience of Occupation, 1941–1944* (New Haven, Yale University Press, 1993), Chapter 3.
50. Victor Gollancz, *Our Threatened Values* (London, Victor Gollancz, 1946).
51. Lieutenant Colonel W. Byford-Jones, *Berlin Twilight* (London, Hutchinson, 1947), p. 145.
52. Maggie Black, *A Cause for our Times: Oxfam the First Fifty Years* (Oxford, Oxfam and Oxford University Press, 1992).
53. Mark Duffield, *Development, Security and Unending War: Governing the World of Peoples* (Cambridge, Polity, 2007), p. 220.
54. Samuel P. Huntington, *The Clash of Civilisations and the Remaking of World Order* (London, Free Press, 2007), pp. 310–312.
55. On the receptivity of governments to pressure groups, see Moodie and Studdert-Kennedy, *Opinions, Publics and Pressure Groups*, p. 72.
56. Drescher in J. Walvin, *Slavery and British Society1776–1846* (London, Macmillan, 1982), p. 30.
57. 'Pain relief bid to head off wool ban', *The Age* (Melbourne), 15 March 2008; 'Únravelling our wool crisis', loc. cit.

4　The Media and War

1. M. J. Armitage and R. A. Mason, *Air Power in the Nuclear Age: 1945–1984* (Basingstoke, Macmillan, 1985), Chapters 2 and 5.
2. Kate Adie, *The Kindness of Strangers* (London, Headline, 2002), p. 195 ff.
3. Elizabeth Knowles (ed.), *The Oxford Dictionary of Quotations* (Oxford, Oxford University Press, 1999), p. 441. Sheena Ashford and Noel Timms, *What Europe Thinks: A Study of Western European Values* (Aldershot, Dartmouth, 1992), p. 16.
4. 'Media coverage of Iraq conflict', MORI http://www.mori.com/polls/2003/iraqmedia.shtml
5. The newspapers had carried articles on wars before this but usually relied on reports from officers serving in the armed forces, to the fury of their commander. See Lieutenant Colonel Gurwood, *Selections from the Dispatches and General Orders of the Duke of Wellington* (London, John Murray, 1841), p. 319.
6. J. B. Atkins, *The Life of Sir William Howard Russell: The First Special Correspondent* (London, 1911), pp. 158–160.
7. See, for example, Stendhal, *The Charterhouse of Parma* (London, Zodiac Press, 1980). Chris Hedges, *War is a Force that Gives us Meaning* (New York, PublicAffairs, 2002).
8. Taken from the quotations at the beginning of Lloyd's book.
9. V. R. Raghavan, 'War as spectator sport', *The Hindu*, 13 April 2003.
10. R. N. Stromberg, *Redemption By War: The Intellectuals and 1914* (Lawrence, The Regents Press of Kansas, 1982).
11. Ellis Ashmead-Bartlett, *Port Arthur: The Siege and Capitulation* (Edinburgh, William Blackwood, 1907), p. 484.
12. Francis McCullagh, *With The Cossacks* (London, Eveleigh Nash, 1906), p. 377.
13. M. Herr, *Dispatches* (New York, Alfred A. Knopf, 1977), p. 214.

14. Morris, *First Aid to the Battlefront*.
15. F. A. McKenzie, *Tokyo to Tiflis: Uncensored Letters from the War* (London, Hurst and Blackett, 1905), p. 247.
16. Alan Moorehead, *The End in Africa* (London, Hamish Hamilton, 1943), pp. 97 and 155.
17. Ibid., pp. 178, 184 and 193.
18. Ibid., p. 168.
19. 'The cavalry action at Balaklava', report of 25 October 1854, published in *The Times*, 14 November 1854.
20. 'Tokyo report on vast damage by new bomb: Parachute said to have been used: New Super Fortress attack', *The Times*, 8 August 1945.
21. John Lanchester, 'Riots, Terrorism etc', *London Review of Books*, 6 March 2008.
22. Stephen Badsey, *The Media and International Security* (London, Frank Cass, 2000), pp. 218–222.
23. P. Knightley, *The First Casualty* (New York, Harcourt Brace Janovich, 1975), p. 109.
24. H. G. Wells, *Mr Britling Sees it Through* (London, Hogarth Press, 1994, first published 1916).
25. Gavin Roynon (ed.), *Home Fires Burning: The Great War Diaries of Georgina Lee* (Stroud, Sutton, 2006), p. 199.
26. Mark Pottle (ed.), *Champion Redoubtable: The Diaries and Letters of Violet Bonham Carter 1914–1945* (London, Phoenix, 1999), p. 81.
27. Steve Tatham, *Losing Arab Hearts and Minds: The Coalition, Al Jazeera and Muslim Public Opinion* (New York, Front Street Press, 2006).
28. 'Five weeks of the whirlwind', *The Guardian*, 10 May 1982.
29. Eric Hobsbawm, 'A requisition order on patriotism', *The Guardian*, 20 December 1982. See also Peter Jenkins, 'Already the means to ends are disproportionate', *The Guardian*, 5 May 1982.
30. 'Spotlight on Milosevic', *The Times*, 1 May 1993; 'The folly of betraying Bosnia', *The Independent*, 26 July 1993; 'Enough is enough', *The Guardian*, 4 August 1993; 'Sarajevo action now!' *The Independent*, 1 October 1993. But see also Simon Jenkins, 'The war the West avoided', *The Times*, 9 June 1993.
31. Admiral Sandy Woodward with Patrick Robinson, *One Hundred days: The Memoirs of the Falklands Battle Group Commander* (London, HarperCollins, 1992), p. 348.
32. Edward Luttwak, Blood for oil: Bush's growing dilemma', *The Independent*, 27 August 1990; 'Advocate for a nightmare scenario', *The Independent*, 20 December 1990; 'germ war casualties would not go home', *The Independent*, 11 January 1991.
33. Philip Towle, *Pundits and Patriots: Lessons from the Gulf War* (London, Institute for European Defence and Strategic Studies, 1991).
34. On Northern Ireland, see Desmond Hamill, *Pig in the Middle: The Army in Northern Ireland 1969–1985* (London, Methuen, 1985); on the partisan warfare in Yugoslavia, see Milovan Djilas, *Wartime: With Tito and the Partisans* (London, Secker and Warburg, 1980).
35. Philip Towle, 'The British debate about European conflicts' in Lawrence Freedman (ed.), *Military Intervention in European Conflicts* (Oxford, Political Quarterly/Blackwell, 1994), p. 94 ff.

36. John Pilger, 'Blair has made Britain a target', *The Guardian*, 21 September 2001 and Peter Preston, 'All domestic policy now has an international dimension', *The Guardian*, 7 January 2002.

37. Jonathan Steele, 'No parallel with Kosovo war', *The Guardian*, 1 November 2001. See also Simon Jenkins, 'The real hawks would not dispatch the bombers', *The Times*, 3 October 2001.

38. 'Afghan army chief sacked over coalition strike blamed for deaths of 89 civilians', *The Times*, 25 August 2008; 'Harrowing video film backs Afghan villagers' claims of carnage by US troops', *The Times*, 8 September 2008.

5   War and Literature

1. Thomas More, *Utopia and a Dialogue of Comfort* (London, Dent, 1962), pp. 107–117.

2. Jonathan Swift, *Gulliver's Travels* (Watford, Bruce Publishing, undated), pp. 52 and 246.

3. Alfred Lord Tennyson, *The Poetical Works of Alfred Lord Tennyson* (London, Peacock, Mansfield and Britton, undated), p. 101.

4. Sir John Slessor, *The Central Blue: Recollections and Reflections* (London, Cassell, 1956). See also H. Bruce Franklin, 'Fatal fiction: A weapon to end all wars', in Nancy Anisfield (ed.), *The Nightmare Considered: Critical Essays on Nuclear War Literature* (Bowling Green, Ohio, Bowling Green University Press, 1991), pp. 5–14.

5. Lockley's Hall's merits as an artistic work are much weaker, see Christopher Ricks, *Tennyson* (Macmillan), p. 164 ff.

6. John Ruskin, lecture to the Royal Military Academy, Woolwich in 1865, reproduced in John Ruskin, *The Crown of Wild Olive* (London, George Allen, 1907).

7. I. F. Clarke, *Voices Prophesying War: Future Wars 1763–3749* (Oxford University Press, 1992).

8. Rudyard Kipling, *Barrack Room Ballads, Departmental Ditties and Other Ballads and Verses* (New York, Alex Grosset, 1899); Rudyard Kipling, *The Five Nations* (London, Methuen, 1903).

9. T. S. Eliot (ed.), *A Choice of Kipling's Verse* (London, Faber and Faber, 1941), pp. 136 and 298.

10. Edmund Wilson, 'The Kipling that nobody read', *The Wound and the Bow* (London, Methuen, 1961), pp. 94–161.

11. Franklin, 'Fatal Fiction', pp. 11–12.

12. T. H. E. Travers, 'Future warfare: H. G. Wells and British military theory, 1895–1916' in Brian Bond and Ian Roy (eds), *War and Society* (London, Croom Helm, 1974), pp. 67–87. Wells' tanks were much larger than they proved to be in the First World War and he saw them walking on legs rather than propelled by tracks.

13. Edward Mead Earle, 'H. G. Wells, British patriot in search of a world state', in E. M. Earle (ed.), *Nationalism and Internationalism* (New York, Columbia University Press, 1950), pp. 79–121. See also G. R. Searle, *The Quest for National Efficiency* (Oxford, Basil Blackwell, 1971), p. 151.

14. Wells, *Mr Britling Sees it Through*.

15. Tennyson, 'Locksley Hall – Sixty years after' in Tennyson, *Poetical Works* (London, Peacock, Mansfield and Britton, undated), p. 565.
16. Ernest Raymond, *Tell England: A Study in a Generation* (London, Cassell, 1922) was reprinted 14 times in its first year and six in its second; Private 19022 (Manning), *Her Privates We* (London, Peter Davies, 1930) was reprinted four times in the first month after publication.
17. For a recent example of the continued grief over the war, see Les Carlyon, *The Great War* (Sydney, Picador, 2007).
18. Bond, *The Unquiet Western Front*.
19. Wells was not enthusiastic about the film, see David C. Smith (ed.), *The Correspondence of H. G. Wells* (London, Pickering and Chatto, 1998), Volume 4, p.121, letter dated sometime in 1936.
20. H. G. Wells, *The Shape of Things to Come: The Ultimate Revolution* (Harmondsworth, Penguin, 2005), first published 1933, pp. 180–198.
21. 'New H. G. Wells film: "Things to Come"', *The Times*, 21 February 1936.
22. Nevil Shute, *What Happened to the Corbetts* (London, Pan Books, 1965), p. 214.
23. Other classic representations of the communist world included Arthur Koestler, *Darkness at Noon* (London, Jonathan Cape, 1940); Czeslaw Milosz, *The Captive Mind* (London, Secker and Warburg, 1953); Robert Conquest, *The Great Terror* (Basingstoke, Macmillan, 1968) and Alexander Solzhenitsyn, *The Gulag Archipelago 1918–1956* (London, Collins, Harvill, Fontana, 1974).
24. Benoit J. Suykerbuyk, *Essays from Oceania and Eurasia: George Orwell and 1984* (Antwerpen, University Instelling, 1984), pp. 75–76.
25. Shute, *On the Beach* (New York, Signet, 1958), pp. 230 and 238.
26. Blurb on the jacket of the Signet edition of *On the Breach*.
27. Edward Teller with Judith L. Shoolery, *Memoirs: A Twentieth-Century Journey in Science and Politics* (Cambridge Mass, Perseus, 2001), p. 445 and note 19. 'Edward Teller: Proponent of the H-bomb whose zeal for weapons of mass destruction as the best guarantee of security knew no bounds'. Obituary in *The Times*, 11 September 2003.
28. *Public Opinion Quarterly*, 1945–1946, p. 530; Cantril and Strunk, pp. 21–22.
29. Aleksander Fursenko and Timothy Naftali, *Khrushchev's Cold War*.
30. Tom W Smith, 'The polls – a report – nuclear anxiety', *Public Opinion Quarterly*, Winter 1988.
31. Igor Korchilov, *Translating History: Thirty Years on the Front Lines with a Top Russian Interpreter* (New York, Lisa Drew/Scribner, 1997), p. 74.
32. *Documents on Disarmament: 1957–1959* (Washington, Department of State, 1960), pp. 1185 and 1474 ff.
33. Howard Simons, 'World-wide capabilities for production and control of nuclear weapons', *Daedalus*, Volume 88, Summer 1959. It is notable how few armchair strategists refer to fictional descriptions of the problems they study; for one exception, see the reference to Shute in Michael Mandelbaum, *The Nuclear Revolution: International Politics before and after Hiroshima* (Cambridge, Cambridge University Press, 1981), p. 225.
34. For an analysis of the way the pendulum swings between optimism and pessimism, see Geoffrey Blainey, *The Great Seesaw: A New View of the Western World* (Basingstoke, Macmillan, 1988).

6 The Rise of the Armchair Strategists

1. Gwyn Prins and Hylke Tromp, *Foundation of War Studies: The Future of War* (The Hague, Kluwer Law International, 2000).
2. Brian Bond (ed.), I. S. Bloch, *Is War Now Impossible? Being and Abridgement of the War of the Future in its Technical, Economic and Political Relations* (Aldershot, Gregg Revivals, 1991).
3. Ibid., Chapter 5, p. 294 ff.
4. Adam Smith, *An Inquiry into the Nature and Causes of the Wealth of Nations* (London, Dent, 1912, first published 1776), Volume 2, pp. 402 and 408.
5. Morley, *Life of Richard Cobden*, pp. 532–533.
6. Julian S. Corbett, *Some Principles of Maritime Strategy*, with an introduction and notes by Eric J. Grove (London, Brassey's, 1988), 'attack and defence of trade', p. 261 ff. For a recent examination of Corbett's work see James Goldrick and John B. Hattendorf, *Mahan is Not Enough* (Newport, Rhode Island, Naval War College Press, 1993).
7. Viscount Jellicoe, *The Crisis of the Naval War* (London, Cassell, 1920), p. vii. For the arguments in Germany about the introduction of unrestricted submarine warfare, see von Tirpitz, *My Memoirs by Grand Admiral von Tirpitz* (London, Hurst and Blackett, 1919), Volume 2.
8. The pamphlet was originally called *Europe's Optical Illusion*, see the account in Norman Angell, *After All: The Autobiography of Norman Angell* (London, Hamish Hamilton, 1951), part 11.
9. Ibid., pp. 163–164.
10. Morley, *Richard Cobden*; Keith Robbins, *John Bright* (London, Routledge and Kegan Paul, 1979).
11. Giichi Ono, *Expenditures of the Sino-Japanese War* (New York, Oxford University Press, 1922).
12. Philip Towle, *Democracy and Peacemaking: Negotiations and Debates 1815–1973* (London and New York, Routledge, 2000), Chapter 5.
13. John Viscount Morley, *Memorandum on Resignation August 1914* (London, Macmillan, 1928), p. 5.
14. Grey, *Twenty-Five Years*, p. 21.
15. Angell, *After All*, pp. 179–186.
16. Ibid., p. 318.
17. See, for example, Arnold J. Toynbee, *Survey of International Affairs 1920–1923* (London, Humphrey Milford/ Oxford University Press, 1925).
18. Vincent Sheean, *In Search of History* (London, Hamish Hamilton, 1935); Peter Fleming, *News from Tartary: A Journey from Peking to Kashmir* (London, Jonathan Cape, 1936); Valentine Williams, *The World of Action* (London, Hamish Hamilton, 1938).
19. For periodical literature, see, for example, John Bull, 'The Rhine problem', and Augur, 'Germany in Europe', *Fortnightly Review*, Volume 121, 1927, pp. 310 and 577; T. Okamoto, 'American-Japanese Issues and the Anglo-Japanese Alliance', *Contemporary Review*, 1921, Volume 119, p. 354. For longer accounts, see Amleto Vespa, *Secret Agent of Japan* (London, Left Book Club/ Victor Gollancz, 1938); Philip Gibbs, *Across the Frontiers* (London, Right Book Club, 1939).

20. E. H. Carr, *The Twenty Years' Crisis 1919–1939* (London, Macmillan, 1946), p. vii.

21. Edgar Mowrer, *Germany Puts the Clock Back* (Harmondsworth, Penguin,1933); R. H. Bruce Lockhart, *Retreat from Glory* (London, Putnam, 1934); John Gunther, *Inside Europe* (London, Hamish Hamilton, 1936); Douglas Reed, *Insanity Fair* (London, Jonathan Cape, 1938).

22. Bruce Lockhart, *Retreat*, p. 290; Mowrer, *Germany*, p. 261; W. H. Chamberlain, *Japan over Asia* (London, Right Book Club, 1938), p. 303.

23. See the Preface to *The Armaments Year Book; General and Statistical Information in regard to Land, Naval and Air Armaments* (Geneva, League of Nations, 1932), the series began in 1926.

24. Lorne S. Jaffe, *The Decision to Disarm Germany* (London, Allen and Unwin, 1985), p. 28 ff. For a balanced recent analysis of the post-war literature, see Bond, *The Unquiet Western Front*.

25. G. Lowes Dickinson, *War: Its Nature, Cause and Cure* (London, George Allen and Unwin, 1923), p. 7.

26. A. A. Milne, *Peace with Honour* (London, Methuen, 1936), p. 194 ff.

27. William H. Honan, *Bywater: The Man who Invented the Pacific War* (London, Macdonald, 1990).

28. Ibid., Chapter 9.

29. Hector C. Bywater, *Navies and Nations: A Review of Naval Developments since the Great War* (London, Constable, 1927), p. 218.

30. Ibid., pp. 206–207.

31. John Barnes and David Nicholson (eds), *Empire at Bay*, p. 754.

32. Hector C. Bywater, *Sea-power in the Pacific* (London, Constable, 1934), p. X1X.

33. See, for example, Malcolm Kennedy, *The Problem of Japan* (London, Nisbet, 1935). For Churchill's views in the 1920s, see *Robert Rhodes James, Churchill: A Study in Failure 1900–1939* (London, Weidenfeld and Nicolson, 1970), p. 165.

34. Francis W. Hirst, *Armaments: The Race and the Crisis* (London, Cobden-Sanderson, 1937).

35. Maxine Block (ed.), *Current Biography: Who's News and Why 1943* (New York, H. W. Wilson, 1944), pp. 811–813.

36. Max Werner, *The Military Strength of the Powers*, (London, Victor Gollancz, 1939).

37. Ismay papers, Kings' College, London, Ismay 5/3, letter of 19 July 1940 to Sir Kenneth Crossley.

38. Compare Donald Cameron Watt, 'British intelligence and the coming of the Second World War in Europe', in Ernest R. May (ed.), *Knowing One's Enemies* (Princeton, Princeton University Press, 1984), p. 254 and Wesley K. Wark, *The Ultimate Enemy: British Intelligence and Nazi Germany, 1933–1939* (Oxford, 1986), p. 101.

39. Max Werner, *Battle for the World: the Strategy and Diplomacy of the Second World War* (London, Victor Gollancz, 1941) and *The Great Offensive: The Strategy of Coalition Warfare* (London, Victor Gollancz, 1943).

40. Brian Bond, *Liddell Hart: A Study of his Military Thought* (London, Cassell, 1977), Chapter 2.

41. For a critical analysis of Liddell Hart's views, see John J. Mearsheimer, *Liddell Hart and the Weight of History* (London, Brassey's, 1988), p. 130. For a more nuanced view, see Bond, *Liddell Hart*, p. 105.

42. David Dilks (ed.), *The Diaries of Sir Alexander Cadogan 1938–1945* (London, Cassell, 1971), p. 164, entry for 28 March 1939.
43. F. H. Hinsley, *Hitler's Strategy* (Cambridge, Cambridge University Press), Chapter 1.
44. Liddell Hart, *Memoirs*, p. 228.
45. Ibid., p. 220.
46. J. M. Spaight, *Aircraft in Peace and the Law* (London, Macmillan, 1919).
47. Douhet, *Command*, pp. 29, 32, 52–54, 196.
48. J. M. Spaight, *Air Power in the Next War* (London, Geoffrey Bles, 1938), pp. 56, 103.
49. Ibid., pp. 106–111.
50. For the Spanish Civil War, see Ibid., pp. 79–92.
51. Ibid., p. 142 ff. See also J. M. Spaight, *Can America Prevent Frightfulness from the Air?* (London, John Lane, 1939), p. 14.
52. Uri Bialer, *The Shadow of the Bomber: The Fear of Air Attack and British Politics 1932–1939* (London, Royal Historical Society, 1980).
53. For Lippmann, see Francine Curro Cary, *The Influence of War on Walter Lippmann* (Maddison, State Historical Society of Wisconsin, 1967); Stephen D. Blum, *Walter Lippmann: Cosmopolitan in a Century of Total War* (Ithaca, Cornell University Press, 1984); Barry D. Riccio, *Walter Lippmann: Odyssey of a Liberal* (New Brunswick, Transaction Publishers, 1994).
54. Walter Lippmann, *US War Aims* (London, Hamish Hamilton, 1944), p. 42. See also Walter Lippmann, *US Foreign Policy* (London, Hamish Hamilton, 1943).
55. The only exception was the Dutch Barrier in the 18th century, see R. Geike and E. Montgomery, *The Dutch Barrier 1705–1719* (Cambridge, Cambridge University Press, 1930).
56. Lippmann, *War Aims*, pp. 72 and 119.
57. Robert Kagan, 'One year after: A grand strategy for the West?' *Survival*, Winter, 2002–2003, p. 139.
58. Lippmann, *War Aims*, pp. 38 and 97.
59. Edward Hallett Carr, *Conditions of Peace* (London, Macmillan, 1942).
60. Francis Fukuyama, *The End of History and the Last Man* (London, Penguin, 1992).
61. Peter Hore (ed.), *Patrick Blackett: Sailor, Scientist, Socialist* (London, Frank Cass, 2003).
62. P. M. S. Blackett, *Military and Political Consequences of Atomic Energy* (London, Turnstile Press, 1948), Chapter 10.
63. Edward Teller with Judith L. Shoolery, *Memoirs*, p. 245. Richard J. Aldrich, *The Hidden Hand: Britain, America and Cold War Intelligence* (London, John Murray, 2001), pp. 119 and 419. 'Names on Orwell's blacklist released', *The Times*, 25 July 2003.
64. Blackett, *Military and Political Consequences*, p. viii.
65. H. E. Wimperis, *International Affairs*, April 1949, p. 199.
66. KHT, *Royal Engineers Journal*, September 1948, p. 62.
67. Stephen King-Hall, *Defence in the Nuclear Age* (London, Victor Gollancz, 1958), p. 13.
68. Major General Sir Charles Gwynn, *Imperial Policing* (London, Macmillan, 1934), p.5.

69. Alfred Draper, *The Amritsar Massacre: Twilight of the Raj* (London, Buchan and Enright, 1981); Nigel Collett, *The Butcher of Amritsar: General Reginald Dyer* (London, Hambledon and London, 2005).

70. Henri Alleg, *The Question* (London, John Calder, 1958).

71. Robert Thompson, *Defeating Communist Insurgency: Experiences from Malaya and Vietnam* (London, Chatto and Windus, 1974), particularly Chapter 4; Sir Robert Thompson, *Make for the Hills: Memories of Far Eastern Wars* (London, Leo Cooper, 1989); 'Sir Robert Thompson', obituary in *The Times*, 20 May 1992.

72. Howard, M. and Paret, P. (eds), *Carl von Clausewitz on War* (Princeton, Princeton University Press, 1984), p. 86.

73. Geoffrey Blainey, *The Causes of Wars*.

74. Stefan Halper and Jonathan Clarke, *The Silence of the Rational Centre* (New York, Basic Books, 2007).

7   The Professional Military

1. *Falkland Islands Review: Report of a Committee of Privy Counsellors under Lord Franks*, Cmnd 8787 (London, HMSO, 1983).

2. Margaret Thatcher, *The Downing Street Years* (New York, Harper/Collins, 1993), p. 179.

3. J. A. Spender, *The Public Life* (London, Cassell, 1925), Volume 2, p. 45; Lord Strang, *Britain in World Affairs: Henry V111 to Elizabeth 11* (London, Faber and Faber and Andre Deutsch, 1961), pp. 181–183; Jasper Ridley, *Lord Palmerston*, pp. 569–574.

4. Alfred Vagts, *A History of Militarism Civilian and Military* (London, Hollis and Carter, 1959), p. 335.

5. Field Marshal Lord Milne, CIGS 1926–1933, foreword to Sir George Arthur, *From Wellington to Wavell* (London, Hutchinson, undated).

6. Michael Howard and Peter Paret (eds), *Carl von Clausewitz on War* (Princeton, Princeton University Press, 1984), pp. 605–608.

7. Roderick Macleod (ed.), *The Ironside Diaries 1937–1940* (London, Denis Kelly, 1962).

8. Selwyn Lloyd, *Suez: A Personal Account* (London, Jonathan Cape, 1978), p. 108.

9. Keith Kyle, *Suez* (London, Weidenfeld and Nicolson, 1991), p. 202.

10. Thatcher, *Downing Street Years*, p. 817.

11. Desmond Hamill, *Pig in the Middle*.

12. Colin Powell with Joseph E. Persico, *My American Journey* (New York, Ballantine, 1996); David Halberstam, *War in a Time of Peace: Bush, Clinton and the Generals* (London, Bloomsbury, 2002); Bob Woodward, *Bush at War* (New York, Simon and Schuster, 2002).

13. Knowles (ed.), *Oxford Dictionary of Quotations*, p. 642.

14. Note the comments by the great 19th-century Liberal Richard Cobden on this point in John Morley, *The Life of Richard Cobden* (London, T. Fisher Unwin, 1881), p. 535.

15. For some recent examples from the United States which demonstrate the caution shown by senior officers, see Colin Powell with Joseph E. Persico,

My American Journey (New York, Ballantine, 1996), p. 561; General Wesley K. Clark, *Waging Modern War* (New York, Public Affairs, 2001), pp. 436–437; David Halberstam, *War in a Time of Peace*, p. 377; Madeleine Albright with Bill Woodward, *Madam Secretary: A Memoir* (London, Macmillan, 2003), p. 395.

16. J. W. Fortescue, *British Statesmen of the Great War: 1793–1814* (Oxford. Clarendon Press, 1911).

17. For Napoleon's views, see Philip J. Haythornthwaite et al., *Napoleon: The Final Verdict* (London, Arms and Armour, 1996), pp. 288 and 301.

18. For an idea of Wellington's approach, see Lieutenant Colonel Gurwood, *Selections from the Dispatches and General of Orders of the Duke of Wellington*. On the occupation of France, see Thomas Dwight Veve, *The Duke of Wellington and the British Army of Occupation in France 1815–1818* (Westport, Greenwood University Press, 1992).

19. Knowles, *Oxford Dictionary of Quotations*, p. 220 attributes it to Clemenceau, Briand or Talleyrand.

20. John Winton, *Convoy: The Defence of Sea Trade 1890–1990* (London, Michael Joseph, 1983), Chapters 6 and 7.

21. David Lloyd George, *War Memoirs*, Volume 1, p. 75.

22. Ibid., pp. 359 and 382.

23. Ibid., pp. 2039–2041.

24. Alan Clark, *The Donkeys* (London, Hutchinson, 1961).

25. John Terraine, *The Smoke and the Fire: Myths and Anti-Myths of War* (London, Sidgwick and Jackson, 1980), pp. 132–140. See also Bond, *Unquiet Western Front*, pp. 78–79.

26. On tanks, see also Prior, *Churchill's World Crisis*, Chapter 13. For a balanced recent assessment of Haig's attitude to tanks and other issues, see Gary Mead, *The Good Soldier: A Biography of Douglas Haig* (London, Atlantic Books, 2007).

27. On the financial situation, see M. J. Daunton, 'How to pay for the war: State, society and taxation in Britain, 1917–1924', *English Historical Review*, September 1996; Kathleen Burk, Britain, *America and the Sinews of War*, 1914–1918 (Boston, George Allen and Unwin, 1985); Edwin R. Seligman, 'The cost of war and how it was met', *American Economic Review*, December 1919.

28. Danchev and Todman, *Allenbrooke Diaries*, entry for 28 September 1939, p. 3.

29. Ibid., entry for 14 June 1940, p. 81.

30. Stephen Roskill, *Churchill and the Admirals* (London, Collins, 1977). On Singapore, see Ivan Simpson, *Singapore Too Little Too late* (London, Leo Cooper, 1970) and Major-General S. Woodburn-Kirby, *Singapore: The Chain of Disaster* (London, Cassell, 1971).

31. Fitzroy Maclean, *Eastern Approaches* (London, Four Square, 1967); F. Spencer Chapman, *The Jungle is Neutral* (London, Chatto and Windus, 1950); John Cross, *Red Jungle* (London, Robert Hall, 1975); Richard Hillary, *The Last Enemy* (Basingstoke, Macmillan, 1942); Johnnie Johnson, *Wing Leader* (London, Chatto and Windus, 1956); George MacDonald Fraser, *Quartered Safe Out Here* (London, Harvill, 1992).

32. Stanley S. Pavillard, *Bamboo Doctor* (London, Macmillan, 1960); Ernest Gordon, *Miracle on the River Kwai* (London, Collins, 1963); John Fletcher-Cooke, *The Emperor's Guest 1942–45* (London, Leo Cooper, 1972); Thomas Pounder, *Death Camps of the River Kwai* (Cornwall, United Writers, 1977).

33. Sheena Ashford and Noel Timms, *What Europe Thinks*, p. 16.
34. Philip de Pirey, *Operation Waste* (London, Arco Publishing, 1954); A. Horne, *A Savage War of Peace: Algeria 1954–1962* (London, Macmillan, 1977); Lieutenant General W. R. Peers, *The My Lai Inquiry* (New York, Norton, 1979).

8   Parliament and War

1. *HoC*, 3 April 1982, column 634; *HoL* 14 April 1982, column 290.
2. *HoC*, 2 August 1956, column 1606.
3. Ibid., 3 August 1914, columns 1815–1817.
4. *HoL*, 29 August 1939, column 909.
5. John M. Sherwig, *Guineas and Gunpowder: British Foreign Aid in the War with France 1793–1815* (Cambridge, Mass, Harvard University Press, 1969).
6. *HoC Debates*, debate of 12 February 1793, columns 345–460.
7. Ibid., 3 August 1914, columns 1833–1884.
8. For an attack on the Liberal and Labour speeches, see Barnes and Nicholson, *Amery Diaries*, p. 106.
9. *HoC*, 1793; *HoC*, Volume CXXX11, March–May 1854; *HoC*, February–March 1857; *HoC*, October 1899; *HoC*, July–August 1914; *HoC*, August–October 1939; *HoC*, July 1950.
10. See the speeches by James Fox, *HoC*, 12 February 1793, columns 363–375, and Sheridan, columns 387–396; *HoC*, debate of 31 March 1854, speech by John Bright, columns 243–271; *HoC*, debate of 3 August 1914, speeches by Ramsay Macdonald, columns 1829–1830, Josiah Wedgwood, column 1837 and Arthur Ponsonby, columns 1841–1842.
11. *HoL*, 23 May 1815, speech by Earl Grey, columns 344, 349–351.
12. Robert Rhodes James (ed.), *Churchill Speaks 1897–1963* (Leicester, Windward, 1981).
13. *HoC*, 1 September 1939, column 133, speech by Arthur Greenwood; 2 September 1939, columns 282–286 and 3 September, columns 291–302.
14. William Pitt, *Orations on the French War* (London, J. M. Dent, 1906), p. 51.
15. 'British Institute of Public Opinion Survey' *Public Opinion Quarterly*, 1943, p. 176.
16. *HoC*, 2 November 1815, column 551.
17. *HoC*, loc cit., columns 578–581; debate of 15 November 1915, speech by T. P. O'Connor, columns 1571–1574. Beresford's view was directly contrary to what Clausewitz had advised, see *On War*, p. 608.
18. See the rebuttal of Beresford by Sir Thomas Whittaker, columns 581–582. For the debates in the Second World War, see *HoC*, 5th Series, Volume 397, February–March 1944, debate of 23 February 1944, columns 863, 871, 883 and 886.
19. *Hoc*, 2 August 1956, speeches by H. Legge-Bourke, columns 1681–1683 and by Desmond Donnelly, columns 1701–1707.
20. Philip Bobbitt, Lawrence Freedman and Gregory F. Treverton, *US Nuclear Strategy* (London, Macmillan, 1989); George Kennan, *The Nuclear Delusion* (London, Hamish Hamilton, 1984), p. 8; P. M. S. Blackett, *Atomic Weapons and East-West Relations* (Cambridge, Cambridge University Press, 1956); John Strachey, *On the Prevention of War* (London, Macmillan, 1962), p. 90 ff.

21. A. J. R. Groom, *British Thinking about Nuclear Weapons* (London, Frances Pinter, 1974). For a classic statement of the case for disarmament, see Philip Noel-Baker, *The Arms Race: A Programme for World Disarmament* (London, Atlantic Books, 1958).

22. Robin Day, 'Troubled reflections of a TV Journalist', *Encounter*, May 1970; Robert Elegant, 'How to lose a war', *Encounter*, August 1981; Susan L.Carruthers, *The Media at War* (New York, St Martin's Press, 2000), pp. 110–119; Miles Hudson and John Stanier, *War and the Media* (Stroud, Sutton, 1999), p. 99 ff.; Peter Young and Peter Jesser, *The Media and the Military: From the Crimea to Desert Strike* (Basingstoke, Macmillian, 1997), Chapter 5.

23. *Statement on Defence Estimates 1983*, Cmnd 8951-1 and 8951-11. The format remained the same until the advent of the Blair government which dramatically shorted the papers, see *Modernising Defence: Annual Report of Defence Activity 1998/99*, Ministry of Defence, 1999.

24. Count Puckler, *How Strong is Britain?* (London, Right Book Club, 1939), p. 8.

25. *HoL Debates*, 20 May 1982, column 813.

26. Hudson and Stanier, *War and the Media*, p. 176; Carruthers, *The Media at War*, p. 130. On Goose Green, see Lawrence Freedman and Virginia Gamba-Stonehouse, *Signals of War* (London, Faber and Faber, 1991), p. 371. See also Valerie Adams, *The Media and the Falklands Campaign* (Basingstoke, Macmillan, 1986), p. 8 ff.

27. For a discussion of the media which takes the view that decreasing importance of war gives the media freedom to report as it wishes, see Peter Young and Peter Jesser, *The Media and the Military from the Crimea to Desert Strike* (Basingstoke, Macmillan, 1997).

28. *HoC*, 6 September 1990, column 738.

29. Ibid., 25 September 1992, columns 119–122.

30. Ibid., 6 September, columns 774 and 821.

31. Loc cit., columns 756 and 762.

32. Loc cit., 7 September, speech by Tom King, columns 836–844.

33. *HoC*, 25 September 1992, columns 116–122.

34. Loc cit., columns 153–154.

35. *HoC, 6th Series*, Volume 328, March 1999, debate of 25 March 1999, columns 541–543, 548.

36. Loc cit., columns 545, 553 and 587.

37. *HoL*, 10 July 2006, columns 519 and 520.

38. *HoC*, 18 March 2003, columns 760–773.

39. William Pitt, *Orations on the French War* (London, J. M. Dent, 1906), p. 369.

40. 'Britain's answer to Japan', *The Times*, 9 December 1941.

41. *Hoc*, 26 August 1968, columns 1274–1420.

42. *HoL*, 13 April 1999, columns 636 and 641.

43. Tam Dalyell, 'In the name of democracy', *The Times*, 6 January 2003; 'MPs may be denied debate in order to retain element of surprise, says Hoon', *The Times*, 7 February 2003; 'Labour mutiny leaves Blair out on a limb', *The Times* and 'Rebel vote stuns Blair', *Guardian*, 27 February 2002. For the actual debates, see *HoC*, 17 March 2003, column 703–728; *HoC*, 18 March, columns 760–909.

44. *HoL*, 17 March 2003, columns 68–124, and especially columns 70, 99 and 114.
45. Pitt, *Orations*, p. 46.
46. *HoC*, 25 March, columns 551, 580 and 585.
47. Loc cit., column 595.
48. *HoC*, 25 October 2006, column 416WH.
49. Loc. Cit., columns 417WH, 424WH and 428WH.
50. *HoC*, 6 September, columns 774 and 821. See also 'House call', *The Times*, 6 August 2002.
51. For one example of such guilt, see Arnold Wilson, *More Thoughts and Talks* (London, Longmans Green, 1939), p. 166. Wilson assuaged his guilt by entering the RAF even though he was over-age. He was killed in France in 1940. For the backlash during the Falklands, see Adams, *The Media and The Falklands*, p. 8 ff.
52. Loc cit., columns 756 and 762.
53. *HoC*, 25 March 1999, columns 544 and 566.
54. Matthew Parris, 'The Americans can do without us', and 'Ingram scoffs at advice of Tory "generals"', *The Times*, 27 October 2001; William Rees-Mogg, 'A war in Iraq is easy: the problem will be the peace', *The Times*, 23 December 2002; for Eyal's views, see Simms, *Unfinest Hour: Britain and the Destruction of Bosnia* (London, Allen Lane, 2001), p. 253.
55. On Healey, see Bruce Reed and Geoffrey Williams, *Denis Healey and the Policies of Power* (London, Sidgwick and Jackson, 1971) and Denis Healey, *The Time of My Life* (London, Michael Joseph, 1989), pp. 45, 246–247. See also Healey's comments in *The RAF Historical Society Journal*, Number 31, 2004, pp. 14 and 15. Curiously he disparaged the contributions by armchair strategists but also held up the Chief Scientific Adviser Solly Zuckerman as one of the two ablest men in the Ministry of Defence in the 1960s. Zuckerman had no direct military experience.
56. *HoC*, 17 October, column 61.
57. *HoC*, *5th Series*, Volume 477, July 1950, debate of 1 July 1950, column 578.
58. Michael Ignatieff has suggested that Western peoples may fail to restrain their leaders if they watch conflict voyeuristically on their televisions but suffer no casualties. See Michael Ignatieff, *Virtual War: Kosovo and Beyond* (London, Chatto and Windus, 2000), pp. 4 and 163.
59. For British attitudes towards bombing enemy cities during the Second World War, see J. M. Spaight, *Volcano Island* (London, Geoffrey Bles, 1943) and Robert Neillands, *The Bomber War: Arthur Harris and the Allied Bombing Offensive, 1939–1945* (London, John Murray, 2001), p. 371 ff.
60. Robert Buzzanon, *Masters of War: Military Dissent and Politics in the Vietnam Era* (Cambridge, Cambridge University Press, 1996).
61. Colin Powell with Joseph E. Persico, *My American Journey* (New York, Ballantine Books, 1996), p. 249.
62. James Holloway 111, *Aircraft Carriers at War: A Personal Retrospective of Korea, Vietnam, and the Soviet Confrontation* (Annapolis, Naval Institute Press, 2007), pp. 416–418.
63. For Powell's views, see Bob Woodward, *Bush at War* (New York, Simon and Schuster, 2002), p. 331 ff. See also David Halberstam, *War in a Time of Peace: Bush, Clinton and the Generals* (London, Bloomsbury, 2002).

9 The Public Debate

1. For an excellent study of a number of Western states, see Philip Everts and Pierangelo Isernia, *Public Opinion and the International Use of Force.*
2. *MPs and Defence: A Survey of Parliamentary Knowledge and Opinion*, Institute for European Defence and Strategic Studies (London, 1988).
3. Hobson, *Jingoism*, p. 3.
4. Ibid., p. 38.
5. Playne, *Neuroses of the Nations*, p. 5 and *The Pre-War Mind in Britain* (London, George Allen and Unwin, 1928).
6. Lloyd George, *War Memoirs*, Volume 1, p. 39.
7. Lord Frederic Hamilton, *My Yesterdays: Here, There and Everywhere* (London, Hodder and Stoughton, undated), 18th edition, p. 274.
8. Walter Lippmann, *Public Opinion*, first published 1922.
9. Sir Charles Petrie, *Twenty Years' Armistice-And After: British Foreign Policy since 1918* (London, Eyre and Spottiswoode, 1940), p. 190.
10. 'British Institute of Public Opinion', *Public Opinion Quarterly*, 1940, pp. 77–80.
11. *Public Opinion Quarterly*, loc cit.; George H. Gallup, *The Gallup International Public Opinion Polls: Great Britain 1937–1975* (New York, Random House, 1976), Volume 1, pp. 1–10. Many of the early polls only count those who responded and ignore the 'don't knows', thus distorting the proportions supporting various opinions.
12. Aldous Huxley, *Ends and Means: An Enquiry into the Nature of Ideals and into the Methods employed for their Realisation* (London, Chatto and Windus, 1938).
13. Gallup, *Opinion Polls*, p. 21.
14. *Public Opinion Quarterly*, 1941, pp. 156 and 313.
15. Gallup, *Opinion Polls*, pp. 8, 25, 33 and 42.
16. Ibid., p. 41. For attitudes towards the Churchill government, see *Public Opinion Quarterly*, 1942, p. 156. See also John Charmley, *Churchill: The End of Glory* (New York, Harcourt Brace, 1993), Chapters 42 and 43.
17. Gallup, *Opinion Polls*, pp. 237, 239, 248 and 257.
18. Jean Owen, 'The public and newspaper appraisals of the Suez Crisis', *Public Opinion Quarterly*, 1957–1958, pp. 350–354. Gallup, *Opinion Polls*, pp. 383, 384, 391 and 395.
19. E. P. Thompson, 'Why neither side is worth backing', *The Times*, 29 April 1982.
20. The Falklands War – Panorama Survey 1 by MORI in http://www.com/polls/trends/falklands panorama1. shtml and The Falklands War-Trends – *Daily Star* Survey 26 April 1982/*Sunday Times* Survey 30 April 1982.
21. The Falklands War, loc cit., p. 13.
22. John E. Mueller, *War, Presidents and Public Opinion* (New York, John Wiley, 1973), pp. 270–274.
23. Richard Sobel, *The Impact of Public Opinion on US Foreign Policy since Vietnam* (New York, Oxford University Press, 2001), p. 14. See also Ole R. Holsti's comments, p. ix.
24. Everts and Isernia, *Public Opinion.*
25. Francis A. Beer, *Peace Against War: The Ecology of International Violence* (San Francisco, W. H. Freeman, 1981), p. 16.

26. Anatol Lieven, 'Don't pick a fight you can't finish Mr Miliband', *The Times*, 26 August 2008 and Robert Skidelsky, 'Miliband must stop playing with fire', *The Times*, 28 August 2008.
27. 'War on Afghanistan', poll 11 October 2001, http://www.mori.com/polls/2001/granada p. 2. See also the later poll, '72 per cent of Britons are expecting terror attack', *The Times*, 7 April 2004.
28. Viscount d'Abernon, *An Ambassador of Peace* (Hoddern and Stoughton, London, 1929).
29. Everts and Isernia, *Public Opinion*, p. 260 ff.
30. 'Percentages for Blair and IDS rise in the first week of the war', MORI, 28 March 2003, http://www.mori.com/polls/2003.

10   Iraq and Afghanistan

1. 'Blair issues Africa action call', BBC 31 May 2007, http://nws.bbc.co.uk/1/hi/uk_politics/6706623, downloaded 24 March 2008.
2. As exemplified by the one day conference held at the Royal United Services Institute on 18 March 2008 on 'Reforming Britain's War Powers'.
3. Sifry and Cerf, *The Iraq War Reader*, pp. 268–271.
4. Powell, *My American Journey*, Chapters 4 and 6.
5. For an analysis of the weakness of some of these constraints, see Stefan Halper and Jonathan Clarke, *The Silence of the Rational Centre* (New York, Basic Books, 2007). For US foreign policy in this period, see Micah L. Sifry and Christopher Serf, *The Iraq War Reader: History, Documents, Opinions* (New York, Touchstone, 2003).
6. Khaled Ahmed, 'Dubious appeal of facing two enemies', *The Friday Times* (Lahore), 27 June to 3 July 2008, p.8; Field Marshal Lord Roberts, *Forty-One Years in India from Subaltern to Commander-in-Chief* (London, Richard Bentley, 1897), volume 2.
7. See particularly Blair's speech to Parliament, *HoC Debates*, 18 March 2003, columns 760-774.
8. For a refutation of the second claim, see Scott McClellan, *What happened: Inside the Bush White House and Washington's Culture of Deception* (New York, PublicAffairs, 2008). McClellan was Bush's White House press secretary.
9. Nor were the Americans the only ones who suffered from this illusion, see the comments by the leader of the Conservatives, Ian Duncan Smith, *HoC*, 18 March 2003, column 776.
10. Aylmer Haldane, *The Insurrection in Mesopotamia, 1920* (Edinburgh, Blackwood, 1922).
11. Ben Anderson, 'Diary', *London Review of Books*, 3 January 2008, pp. 40–43; 'Tough guy feels the fear', *The Times*, part 2, p. 19, 22 January 2008, but see also Richard Holmes, *Dusty Warriors: Modern Soldiers at War* (London, Harper Press, 2006), particularly pp. 348-352.
12. 'Iraq and Afghan missions not clear, says field marshal', *The Times*, 23 October 2006; Martin Samuel, 'You voted for this ridiculous war, Reid. So go fight it', *The Times*, 21 August 2007.

13. House of Lords, Select Committee on the Constitution, *Waging War: Parliament's Role and Responsibility*, HL Paper 236-1 (London, Stationary Office), Volume 1, p. 20.

14. Scott McClellan, *What Happened: Inside the Bush White House and Washington's Culture of Deception* (New York, PublicAffairs, 2008), p. 140.

15. See James A. Baker et al., *The Iraq Study Group Report* (New York, Vintage Books, 2006) for a call to cooperate with regional governments.

16. There had been some attempts at democracy in Afghanistan but these had often proved abortive, see Sarfaz Khan, Mohammad Shafi and Ijaz Khan, 'Insights into electoral history in Afghanistan', *Journal of Law and Society*, Peshawar, July 2006.

17. 'Government "gave public false hopes" of achieving Iraq goals', *The Times*, 8 October 2007.

18. On the esteem felt for the armed forces, see Ashford and Timms, *What Europe Thinks*, p. 16.

19. *The 9/11 Commission Report: Final Report of the National Commission on Terrorist Attacks upon the United States* (New York, W.H.Norton, undated); Michael Howard, 'Are we at war?' *Survival*, August–September 2008, p. 248.

20. They also complain that Ministers lack military experience but such experience at a junior level is rarely helpful; see the contemptuous comments by Admiral James L. Holloway in *Aircraft Carriers at War* about President Carter, pp. 383, 394–415.

21. *Waging War*, HL Paper 236-1, Stationary Office, London, Volume 2, p. 3, evidence by Clare Short.

22. 'Iraq military campaign objectives', in Annex C of *Review of Intelligence of Weapons of Mass Destruction*, Report of a Committee of Privy Counsellors, Chairman Lord Butler of Brockwell, HC 898, 14 July 2004, p. 146.

23. 'Iraq Military Campaign Objectives', in Annex C of *Review of Intelligence*, p. 177.

24. David Woodward, *Sunk: How the Great Battleships were Lost* (London, George Allen and Unwin, 1982), Chapter 4.

25. *Review of Intelligence of Weapons of Mass Destruction*, p. 106.

26. For the legal arguments, see Mary Ellen O'Connell, *The Myth of Preemptive Self-Defense* (Washington, American Society of International Law Task Force on Terrorism, August 2002); *Would an Invasion of Iraq be a 'Just War'?* (Washington, United States Institute of Peace, January 2003); David M. Ackerman et al., *International Law and the Preemptive Use of Force Against Iraq* (Washington, Congressional Research Service, 17 March 2003); Lord Alexander of Weedon, *Iraq: Pax Americana and the Rule of Law* (London, Justice/International Commission of Jurists, 2003).

27. Benedikt Birnberg, 'Legal advice on the war in Iraq', *The Times*, 29 March 2005; See also 'History and precedent on Iraq advice', *The Times*, 4 April 2005; 'Impact of the Attorney-General's legal opinion on Iraq War', *The Times*, 30 April 2005

28. *Review of Intelligence of Weapons of Mass Destruction*, p. 102.

29. *Hoc*, 18 March 2003, column 864.

30. Loc cit., column 854.

31. Loc cit., column 832.

32. Loc cit., column 858.

33. Loc cit., columns 804, 876, 887.
34. *Waging War*, Volume 2, p. 3.
35. *Waging War*, Volume 2, p. 202.
36. 'National turnout', *The Times*, 6 May 2005. See also *Whitaker's Almanac 2005* (London, A and C Black, 2004), p.146.
37. Other European parliaments suffered from the same lack of public prestige, see '"Beach-towel" brigade steal the limelight as parliament is left in the shade', *The Times*, 6 June 2001.
38. *Waging War*, Volume 1, p. 43.
39. *Falkland Islands Review, Report of a Committee of Privy Counsellors*, Cmnd 8787, (London, HMSO, January 1983), p. 18.
40. *Waging War*, Volume 2, p. 62.
41. Oddly enough many MPs seemed unaware of this and thought that their debate on 18 March 2003 was unique, see *HoC Debates*, 18 March 2003, column 829.
42. *Statement on Defence Estimates: Britain's Defence for the 1990s*, Volume 1, Cm 1559-1 (London, HMSO, 1991), p. 11.
43. Simon Jenkins, 'When Blair calls in the poodles, we have only the press wolves to save us', *The Times*, 8 December 2004.
44. 'A new elected house', letter from Lord Howe of Aberavon in *The Times*, 12 February 2008.
45. 'I never believed in elections for the Lords, admits Blair', *The Times*, 19 June 2007.
46. 'To war or not to war?' *The Times*, 11 March 2003 reporting Populus/Times polls.
47. 'Opposition to war', *The Times*, 15 March 2003.
48. 'PM's style of government to be called into question', *Evening Standard*, 9 July 2004; 'Archbishop accuses Labour of Damaging Democracy', *The Times*, 21 April 2004; William Rees-Mogg, 'Are we fools led by liars?' *The Times*, 28 February 2005.

11   Do Debates on War Matter?

1. K. R. M. Short, *Western Broadcasting over the Iron Curtain* (Croom Helm, London, 1986), p. 6; Philip M. Taylor, *Munitions of the Mind: A History of Propaganda from the Ancient World to the Present Day* (Manchester University Press, Manchester, 2003), Chapter 24.
2. Wilson, *Patriotic Gore*, pp. xi–xii.
3. Ibid., particularly Chapters 1, 3, 11 and 12. Only, perhaps, in his handling of the 'reconstruction' of the South after the Civil War is Wilson unbalanced.
4. *The Essential Left: Four Classic Texts on the Principles of Communism* (Unwin, London, 1962), pp. 1–48.
5. 'Disease made Marx boil with anger', *The Times*, 31 October 2007.
6. Leo Tolstoy, *The Kingdom of God and Peace Essays*, (London, Oxford University Press/Humphrey Milford, 1939).
7. L. N. Tolstoy, *War and Peace*, Penguin, Harmondsworth, 1961, Volume 2, p. 1407.

8. 'India, US agree on amended NSG draft waiver', *The Hindu*, 31 August 2008: 'Waiver enables member states to provide India with full civil nuclear cooperation', *The Hindu*, 7 September 2008.

9. W. Trotter, *Instincts of the Herd in Peace and War*.

10. Correlli Barnett, *The Collapse of British Power* (Gloucester, Alan Sutton, 1987), p. 21.

11. Amongst the massive literature on appeasement, see R. A. C. Parker, *Chamberlain and Appeasement: British Policy and the Coming of the Second World War* (Basingstoke, Macmillan, 1993).

12. On Bosnia, see, for example, Brendan Simms, *Unfinest Hour*.

13. 'It's like the junta are taking a gun and shooting their own people', *The Times*, 13 May 2008.

14. David Aaronovitch, 'The Junta has handed us the right to intervene', *The Times*, 13 May 2008; 'Burma's agony is a test of the UN's moral authority', *The Times*, 12 May 2008.

15. Matthew Parris, 'Is Mugabe the real problem in Zimbabwe?' *The Times*, 28 June 2008.

16. Peter Lennox, 'Why the Nobel Peace Prize causes so much conflict', *The Times*, 13 October 1981.

17. L. S. Amery, *My Political Life: The Unforgiving Years* (London, Hutchinson,1955), p. 286, quoting Amery's own speech attacking the Munich settlement.

18. Sir J. R. Seeley, *The Expansion of England* (London, Macmillan, 1900, first published 1883), p. 251 ff.

19. Randall Davidson, *Captains and Comrades of the Faith* (London, Society for Promoting Christian Knowledge, 1916), p. 72.

20. Richard J. Barnet, *Intervention and Revolution: The United States in the Third World* (London, Paladin, 1972), p. 20; Michael Ignatieff, *Empire Lite: Nation-Building in Bosnia, Kosovo and Afghanistan* (London, Vintage, 2003), p. 43. For a sympathetic Indian view of imperialism, see Nirad C. Chaudhuri, *Thy Hand Great Anarch! India 1921–1952* (London, Hogarth Press, 1990) and for Gandhi's own ideas, see the interview in Upton Close, *The Revolt of Asia: The End of the White Man's World Dominance* (New York, Putnam's, 1927).

21. Ronald Robinson, John Gallagher with Alice Denny, *Africa and the Victorians: The Official Mind of Imperialism* (London and Basingstoke, Macmillan, 1981), p. 20.

22. Quoted in I. D. Westerman, *Provincial Reconstruction in Afghanistan* (Cambridge, unpublished M.Phil. thesis, 2008), p. 25.

23. J. A. Spender, *The Public Life* (London, Cassell, 1925), Volume 2, pp. 154–156.

24. Ridley, *Palmerston*, p. 255.

25. George Gallup, jr., *The Gallup Poll: Public Opinion 2001* (Wilmington, Scholarly Resources, 2002), p. 43. There is a much larger group who dislike Israel than is the case with the Philippines or Taiwan, but the public rallied round Israel when it was involved in a general war with the Arabs, see Connie de Boer, 'The polls: Attitudes towards the Arab-Israeli conflict', *Public Opinion Quarterly*, Spring 1983.

26. Bob Woodward, *The Commanders* (New York, Simon and Schuster, 1991), p. 226.

27. Margaret Thatcher, *The Downing Street Years* (New York, HarperCollins, 1993), pp. 818–819.

Chronology

Publications	Political and Military Events
1516 Thomas More's *Utopia*	
1547 First Edition of *Homilies*	
	1642–1646 Civil War
1644 John Milton's *Tractate on Education*	
	1688 'Glorious Revolution' against James II
1726 Jonathan Swift's *Gulliver's Travels*	**1745** Last Stuart Uprising
	1772 Liberation of Slaves in England
1778 Adam Smith's *Wealth of Nations*	
1784 James Ramsay's *Essay on the Treatment and Conversion of African Slaves in the British Colonies*	**1789** French Revolution begins
	1793 Britain joins war against French Revolutionaries
	1807 Slave trade banned on British ships
	1815 End of French Wars
	1832 Great Reform Bill extends voting rights
	1834 Slaves freed in West Indies
	1839 Anti-Corn Law League founded

1842
Alfred Tennyson's
Locksley Hall

1859
Charles Darwin's
Origin of Species

1854–1855
Crimean War

1855
Stamp Duty on newspapers abolished

1861–1865
American Civil War

1864
Red Cross founded

1868
St Petersburg Declaration bans use of
expanding bullets

1870–1871
Franco-Prussian War

1870
Free Universal Education

1871
George Chesney's
Battle of Dorking

1880
Compulsory Education for all

1898
Ivan (Jean de) Bloch's
War of the Future

1899
First Hague Peace Conference

1899–1902
Boer War

1901
J. A. Hobson's
Psychology of Jingoism

1904–1905
Russo-Japanese War

1909
Norman Angell's
Great Illusion

1914–1918
First World War

1916
W. Trotter's
*Instincts of the Herd in Peace and
War*

1914
Union of Democratic Control founded

1915
Women's League for International Peace
and Freedom founded

1925
Hector Bywater's
Great Pacific War

1933
H. G. Wells'
Shape of Things to Come

1934
Peace Pledge Union founded

1936
Germany reoccupies Rhineland

1937
Public opinion polls begin in UK

1938
J. M. Spaight's
Air Power in the Next War

1938
Munich Settlement

1939
Max Werner's
Military Strength of the Powers

1939–1945
British involvement in the Second
World War

1942
Oxford Committee for Famine Relief
founded

1943 and 1944
Walter Lippmann's
US Foreign Policy and *US War Aims*

1947
First OXFAM shop

1948
P. M. S. Blackett's
Military and Political Implications of Atomic Energy

1949
George Orwell's
Nineteen Eighty-Four

1950
Korean War

1956
Suez operation

1957
Nevil Shute's
On the Beach

1958
CND founded

1958
Stephen King-Hall's
Defence in the Nuclear Age

1959
Irish Foreign Minister Aiken launches
anti-proliferation Initiative

1964–1973
US military involvement in Vietnam War

1974
Robert Thompson's
Defeating Communist Insurgency

1982
Falklands war between Britain and
Argentina. Parliament supplied with
information on military deployments

1990–1991
First Gulf War

1992
British peacekeepers sent to Bosnia

1999
NATO's bombing of Serbia over Kosovo issue

2001
Terrorist attack on Twin Towers and
Pentagon
US intervention in Afghanistan

2003
Second Gulf War
First extensive debates in House of Lords on
legality of the War

2005
Terrorist attack on London underground

Selected Biographies

Alexander Field Marshal Harold, 1891–1969, served in France in the First World War, commanded in Burma 1942, Middle East 1942–1943, invasion of Sicily 1943, supreme commander Mediterranean 1943–1945, Minister of Defence 1952–1954.

Alanbrooke Viscount, 1883–1963, army officer, served in the First World War, fought in Dunkirk campaign 1940, CIGS 1941, chairman Chiefs of Staff Committee 1941–1945. He will be remembered for the way in which he limited Churchill's wildest enthusiasms and defended the Services against his criticisms.

Alison Archibald, 1792–1867, Scottish journalist and writer, author of histories of Europe during the French Revolution and afterwards.

Amery Leopold Stennett, 1873–1955, MP for Sparkbrook in Birmingham 1911–1945, Colonial Secretary 1924, Secretary of State for India 1940–1945. One of the ablest politicians of his generation, his greatest contribution was his defence of India's interests against Churchill.

Angell Norman, 1872–1967, author of a number of anti-war books including *The Great Illusion* and his Autobiography, *After All*. Awarded the Nobel Peace Prize in 1933. A household name, he emphasised the economic destructiveness of warfare.

Ashdown Paddy, 1941–, served Royal Marines in Malaysia and Northern Ireland, worked in the Foreign Office, Liberal MP 1983, 1988 leader of Liberal and Social Democratic party.

Bacon Francis, 1561–1626, lawyer, politician and essayist. Solicitor General 1607, Attorney General 1613, 1618 Lord Chancellor. A brilliant writer and lawyer, he advanced his legal career by his devious political manoeuvres.

Baring Maurice, 1874–1946, writer and journalist, diplomat 1898–1904, foreign correspondent for *The Times*, 1904–1914, served in Royal Flying Corps in the First World War and was a friend of the founder of the RAF, Lord Trenchard. Author of poetry, novels, history.

Barker Ernest, politicial scientist, Principal of King's College London 1920–1927, Professor of Political Science, Cambridge 1928–1939. Author of *The Character of England* 1947, *Reflections on Government* 1942, *Principles of Social and Political Theory* 1952.

Beaverbrook Lord, 1879–1964, born Maxwell Aitken in Canada but worked primarily in Britain after 1910, Newspaper owner and MP 1911–1916, owner of *The Daily Express*, which he built up into a leading newspaper. Minister of Information 1918 and Minister of Supply 1941–1942. A brilliant newspaperman, he was distrusted for his political manoeuvres.

Bell George, 1883–1958, Anglican cleric, Bishop of Chichester, chaplain to Archbishop Davidson, first chairman central committee of World Council of Churches, chairman Church of England Council on Foreign Relations 1945–1958. Author *Christianity and World Order 1940*. He will be remembered for his determined defence of Christian values against political and military convenience.

Bell Martin, 1938–, journalist and politician, reported for BBC in Bosnia and elsewhere, stood on an anti-sleaze platform to become MP for Tatton in 1997.

Benn Tony, 1925–, Labour politician, MP for Bristol 1950–1960 and 1963–1983, MP for Chesterfield 1984–2001, Minister of Technology 1966–1970, author of a number of books on political affairs and famous for his radical critiques of political events.

Blackett Patrick, 1897–1974, naval officer, author and physicist, served in the Royal Navy in the First World War, discovered the positron 1934, pioneered operational research in the Second World War for the Royal Navy, Professor at Manchester University 1933–1937, Imperial College 1953–1965. Nobel prize for physics 1948.

Blair Tony, 1953–, Labour politician and lawyer, MP for Sedgefield 1983–2007, leader of opposition 1994–1997, Prime Minister 1997–2007. He will be remembered for moving the Labour party sharply to the right, for his election victories and for his close association with the United States under George W. Bush.

Bloch Ivan (also Jean de), 1836–1902, born in Poland, banker and railway financier, attended first Hague Peace Conference at The Hague 1899, famous for *La Guerre Future* which he had researched for years and published in Paris in 1898, which forecast the stalemate of the trenches.

Blunt Anthony, 1907–1983, surveyor of the Queen's pictures 1945–1972 and Soviet spy. Director of the Courtauld Institute 1947–1974. Unmasked as Soviet spy 1979 and his knighthood was annulled.

Bond Brian, 1936–, military historian, Professor of Military History at King's College, London 1986–2001, author of numerous books on military history including *British Military Policy Between the Wars* and *War and Society in Europe 1870–1970*.

Boyce Michael Cecil Baron, 1943–, submariner, Commander in Chief Fleet 1997–1998, First Sea Lord 1998–2001, Chief of Defence Staff 2001–2003.

Bright John, 1811–1889, radical politician and free trader, member of Anti-Corn Law League, MP for Durham, attacked Crimean War, MP for Birmingham 1857, 1868 President of the Board of Trade. A world figure, he gave his name to a town in Australia and received many other tributes.

Brougham Henry, 1778–1868, lawyer and politician, critic of slave trade, legal reformer; Lord Chancellor 1830–1834, contributor to the *Edinburgh Review*.

Brown Gordon, 1951–, Labour politician, Chancellor of Exchequer 1997–2007, Prime Minister 2007–.

Bush George Herbert Walker, 1924–, US Republican politician, served in US Navy in Second World War, Senator for Texas, Permanent Representative at the UN 1971–1973, Director of CIA 1976, Vice-President of US 1980–1988, President 1988–1992.

Bush George Walker, 1946–, US Republican politician, Governor of Texas 1986–1988, President of US 2001–2008. Elected on a semi-isolationist platform he reversed his policies after 9/11 and will be remembered as the President who launched the wars in Afghanistan and Iraq.

Bywater Hector, 1884–1940, journalist specialising in naval affairs particularly in the Pacific. Worked for *The Daily Telegraph* and other newspapers, and published a number of books on naval affairs.

Cameron James, 1911–1985, journalist with *Daily Express* and *New Chronicle*, television presenter and radical.

Chamberlain Neville, 1869–1940, Conservative MP for Birmingham 1918–1940, Chancellor of the Exchequer 1931–1937, Prime Minister 1937–1940. Though he has his defenders, his name will always be associated with appeasement and the Munich settlement.

Chaucer Geoffrey, 1345–1400, poet, served in army in France 1359, sent on royal missions to Italy 1372–1373, 1377 to France and elsewhere. Author of *Troilus and Cressida, Canterbury Tales* and so on, 1386 lost his official positions and remained impoverished and out of favour until 1399, often called first great English poet. His work offers a unique insight into the life of his period.

Chesterfield Lord, 1694–1773, essayist. Politician, MP 1715–1723, Lord Lieutenant of Ireland 1745, 1746 one of the principal secretaries of state. Remembered for his letters.

Churchill Winston 1874–1965, Conservative MP 1900, Liberal MP 1906, Home Secretary 1910, First Lord of the Admiralty 1911–1915, 1917 Minister of Munitions, 1939 First Lord of Admiralty, Prime Minister 1940–1945 and 1951–1955. Widely regarded as one of Britain's greatest wartime leaders alongside Marlborough and the Elder Pitt. Author of a number of historical and biographical works.

Clarendon. 4th Earl, 1800–1870, ambassador to Madrid, President of Board of Trade 1846, Irish Viceroy 1847–1852, Secretary of State for Foreign Affairs 1853–1855, 1865 and 1868.

Clarke Kenneth, 1940–, Conservative politician, Chancellor of the Exchequer 1993–1997. Well known for his enthusiasm for the European Union within the Conservative party, though this may have kept him from its leadership.

Clarkson Thomas, 1760–1846, anti-slavery campaigner, collected together the information which William Wilberforce used in the campaign. Published a two-volume history of the campaign.

Cobden Richard, 1804–1864, apostle of free trade, most prominent member of Anti-Corn Law League, MP for the West Riding of Yorkshire, suffered for his opposition to the Crimean and Opium Wars.

Colet John, 1467–1519, theologian, visited Italy 1493–1496, Dean of St Paul 1505, endowed St Paul's School in London.

Constantine 1, 274–337, fought in Egypt and Persia, succeeded his father as Emperor of Western Roman Empire in 306, 313 gave civil rights to Christians, made Christianity state religion 324, defeated Eastern Emperor and moved capital to 'Constantinople' in 330.

Darwin Charles, 1808–1892, originator of the theory of natural selection, accompanied scientific survey on HMS Beagle 1831–1836 to Brazil, Argentina, Chile, Australia and New Zealand. Author of *Journal of Researches into the Geology and Natural History of the Various Countries Visited by HMS Beagle* (normally, *The Voyage of the Beagle*) 1839, *The Origin of the Species by means of Natural Selection* 1859, *The Descent of Man and Selection in Relation to Sex* 1871. Regarded as one of Britain's greatest scientists.

Davidson Randall 1848–1930, Anglican clergyman, Archbishop of Canterbury 1903–1928, improved relations between Anglican and Orthodox Churches.

Dunant Jean Henri, 1828–1910, founded Red Cross after seeing wounded at the battle of Solferino in 1864. Later went bankrupt and disappeared from public roles, but awarded the first Nobel Peace Prize in 1901.

Edward V11, 1841–1910, King of Great Britain 1901–1910, playboy lifestyle before he came to the throne, visited a number of continental countries as King, helping to cement Entente with France and Russia.

Ferdinand Franz, 1863–1914, nephew to the Emperor Franz Joseph and heir to Austro-Hungarian throne. Most famous for his death; his assassination in July 1914 by a Balkan nationalist sparked the First World War.

Fox Charles James, 1749–1806, radical politician. MP at 19, 1773 commissioner of the Treasury, quarrelled with George 111 and later with William Pitt, opponent of French Wars, Foreign Secretary 1806.

Fox George, 1624–1691, founder of the Quakers, originally a shoemaker, he wandered the country preaching and inveighing against priests, lawyers, social conventions and soldiers, imprisoned several times for his views, visited West Indies, America, Netherlands and Germany. Founded 'Friends of Truth' or Quakers.

Fuchs Klaus, 1911–1988, German-born physicist and spy for Soviet Union. Fled from Germany to Britain 1933, worked on atomic bomb project 1943–1945 and at Harwell post war. Sentenced to 14 years for passing information on Manhattan project to Russia 1950. Worked in East Germany after release.

Fuller J. F. C., 1878–1966, soldier and military analyst, served in the Boer War and First World War, advocate of armoured warfare, retired from army 1933 and wrote numerous books on history and warfare.

Gort John, Viscount, 1884–1946, army officer, joined 1905 and served in First World War, CIGS 1937–1939, commanded British forces in Europe 1939–1940, Gibraltar 1940–1942 and Malta 1942–1944.

Grey Edward 1862–1933, Liberal politician. MP 1885, Under-Secretary at the Foreign Office 1894, Foreign Secretary 1905–1916. Played a major role in Britain's foreign policy before the First World War, ineffective during the war years, he took up the League of Nations cause after retirement.

Grotius Hugo, 1583–1645, Dutch theologian and jurist, fled to Paris 1621, author of highly influential *De Jura Belli et Pacis* 1625, Swedish ambassador at French court 1634–1645.

Halifax Earl, 1881–1959, Viceroy of India 1926–1931, Foreign Secretary 1938–1940, Ambassador to the USA 1941–1946. He was closely associated with Neville Chamberlain's policy of appeasement.

Hazlitt William, 1778–1830, English journalist and essayist, wrote on poetry and social and political affairs; author of *Reply to Malthus* 1807, *Table Talk* 1821, *Life of Napoleon Bonaparte* 1828–1839; one of the most famous radical commentators of his time.

Healey Denis 1917–, Baron, Labour politician, served in army in the Second World War, MP for Leeds 1952, Secretary of State for Defence 1964–1970, Chancellor of the Exchequer 1974–1979. Known for his forthright views and position on the right of the Labour party.

Hobson John Atkinson 1858–1940, economist and writer, his theories of Imperialism influenced Lenin, author of the *Imperialism* 1902 and the *Science of Wealth* 1911 amongst many other books.

Homer, 8th century BC Greek poet, author of epics of *The Illiad* on the siege and fall of Troy and *The Odyssey* on Odysseus's wanderings after the fall of the city, little known about his life.

Hoover Herbert, 1874–1964, mining engineer, organised relief movement in Europe during the First World War and after the Second World War. His Presidency of United States from 1928–1932 was regarded as a failure because of the Great Depression and his role saving Europeans from starvation was overshadowed.

Howard Sir Michael, 1922–, military historian, served in the Second World War, Professor of War Studies, King's College, London 1963–1968, Chichele Professor History of War at Oxford University 1977–1980, Regius Professor of Modern History 1980–1989, author of numerous books on military history.

Hurd Douglas, Baron, 1930–, Conservative politician, HM Diplomatic Service 1952–1966, MP for Mid Oxon 1974–1983, MP for Witney 1983–1997, Secretary of State for Foreign Affairs 1989–1995. Author of a number of novels and books on politics.

Ironside William Edmund, 1880–1959, army officer, served in the First World War, commanded allied forces Archangel 1919, served in India 1928–1936 CIGS 1939–1940, commander in chief home forces 1940.

Kipling Rudyard, 1865–1936, poet, novelist and journalist; employed as journalist in India 1880–1889; author of *Kim* 1901, *Just So Stories*. Awarded Nobel Prize for literature 1907. Kipling was immensely famous at the end of the 19th century and some of his non-political poetry has enjoyed a revival in recent years.

Lang Cosmo, 1864–1945, Anglican clergyman, Archbishop of York 1909–1928, Archbishop of Canterbury 1928–1942.

Lansbury George, 1859–1940, Christian socialist and pacifist, MP 1910–1912, editor *Daily Herald* 1919–1922, leader of Labour party 1932–1935, resigned when party supported sanctions against Italy over its invasion of Abyssinia.

Leach Sir Henry Admiral of the Fleet, 1923–, served in the Royal Navy during the Second World War, First Sea Lord 1979–1982.

Liddell Hart Sir Basil, 1895–1970, military historian, served in the First World War, military correspondent of *The Daily Telegraph*, 1925–1935 and of *The Times*, 1935–1939, one of the best-known military commentators of the period and author of numerous books on history and strategy.

Lippmann Walter, 1899–1974, journalist with *New York World* and *Herald Tribune*. Author of *US Foreign Policy* 1943, *US War Aims* 1944, *The Cold War* 1947 and numerous other books on politics and world affairs. He was the best-known liberal US political commentator for many years, his influence stretching from the Paris peace conference to the Vietnam War.

Lloyd George David, Liberal politician and Prime Minister, Chancellor of the Exchequer 1908, 1909 increased income tax and death duties, Minister of Munitions 1915, split Liberal party when he became Prime Minister 1916–1922.

Mansfield Earl, 1705–1793, Solicitor General 1742, Attorney General 1754, Chief Justice of the King's Bench 1756.

Mill John Stuart, 1806–1873, British philosopher and social reformer, worked for East India company 1823–1858, wrote *System of Logic* 1843, *On Liberty* 1859, Liberal MP 1865.

Milne George Francis, 1866–1948, army officer, served in the Boer War, First World War, CIGS 1926–1933.

Milton John, 1608–1674, poet and essayist, supporter of Paliamentarians during Civil War . Author of *Areopagitica* an attack on censorship 1644, official apologist for the Commonwealth until the restoration of Stuarts, went blind 1652. Author of *Paradise Lost* 1667, *Paradise Regained* 1671. Widely considered greatest British poet of 17th century.

Moorehead Alan, 1910–, born in Australia, worked for British and Australian newspapers, war correspondent 1930–1946, retired to write books; author of *The Russian Revolution*, *The Fatal Impact* and many other historical works.

Morley John, 1838–1923, politician, essayist, biographer of Edmund Burke, Richard Cobden, Gladstone and others, edited *Pall Mall Gazette*, MP for Newcastle 1883–1895. Lord President of Council 1910 until resigned over the declaration of the First World War.

Nasser Gamal Abdul, 1918–1970, Egyptian politician, led revolt against King Farouk 1952, President of Egypt 1956–1970, united Egypt and Syria in short-lived United Arab Republic 1958. Charismatic speaker and leader of the Arab world who presided over military defeats in 1956 and 1967.

Nicholson Michael, 1937–, reporter and television presenter, joined ITN 1963, served as a war correspondent in numerous wars including Nigerian civil war, senior foreign correspondent with ITN 1991–1998.

Nightingale Florence, 1820–1910, nursing reformer, took 38 nurses to Scutari during Crimean War, helped set up training for nurses at St Thomas's and at King's College Hospital. Worked on improvements in army nursing and on health conditions in India. Arguably the most famous 19th-century English woman after Victoria herself

Nott Sir John, 1932–, army officer, banker and Conservative politician, MP for Cornwall St Ives 1966–1983, Secretary of State for Defence 1981–1983.

Owen David, 1938–, Baron, Labour and Social Democrat politician, Labour MP 1966–1981, SDP 1981–1992, Secretary of State for Foreign Affairs 1977–1979, co-chairman of the International Conference on former Yugoslavia 1992–1995.

Pascal Blaise, 1623–1662, brilliant French mathematician, physicist and theologian. Supporter of Jansenists, author of *Lettres Provinciales* 1656–1657 and *Pensees* 1669.

Palmerston Viscount, 1784–1865, politician, MP 1807 and for Cambridge 1811–1831, junior Lord of the Admiralty and Secretary at War 1809–1828, Foreign Secretary 1830–1841 and again 1846–1852. Prime Minister 1855–1858 and 1859–1865. Famous for his robust foreign policy and support for British interests.

Percival John, 1834–1918, Anglican clergyman, President of Trinity College, Oxford 1879–1882, Headmaster of Rugby 1887–1895, Bishop of Hereford 1895–1917.

Philby Kim, 1911–1988, diplomat and Soviet spy, head of Mi6 Soviet counterespionage 1944–1946, First Secretary embassy in Washington 1949–1951, correspondent of *The Observer* from 1956, fled to USSR 1963. Author of *My Silent War* 1968.

Pitt William, 1759–1806, elected as an MP at 21 and become Chancellor of the Exchequer 18 months later, Prime Minister in 1783–1801, and from 1804 to 1806.

Ponsonby Arthur, 1871–1946, lifelong pacifist, Liberal MP before 1914, struggled against the First World War, Labour MP for Sheffield 1922–1930, leader of Labour opposition in Lords 1931–1935.

Powell Colin, 1937–, US army officer, served in Vietnam War, Commander in Chief of US armed forces 1989, Chief of Joint Chiefs of Staff 1989–1993, Secretary of State 2001–2005. His illustrious military career was overshadowed by his subsequent service in the administration of George W. Bush and his inability to restrain its use of military forces.

Rees Mogg, William, Baron, 1928–, editor of *The Times* 1967–1981, columnist, author of books on politics, religion and economics.

Ribbentrop Joachim von, 1893–1946, originally a wine merchant, member of National Socialist party 1932, Hitler's adviser on foreign affairs, 1936 Ambassador to Britain, Foreign Minister 1936–1945, condemned at Nuremberg trials and executed.

Robertson George, 1946–, Baron, Labour politician, Secretary of State for Defence 1997–1999, Secretary General of NATO 1999–2003.

Runcie Robert, 1921–, Anglican clergyman, served in armed forces in the Second World War, Bishop of St Albans 1970, Archbishop of Canterbury 1980–1990.

Russell William Howard, 1820–1907, often described as the first of the war correspondents, made his reputation during the Crimean War; reported also on the Indian Mutiny, American Civil War, Franco-Prussian and the Zulu Wars. He founded *The Army and Navy Gazette* to increase coverage of military affairs. Russell visited India and Egypt as private secretary of the heir to the throne (Edward).

Sharp Granville, 1735–1813, ordnance department, London, 1758–1776, resigned in sympathy with American colonies, fought for freedom of slaves in Britain and advocated the establishment of a home for slaves in Sierra Leone.

Sheppard Hugh Richard, 1880–1937, Vicar of St Martin in the Fields 1914–1927, Dean of Canterbury, 1929–1931, Canon of St Paul's 1934–1937. Encouraged religious broadcasting and pacifist causes.

Short Clare, Labour politician, MP for Birmingham Ladywood since 1983, Secretary of State for International Development 1997–2003, resigned over attack on Iraq 2003.

Shute Nevil, 1899–1960 (real name Norway), aeronautical engineer and novelist, worked on R100 airship, war correspondent 1943–1945, settled in Australia 1945; author of *Slide Rule, A Town Like Alice, On the Beach* and many others.

Smuts Jan, 1870–1950, South African statesman, fought for Boers, served on Boer delegation to peace conference, Minister of Defence Union of South Africa, 1910–1919, supporter of League of Nations, Prime Minister South Africa 1919–1924 and again 1939–1948.

Spaight John Moloney, 1877–1968, lawyer, civil servant and author. Director of Accounts Air Ministry 1930–1934, Principal Assistant Secretary 1934–1937. Author of numerous books on air power and particularly its relationship with international law.

Taylor Sir Teddy, 1937–, Conservative MP for Glasgow Cathcart 1964–1979 and Southend East 1980–1997.

Temple William, 1881–1944, Headmaster of Repton school 1910–1914, Bishop of Manchester 1921, Archbishop of York 1929–1942 Archbishop of Canterbury 1942–1944. Author of *Church and Nation*, 1915, *Christianity and the Social Order*, 1942.

Tennyson Alfred, 1809–1892, educated Cambridge, poet laureate 1850, very widely read and admired, wrote poetry on social issues, including women's education, war, religion and science.

Thatcher Margaret, Baroness. 1925–, Conservative politician, MP for Finchley 1959–1992, Prime Minister 1979–1990, changed the face of Britain by reducing the power of the unions, denationalising industries and allowing the pound to float on international exchanges.

Toussaint L'Ouverture, 1746–1803, born of slave parents in Haiti, freed 1777, joined black insurgents on island 1791, made commander of island by French in 1797 and defeated British and Spanish, but refused to obey Napoleon's order to restore slavery, Defeated and imprisoned by French, died in France.

Vatel Emerich de, 1714–1767, Swiss legal expert, Saxon representative at Bern 1746–1764. Author of *Droit des Gens* 1758.

Vincent Richard Baron, 1931–, Commandant Royal Military College of Science 1980–1983, Master General of the Ordnance 1983–1987, Chief of Defence Staff 1991–1992.

Wells Herbert George 1866–1946, socialist, novelist, essayist and political commentator, author of some hundred books which were translated and read across the world. His science fiction was especially well known and made into a number of films.

Werner Max, 1901–, economist and strategist. Born Aleksandr Shifrin in Kharkov, moved to Western Europe 1923, economic journalist, newspaper editor, fled to Paris from Germany 1933, *Towards the Second World War* published Paris 1938, moved to New York in the Second World War and wrote for *New Republic* and *Reynolds News*.

Wilberforce William, 1759–1833, politician, Evangelist and social reformer, MP for Hull 1780 and 1784 for Yorkshire, 1787 founded association for the reformation of manners, 1788 began his campaign for abolition of slave trade, successful 1807, hopes to secure total abolition of slavery, forced to retire from Parliament by ill health 1825.

Wilkinson Paul, 1937–, academic specialising in the study of terrorism, Professor of International Relations at the University of St Andrews since 1990, author of numerous books on terrorism and its handling by democracies.

Williams Rowan, 1950–, Anglican clergyman, Lecturer in Divinity Cambridge 1980–1986, Bishop of Monmouth 1992–2002, Archbishop of Canterbury 2002–. Author of a number of books of poetry and theology.

Wilson Edmund, 1895–1902, widely read American literary critic. Served in the US army during the First World War, subsequently editor of *Vanity Fair* and associate editor of *New Republic*. Author of *Axel's Castle* 1931, *To the Finland Station* 1940, *The Wound and the Bow* 1941 and *Patriotic Gore* 1962.

Zimmern Alfred, 1879–1957, Wilson Professor of International Relations, Aberystwyth 1919–1921, Professor of International Relations, Oxford 1930–1944.

Sources for these biographies included various editions of *Who's Who: An Annual Biographical Dictionary* (London, Adam and Charles Black); *The Concise Dictionary of National Biography* (Oxford, Oxford University Press, 1982); Magnus Magnusson ansd Rosemary Goring, *Chambers Biographical Dictionary* (Edinburgh, Chambers, 1990); Bruce P. Lenman and Katharine Boyd (eds), *Chambers Dictionary of World History* (Edinburgh, Chambers, 1993); Juliet Gardiner (ed.), The History Today *Who's Who in British History* (London, Collins, 2000); John Ramsden (ed.), The Oxford *Companion to Twentieth Century British Politics* (Oxford, Oxford University Press, 2002).

Bibliography

Adams, V., *The Media and the Falklands Campaign* (Basingstoke, Macmillan, 1986).

Adie, K., *The Kindness of Strangers* (London, Headline, 2002).

Adleman, J. R. and Chih-yu Shi, *Symbolic War: The Chinese Use of Force 1840–1980* (Taipei, National Chengchi University, 1993).

Ainsworth, M. (ed.), *Milton on Education: The Tractate of Education* (New Haven, Yale University Press, 1928).

Albright, M. and Woodward, B., *Madam Secretary: A Memoir* (London, Macmillan, 2003).

Aldrich, R. J., *The Hidden Hand: Britain, America and Cold War Intelligence* (London, John Murray, 2001).

Alleg, H., *The Question* (London, John Calder, 1958).

Angell, N., *After All: The Autobiography of Norman Angell* (London, Hamish Hamilton, 1951).

Anisfield, N. (ed.), *The Nightmare Considered: Critical Essays on Nuclear War Literature* (Bowling Green, Ohio, Bowling Green University Press, 1991).

Armitage, M. J. and Mason, R. A., *Air Power in the Nuclear Age: 1945–1984* (Basingstoke, Macmillan, 1985).

Arthur, Sir George, *From Wellington to Wavell* (London, Hutchinson, 1942).

Ashford, S., and Timms, N., *What Europe Thinks: A Study of Western European Values* (Aldershot, Dartmouth, 1992).

Aydon, C., *Charles Darwin* (London, Constable, 2002).

Ayres, J. (ed.), *Paupers and Pig Killers: The Diary of William Holland A Somerset Parson 1799–1818* (Gloucester, Alan Sutton, 1984).

Baring, M., *With the Cossacks in Manchuria* (Londo, Eveleigh Nash, 1905).

Barker, Sir Ernest, *National Character and the Factors in its Formation* (London, Methuen, fourth and revised edition 1948).

Barnes, J. and Nicholson, D. (eds), *Empire at Bay: The Leo Amery Diaries 1929–1945* (London, Hutchinson, 1988).

Barnet, R. J., *Intervention and Revolution: The United States in the Third World* (London, Paladin, 1972).

Barnett, C., *The Collapse of British Power* (Gloucester, Alan Sutton, 1987).

Baskerville, S., *Not Peace but a Sword: The political Theology of the English Revolution* (London, Routledge, 1993).

Bedoyere, M. de la (ed.), *Objections to Roman Catholicism* (London, Constable, 1964).

Bell, G. K., *Randall Davidson: Archbishop of Canterbury* (London, Geoffrey Cumberlege, Oxford University Press, 1952).

Bethune-Baker, J., *The Influence of Christianity on War* (Cambridge, Macmillan and Bowes, 1885).

Bialer, U., *The Shadow of the Bomber* (London, Royal Historical Society, 1980).

Black, J., *The English Press 1621–1861* (Stroud, Sutton Publishers, 2001).

Black, M., *A Cause for our Times: Oxfam the First Fifty Years* (Oxford, Oxfam and Oxford University Press, 1992).

Blackett, P. M. S., *Military and Political Consequences of Atomic Energy* (London, Turnstile Press, 1948).

——, *Atomic Weapons and East-West Relations* (Cambridge, Cambridge University Press, 1956).

Blainey, G., *The Causes of War* (Melbourne, Sun Books, 1973).

——, *The Great Seesaw: A New View of the Western World* (Basingstoke, Macmillan, 1988).

Bloch, I. S., *Is War Now Impossible? Being and Abridgement of the War of the Future in its Technical, Economic and Political Relations* (Aldershot, Gregg Revivals, 1991).

Block, M. (ed.), *Current Biography: Who's News and Why 1943* (New York, H. W. Wilson, 1944).

Blum, S. D., *Walter Lippmann: Cosmopolitan in a Century of Total War* (Ithaca, Cornell University Press, 1984).

Bobbitt, P., Freedman Lawrence and Treverton Gregory F., *US Nuclear Strategy* (London, Macmillan, 1989).

Bond, B., *Liddell Hart: A Study of his Military Thought* (London, Cassell, 1977).

——, *The Unquiet Western Front: Britain's Role in Literature and History* (Cambridge, Cambridge University Press, 2002).

—— and Roy, I. (eds), *War and Society* (London, Croom Helm, 1974).

Bonney, R. (ed.), *Economic Systems and State Finance* (Oxford, Clarendon Press, 1995.

Bracken, P., *The Command and Control of Nuclear Weapons* (New Haven, Yale University Press, 1983).

Brittain, V., *The Rebel Passion* (London, George Allen and Unwin, 1964).

Brock, P., *Pacifism in Europe to 1914* (Princeton, Princeton University Press, 1992).

Brooke, Lord, *An Eye-witness in Manchuria* (London, Eveleigh Nash, 1905).

Brooks, S. and Gagnon Alain-G, *The Political Influence of Ideas* (Westport, Praeger, 1994).

Bruce, L. R. H., *Retreat from Glory* (London, Putnam, 1934).

Bunyan, J., *The Holy War* (London, Religious Tract Society, 1906).

Burk, K., *Britain, America and the Sinews of War, 1914–1918* (London, George Allen and Unwin, 1985).

Burroughs, E. A., Lord Bishop of Durham, *The Christian Church and War* (London, James Nisbet, 1931).

Bussey, G. and Tims, M., *Women's International League for Peace and Freedom 1915–1965* (London, George Allen and Unwin, 1965).

Butterfield, H., *Christianity and History* (London, George Bell, 1949).

Buzzanco, R., *Masters of War: Military Dissent and Politics in the Vietnam Era* (Cambridge, Cambridge University Press, 1996).

Byford-Jones, Lieutenant Colonel W., *Berlin Twilight* (London, Hutchinson, 1947).

Bywater, H. C., *Navies and Nations: A Review of Naval Developments since the Great War* (London, Constable, 1927).

Calder, A., *The People's War: Britain 1939–45* (London, Jonathan Cape, 1969).

Cantril, H. and Strunk, M., *Public Opinion 1935–1946* (Princeton, Princeton University Press, 1951).

Carr, E. H., *The Twenty Years' Crisis 1919–1939* (London, Macmillan, 1946).

Carruthers, S. L., *The Media at War* (New York, St Martin's Press, 2000).

Cary, F. C., *The Influence of War on Walter Lippmann 1914–1944* (Madison, State Historical Society of Wisconsin, 1967).

Caute, D., *The Fellow Travellers: Intellectual Friends of Communism* (New Haven, Yale University Press, 1988).

Chadwick, O., *The Secularisation of the European Mind in the Nineteenth Century* (Cambridge, Cambridge University Press, 1990).

Chamberlain, W. H., *Japan over Asia* (London, Duckworth, 1938).

Chapman, F. S., *The Jungle is Neutral* (London, Chatto and Windus, 1950).

Church, R. W., *The Message of Peace and Other Sermons* (London, Society for Promoting Christian Knowledge, 1895).

Clark, A., *The Donkeys* (London, Hutchinson, 1961).

Clark, General Wesley K., *Waging Modern War* (New York, Public Affairs, 2001).

Clark, L. L., *Social Darwinism in France* (Alabama, University of Alabama Press, 1985).

Clark, R. W., *Tizard* (London, Methuen, 1965).

Clarke, I. F., *Voices Prophesying War: Future Wars 1763–3749* (Oxford University Press, 1992).

Collett, N., *The Butcher of Amritsar: General Reginald Dyer* (London, Hambledon and London, 2005).

Conquest, R., *The Great Terror* (Basingstoke, Macmillan, 1968).

Corbett, J. S., *Some Principles of Maritime Strategy*, with an introduction and notes by Eric J. Grove (London, Brassey's, 1988).

Coulby, D. and Jones, C., *Education and Warfare in Europe* (Aldershot, Ashgate, 2001).

Coupland, Sir Reginald, *The British Anti-Slavery Movement* (London, Frank Cass, 1964).

Crook, P., *Darwinism, War and History* (Cambridge, Cambridge University Press, 1994).

Cross, J., *Red Jungle* (London, Robert Hall, 1975).

d'Abernon, Viscount, *An Ambassador of Peace* (London, Hodder and Stoughton, 1929).

Danchev, A. and Todman, D. (eds), *War Diaries 1939–1945: Field Marshal Lord Alanbrooke* (London, Weidenfeld and Nicolson, 2001).

Darwin, C., *The Voyage of the Beagle* (Ware, Wordsworth, 1997).

Davidson, R. T., *Occasions: Sermons and Addresses delivered on Days of Interest* (Mowbray, London, 1925).

de Pirey Philip, *Operation Waste* (London, Arco Publishing, 1954).

Dickens, A. G. and Jones, W. R. D., *Erasmus The Reformer* (London, Methuen, 1994).

Dickinson, H. T. (ed.), *Britain and French Revolution, 1789–1815* (Basingstoke, Macmillan, 1989).

Dilks, D. (ed.), *The Diaries of Sir Alexander Cadogan 1938–1945* (London, Cassell, 1971).

Douhet, G., *The Command of the Air*, translated by Dino Ferrari, new edition, Office of Air Force History, Washington, 1983.

Driver, C., *The Disarmers: A Study in Protest* (London, Hodder and Stoughton, 1964).

Duffield, M., *Global Governance and the New Wars: The Merging of Development and Security* (London, Zed Books, 2001).

———, *Development, Security and Unending War: Governing the World of Peoples* (Cambridge, Polity, 2007).

Earle, E., M. (ed.), *Nationalism and Internationalism* (New York, Columbia University Press, 1950).

Eliot, T. S. (ed.), *A Choice of Kipling's Verse* (London, Faber and Faber, 1941).

Everts, P. and Isernia, P., *Public Opinion and the International Use of Force* (London, Routledge, 2001).

Farrar, F. W., *The Fall of Man and Other Sermons* (London, Macmillan, 1868).

Ferguson, N., *The Pity of War* (London, Allen Lane/The Penguin Press, 1998).

Fleming, P., *News from Tartary: A Journey from Peking to Kashmir* (London, Jonathan Cape, 1936).

Fletcher-Cooke, J., *The Emperor's Guest 1942–1945* (London, Leo Cooper, 1972).

Fortescue, J. W., *British Statesmen of the Great War: 1793–1814* (Oxford, Clarendon Press, 1911).

Freedman, L. (ed.), *Military Intervention in European Conflicts* (Oxford, Political Quarterly/Blackwell, 1994).

—— and Gamba-Stonehouse, V., *Signals of War* (London, Faber and Faber, 1991).

Froude, J. A., *Life and Letters of Erasmus* (London, Longmans, Green, 1906).

Fukuyama, F., *The End of History and the Last Man* (London, Penguin, 1992).

Fuller, Major General J. F. C., *The Conduct of War 1789–1961* (London, Eyre and Spottiswoode, 1962).

Fursenko, A. and Naftali, T., *Khrushchev's Cold War* (New York, Norton, 2006).

Gallup, G. H., *The Gallup International Public Opinion Polls: Great Britain 1937–1975* (New York, Random House, 1976).

Garbett, C., *In an Age of Revolution* (London, Hodder and Stoughton, 1952).

Geike, R. and Montgomery, E., *The Dutch Barrier 1705–1719* (Cambridge, Cambridge University Press, 1930).

Gerard, J. W., *My Four Years in Germany* (London, Hodder and Stoughton, 1917).

Gibbs, P., *Across the Frontiers* (London, Michael Joseph, 1938).

Gibson, W., *The Church of England 1688–1832* (London, Routledge, 2001).

Goldrick, J. and Hattendorf, J. B., *Mahan is not Enough* (Newport, Rhode Island, Naval War College Press, 1993).

Gollancz, V., *Our Threatened Values* (London, Victor Gollancz, 1946).

Gordon, E., *Miracle on the River Kwai* (London, Collins, 1963).

Goulding, M., *Peacemonger* (London, John Murray, 2001).

Grane, W. L., *The Passing of War: A Study in Things that Make for Peace* (London, Macmillan, 1912).

Grey, Viscount Grey of Fallodon, *Twenty-Five Years 1892–1916* (London, Hodder and Stoughton, 1923).

Groom, A. J. R., *British Thinking about Nuclear Weapons* (London, Frances Pinter, 1974).

Gunther, J., *Inside Europe* (London, Hamish Hamilton, 1936).

Gurwood, Colonel, *Selections from the Dispatches and General Orders of the Duke of Wellington* (London, John Murray, 1841).

Halberstam, D., *War in a Time of Peace: Bush, Clinton and the Generals* (London, Bloomsbury, 2002).

Haldane, A., *The Insurrection in Mesopotamia, 1920* (Edinburgh, Blackwood, 1922).

Halper, S. and Clarke, J., *The Silence of the Rational Centre* (New York, Basic Books, 2007).

Halsey, H. A., *Change in British Society* (Oxford, Oxford University Press, 1981).

Hamill, D., *Pig in the Middle: The Army in Northern Ireland 1969–1985* (London, Methuen, 1985).

Hamilton, Lord Frederick, *My Yesterdays: Here, There and Everywhere* (London, Hodder and Stoughton, undated 18th edition).

Hamilton, I., *The Happy Warrior: A Life of General Sir Ian Hamilton* (London, Cassell, 1966).

Hancock, W. K. and Browning, M. M., *British War Economy* (London, HMSO, 1949).

Harari, Y. N., *Renaissance Military Memoirs: War, History and Identity 1450–1600* (Woodbridge, Boydell, 2004).

Harfiyah, A. H., Ramsbotham, O., Risaluddin, S. and Wicker, B., *The Crescent and the Cross: Muslim and Christian Approaches to War and Peace* (London, Council of Christian Approaches to Defence and Disarmament, 1999).

Harris, S., *Out of Control: British Foreign Policy and the Union of Democratic Control* (Hull, University of Hull Press, 1996).

Hart, E., *Man Born to Live: Life and Work of Henry Dunant Founder of the Red Cross* (London, Victor Gollanz, 1953).

Hastings, Max, *Going to the Wars* (Basingstoke, Macmillan, 2000).

Haythornthwaite, P. J., et al., *Napoleon: The Final Verdict* (London, Arms and Armour, 1996).

Hazlitt, W., *Table Talk* (London, Humphrey Milford/Oxford University Press, 1925).

Healey, D., *The Time of My Life* (London, Michael Joseph, 1989).

Hedges, C., *War is a Force that Gives us Meaning* (New York, Public Affairs, 2002).

Henderson, Sir Nevil, *Failure of a Mission: Berlin 1937–1939* (London, Hodder and Stoughton, 1940).

Herr, M., *Dispatches* (New York, Alfred A. Knopf, 1977).

Hillary, R., *The Last Enemy* (Basingstoke, Macmillan, 1942).

Hinsley, F. H., *Hitler's Strategy* (Cambridge, Cambridge University Press, 1951).

———, *Power and the Pursuit and the Pursuit of Peace: Theory and Practice in the History of Relations between States* (Cambridge, Cambridge University Press, 1981).

Hirst, F. W., *Armaments: The Race and the Crisis* (London, Cobden-Sanderson, 1937).

Hobson, J. A., *The Psychology of Jingoism* (London, Grant Richards, 1901).

Hoffmann, P., *German Resistance to Hitler* (Cambridge Mass., Harvard University Press, 1988).

Holloway, James 111, *Aircraft Carriers at War: A Personal Retrospective of Korea, Vietnam, and the Soviet Confrontation* (Annapolis, Naval Institute Press, 2007).

Holmes, R., *Dusty Warriors: Modern Soldiers at War* (London, Harper Press, 2006).

Honan, W., H., *Bywater: The Man who Invented the Pacific War* (London, Macdonald, 1990).

Hope-Jones, A., *Income Tax in the Napoleonic Wars* (Cambridge, Cambridge University Press, 1939).

Hore, Peter (ed.), *Patrick Blackett: Sailor, Scientist, Socialist* (London, Frank Cass, 2003).

Horne, A., *A Savage War of Peace: Algeria 1954–1962* (London, Macmillan, 1977).

Howard, M., *Studies in War and Peace* (London, Temple Smith, 1970).

——— and Paret, P. (eds), *Carl von Clausewitz on War* (Princeton, Princeton University Press, 1984).

Hudson, M. and Stanier, J., *War and the Media* (Stroud, Sutton, 1999).

Hurst, M. (ed.), *Key Treaties of the Great Powers* (Newton Abbot, David and Charles, 1972).

Huxley, A., *Ends and Means: An Enquiry into the Nature of Ideals and into the Methods employed for their Realisation* (London, Chatto and Windus, 1938).

Ignatieff, M., *Virtual War: Kosovo and Beyond* (London, Chatto and Windus, 2000).

———, *Empire Lite: Nation-Building in Bosnia, Kosovo and Afghanistan* (London, Vintage, 2003).

Iremonger, F. A., *William Temple: Archbishop of Canterbury, His Life and Letters* (London, Oxford University Press, 1948).

Irvine, W., *Apes, Angels and Victorians: A Joint Biography of Darwin and Huxley* (London, Weidenfeld and Nicolson, 1955).

Jaffe, L., *The Decision to Disarm Germany* (London, Allen and Unwin, 1985).

James, A., *Red Cross International and the Strategy of Peace* (London, Hodder and Stoughton, 1959).

James, R. R. (ed.), *Churchill Speaks 1897–1963* (Leicester, Windward, 1981).

James, C. L. R., *The Black Jacobins: Toussaint L'Ouverture and the San Domingo Revolution* (New York, Vintage, 1963).

Jasper, R., *George Bell: Bishop of Chichester* (London, Oxford University Press, 1967).

Jellicoe, Admiral, *The Crisis of the Naval War* (London, Cassell, 1920).

Jenkins, D., *The British: Their Identity and the Churches* (SCM Press, London, 1975).

Jobson, A., *Suffolk Remembered* (London, Robert Hale, 1969).

Johnson, J., *Wing Leader* (London, Chatto and Windus, London, 1956).

Jupp, P. (ed.), *The Letter-Journal of George Canning 1793–1795* (London, Royal Historical Society, 1991).

Kendall, G., *Religion in War and Peace* (London, Hutchinson, 1947).

Kennan, G. F., *The Nuclear Delusion* (London, Hamish Hamilton, 1984).

Kennedy, M., *The Problem of Japan* (London, Nisbet, 1935).

Ketterer, D. (ed.), *Flashes of the Fantastic* (Westport Cnn., Praeger, 2004).

Keynes, J. M., *Economic Consequences of the Peace* (New York, Harcourt, Brace and Howe, 1920).

King, A. (ed.), *British Political Opinion 1937–2000* (London, Politicos, 2001).

——— and Plunkett, J., *Victorian Print Media* (Oxford, Oxford University Press, 2005).

King-Hall, S., *Defence in the Nuclear Age* (London, Victor Gollancz, 1958).

Kinglake, A. W., *The Invasion of the Crimea* (Edinburgh, William Blackwood, 1878), Volume V11.

Kipling, R., *Barrack Room Ballads, Departmental Ditties and Other Ballads and Verses* (New York, Alex Grosset, 1899).

———, *The Five Nations* (London, Methuen, 1903).

Klemperer, K. von, *German Resistance against Hitler: The Search for Allies Abroad 1938–1945* (Oxford, Clarendon, 1994).

Knightley, P., *The First Casualty* (New York, Harcourt Brace Janovich, 1975).

Knop, W. G., Compiler, *Beware of the English: German Propaganda Exposes England* (London, Hamish Hamilton, 1939).

Knowles, E. (ed.), *The Oxford Dictionary of Quotations* (Oxford, Oxford University Press, 1999).

Koestler, A., *Darkness at Noon* (London, Jonathan Cape, 1940).

Korchilov, I., *Translating History: Thirty Years on the Front Lines with a Top Russian Interpreter* (New York, Lisa Drew/ Scribner, 1997).

Kyle, K., *Suez* (London, Weidenfeld and Nicolson, 1991).

Laslett, P., *The World We Have Lost* (London, Methuen, 1965).

Lester Smith, W. O., *Education* (Harmondsworth, Penguin, 1965).

Lewis, B., *The Crisis of Islam: Holy War and Unholy Terror* (London, Weidenfeld and Nicolson, 2003).

Liddell, Hart B. H., *Memoirs* (London, Cassell, 1965).

Liddon, H. P., Canon of St Paul's, *Sermons Preached on Special Occasions 1860–1889* (London, Longmans Green, 1897).

Lightfoot, J. B., *Cambridge Sermons* (Cambridge and London, Macmillan, 1873).

Lippmann, W., *Public Opinion* (New York, Free Press Paperbacks, 1997, first edition 1922).

———, *US Foreign Policy* (London, Hamish Hamilton, 1943).

———, *US War Aims* (London, Hamish Hamilton, 1944).

Lloyd, G. D., *War Memoirs* (London, Odhams, 1938 edition).

Lloyd, S., *Suez: A Personal Account* (London, Jonathan Cape, 1978).

Lockhart, J. G., *Cosmo Gordon Lang* (London, Hodder and Stoughton, 1949).

Louis, W. R., *Ends of British Imperialism: The Scramble for Empire, Suez and Decolonisation* (London, Tauris, 2006).

Lowes, D. G., *War: Its Nature, Cause and Cure* (London, George Allen and Unwin, 1923).

Loyd, A., *My War Gone by, I Miss it so* (London, Anchor, 2000).

Mac Isaac David (ed.), *The United States Strategic Bombing Survey* (New York, Garland Publishing, 1976).

MacDonald Fraser George, *Quartered Safe Out Here* (London, Harvill, 1992).

Maclean, F., *Eastern Approaches* (London, Four Square, 1967).

Macleod, E. V., *A War of Ideas* (Aldershot, Ashgate, 1998).

Maddison, A., *Dynamic Forces in Capitalist Development: A Long-run Comparative View* (Oxford, Oxford University Press, 1991).

Mandelbaum, M., *The Nuclear Revolution: International Politics before and after Hiroshima* (Cambridge, Cambridge University Press, 1981).

Mandler, P., *The English National Character: The History of an Idea from Edmund Burke to Tony Blair* (New Haven, Yale University Press, 2006).

Martin D. and Mullen, P. (eds), *Unholy Warfare: The Church and the Bomb* (London, Basil Blackwell, 1983).

Matheson, P. E., *The Life of Hastings Rashdall DD* (London, Oxford University Press, 1928).

May, E. R. (ed.), *Knowing One's Enemies: Intelligence Assessment before the Two World Wars* (Princeton, New Jersey, Princeton University Press, 1984).

Mazower, M., *Inside Hitler's Greece: The Experience of Occupation, 1941–1944* (New Haven, Yale University Press, 1993).

McCallum, R. B., *Public Opinion and the Last Peace* (London, Oxford University Press, 1944).

McCarthy, D. J., *The Prisoner of War in Germany* (London, Skeffington, 1918).

McClellan, S., *What happened: Inside the Bush White House and Washington's Culture of Deception* (New York, PublicAffairs, 2008).

McClelland, G., *Embers of War: Letters from a Quaker Relief Worker in War-torn Germany* (London, Tauris, 1997).

McCullagh, F., *With the Cossacks* (London, Eveleigh Nash, 1906).

McKenzie, F. A., *From Tokyo to Tiflis: Uncensored Letters from the War* (London, Hurst and Blackett, 1905).

McPhail, H., *The Long Silence: Civilian Life under the German Occupation of Northern France 1914–1918* (London, Tauris, 2001).

Mead, G., *The Good Soldier: A Biography of Douglas Haig* (London, Atlantic Books, 2007).

Mead, W. R., *God and Gold: Britain, America and the Making of the Modern World* (London, Atlantic Books, 2007).

Mearsheimer, J. J., *Liddell Hart and the Weight of History* (London, Brassey's, 1988).

Mercer, A., *Disease, Mortality and Population in Transition* (Leicester, Leicester University Press, 1990).

Milne, A. A., *Peace with Honour* (London, Methuen, 1936).

Milosz, C., *The Captive Mind* (London, Secker and Warburg, 1953).

Moon, P. (ed.), *Wavell: The Viceroy's Journals* (London, Oxford University Press, 1973).

Moorehead, A., *The End in Africa* (London, Hamish Hamilton, 1943).

Moran, L., *Winston Churchill: The Struggle for Survival* (London, Constable, 1960).

More, T., *Utopia and a Dialogue of Comfort* (London, Dent, 1962).

Morgenthau, H., *I Was Sent to Athens* (New York, Doubleday, 1929).

Morley, J., *Life of Richard Cobden* (London, T. Fisher Unwin, 1906).

Morley, J. V., *Memorandum on Resignation August 1914* (London, Macmillan, 1928).

Morris, P. (ed.), *First Aid to the Battlefront: Life and Letters of Sir Vincent Kennett-Barrington* (Stroud, Sutton, 1992).

Morrison, S., *I Renounce War: The Story of the Peace Pledge Union* (London, Sheppard Press, 1962).

Moss, N., *The Men who Play God: The Story of the Hydrogen Bomb* (London, Victor Gollancz, 1968).

Mowrer, E., *Germany Puts the Clock Back* (Harmondsworth, Penguin,1933).

Mozley, J. B., D. D., *Sermons Preached Before the University of Oxford on Special Occasions* (Oxford. Rivingtons, 1886).

Mueller, J. E., *War, Presidents and Public Opinion* (New York, John Wiley, 1973).

Muir, R., *The Expansion of Europe* (London, Constable, 1935).

Neillands, R., *The Bomber War: Arthur Harris and the Allied Bombing Offensive, 1939–1945* (London, John Murray, 2001).

Nicholas, H. G. (ed.), *Washington Despatches 1941–1945: Weekly Political Reports from the British Embassy* (London, Weidenfeld and Nicolson, 1981).

Nicholson, M., *A Measure of Danger Memoirs of a War Correspondent* (London, Harper Collins, 1991).

Nicolson, H., *Peacemaking 1919* (London, Constable, 1933).

Noel-Baker, P., *The Arms Race: A Programme for World Disarmament* (London, Atlantic Books, 1958).

Ohnuki-Tierney, E., *Kamikaze: Cherry Blossom and Nationalisms* (Chicago, University of Chicago Press, 2002).

Ono, G., *Expenditures of the Sino-Japanese War* (New York, Oxford University Press, 1922).

Overy, R. J., *The Air War 1939–1945* (London, Europa Publications, 1980).

Parker, R., *The Common Stream* (London, Paladin-Grafton, 1976).

Pascal, B., *The Provincial Letters of Blaise Pascal* (London, Griffith Farran, Okeden and Welsh, undated).

Pavillard, S. S., *Bamboo Doctor* (London, Macmillan, 1960).

Peacock, A. T. and Wiseman, J., *The Growth of Public Expenditure in the United Kingdom* (London, George Allen and Unwin, 1967).

Peers, Lieutenant General W. R., *The My Lai Inquiry* (New York, Norton, 1979).

Petrie, Sir Charles, *Twenty Years' Armistice-And After: British Foreign Policy since 1918* (London, Eyre and Spottiswoode, 1940).

Playne, C. E., *The Neuroses of the Nations* (London, George Allen and Unwin, 1925).

———, *The Pre-War Mind in Britain* (London, George Allen and Unwin, 1928).

Pollock, J., *Wilberforce* (London, Constable, 1977).

Powell, C. and Persico, J. E., *My American Journey* (New York, Ballantine, 1996).

Pringle, P. and William, A., *SIOP: Nuclear War from the Inside* (London, Sphere, 1983).

Prins, G. and Hylke, T., *Foundation of War Studies: The Future of War* (The Hague, Kluwer Law International, 2000).

Prior, M., *Campaigns of a War Correspondent* (London, Edward Arnold, 1912).

Private 19022 (Manning), *Her Privates We* (London, Peter Davies, 1930).

Prior, R., *Churchill's World Crisis as History* (Beckenham, Croom Helm, 1983).

Proctor, J. (ed.), *Village Schools: A History of Rural Elementary Education from the Eighteenth to the Twenty-First Century in Prose and Verse* (Oxford, Oxford University Press, 2005).

Puckler, Count Erdmann, *How Strong is Britain?* (London, Routledge, 1939).

Ranki, G., *The Economics of the Second World War* (Vienna, Böhlau Verlag, 1993).

Raviv, A., et al., *How Children Understand Peace and War* (San Francisco, Jossey-Bass Publishers, 1999).

Raymond, E., *Tell England: A Study in a Generation* (London, Cassell, 1922).

Read, Donald, *Cobden and Bright: A Victorian Political Partnership* (London, Edward Arnold, 1988).

Reed, B. and Williams G., *Denis Healey and the Policies of Power* (London, Sidgwick and Jackson, 1971).

Reed, Douglas, *Insanity Fair* (London, Jonathan Cape, 1938).

Rhodes, J. R., *Churchill: A Study in Failure 1900–1939* (London, Weidenfeld and Nicolson, 1970).

Riccio, B. D., *Walter Lippmann: Odyssey of a Liberal* (New Brunswick, Transaction Publishers, 1994).

Richardson, L. F., *Statistics of Deadly Quarrels* (London, Stevens, 1960).

Ricks, C., *Tennyson* (Basingstoke, Macmillan, 1989).

Ridley, J., *Lord Palmerston* (London, Constable, 1970).

Robbins, K., *John Bright* (London, Routledge and Kegan Paul, 1979).

———, *Politicians, War and Diplomacy in British Foreign Policy* (London, Hambledon Press, 1994).

Roberts, Field Marshal Lords, *Forty-One Years in India from Subaltern to Commander-in-Chief* (London, Richard Bentley, 1897).

Roskill, S., *Churchill and the Admirals* (London, Collins, 1977).

Roydon, G. (ed.), *Home Fires Burning: The Great War Diaries of Geogina Lee* (Stroud, Sutton, 2006).

Ruskin, J., *The Crown of Wild Olive* (London, George Allen, 1907).

Russell, F. H., *The Just War in the Middle Ages* (Cambridge, Cambridge University Press, 1975).

Salahi, M. A., *Muhammad: Man and Prophet* (Shaftesbury, Element, 1995).

Sandler, T., *Collective Action: Theory and Applications* (New York, Harvester Wheat-sheaf, 1992).

Schweppenburg, General Baron von, *The Critical Years* (London, Wingate, 1952).

Scribner, *Encyclopedia of American Lives: Notable Americans who died between 1981 and 1985* (New York, Scribner's, 1998).

Searle, G. R., *The Quest for National Efficiency* (Oxford, Basil Blackwell, 1971).

Semmel, B., *Imperialism and Social Reform* (London, George Allen and Unwin, 1960).

Sheean, V., *In Search of History* (London, Hamish Hamilton, 1935).

Sherer, M., *Recollections of the Peninsula* (Staplehurst, Kent, Spellmount Library, 1996).

Sermons or Homilies appointed to be read in Church (London, Prayer Book and Homily Society, 1988).

Sherwig, J. M., *Guineas and Gunpowder: British Foreign Aid in the War with France 1793–1815* (Cambridge, Harvard University Press, 1969).

Sherwood, M., *After Abolition: Britain and the Slave Trade since 1807* (London, Tauris, 2007).

Short, K. R. M. (ed.), *Western Broadcasting over the Iron Curtain* (London, Croom Helm, 1986).

Shute, N., *On the Beach* (New York, Signet, 1958).

———, *What Happened to the Corbetts* (London, Pan Books, 1965).

Sifry, M. L. and Serf, C., *The Iraq War Reader: History, Documents, Opinions* (New York, Touchstone, 2003).

Simpson, I., *Singapore Too Little Too late* (London, Leo Cooper, 1970).

Skidelsky, R., *John Maynard Keynes: Fighting for Freedom, 1937–1946* (London, Penguin, 2002).

Slessor, Sir John, *The Central Blue: Recollections and Reflections* (London, Cassell, 1956).

Smith, A., *An Inquiry into the Nature and Causes of the Wealth of Nations* (London, Dent, 1912).

Smith, D. C. (ed.), *The Correspondence of H.G. Wells* (London, Pickering and Chatto, 1998).

Smith, G. G. (ed.), *The Life and Speeches of John Bright MP* (London, Hodder and Stoughton, 1892).

Sobel, R., *The Impact of Public Opinion on US Foreign Policy since Vietnam* (New York, Oxford University Press, 2001.

Solzhenitsyn, A., *The Gulag Archipelago 1918–1956* (London, Collins/Harvill/Fontana, 1974).

Spaight, J. M., *Aircraft in Peace and the Law* (London, Macmillan, 1919).

———, *Air Power in the Next War* (London, Geoffrey Bles, 1938).

———, *Volcano Island* (London, Geoffrey Bles, 1943).

Stanhope, E., *Letters Written by the Late Right Honourable Philip Dormer Stanhope Earl of Chesterfield to His Son* (London, Dodsley, 1772).

Stendhal, *The Charterhouse of Parma* (London, Zodiac Press, 1980).

Stevenson, D., *1914–1918: The History of the First World War* (London, Allen Lane, 2004).

Strachan, H., *The Politics of the British Army* (Oxford, Clarendon Press, 1997).

Strachey, J., *On the Prevention of War* (London, Macmillan, 1962).

Strang, Lord, *Britain in World Affairs: Henry V111 to Elizabeth 11* (London, Faber and Faber and Andre Deutsch, 1961).

Stromberg, R. N., *Redemption By War: The Intellectuals and 1914* (Lawrence, The Regents Press of Kansas, 1982).

Suykerbuyk, B. J., *Essays from Oceania and Eurasia: George Orwell and 1984* (Antwerpen, University Instelling 1984).

Swartz, M., *The Union of Democratic Control in British Politics during the First World War* (Oxford, Clarendon Press, 1971).

Swift, J., *Gulliver's Travels* (Watford, Bruce Publishing, undated).

Sykes, C., *Troubled Loyalty: A Biography of Adam von Trott zu Solz* (London, Collins, 1968).

Tatham, S., *Losing Arab Hearts and Minds: The Coalition, Al Jazeera and Muslim Public Opinion* (New York, Front Street Press, 2006).

Taylor, R. and Pritchard, C., *The Protest Makers: The British Nuclear Disarmament Movement of 1958–1965, Twenty Years on* (Oxford, Pergamon Press, 1980).

Teller, E. and Brown, A., *The Legacy of Hiroshima* (London, Macmillan, 1962).

Teller, E. with Shoolery, J. L., *Memoirs: A Twentieth-Century Journey in Science and Politics* (Cambridge Mass., Perseus, 2001).

Temperley, H. and Penson, L. M., *Foundations of British Foreign Policy from Pitt (1792) to Salisbury (1902)* (Cambridge, Cambridge University Press, 1938).

Temple, W., *The Life of Bishop Percival* (London, Macmillan, 1921).

Tennyson, Lord, *Poetical Work of Alfred Lord Tennyson* (London, Peacock, Mansfield and Britton, undated).

Terraine, J., *A Time for Courage: The Royal Air Force in the European War 1939–1945* (New York, Macmillan, 1985).

———, *The Smoke and the Fire: Myths and Anti-Myths of War* (London, Sidgwick and Jackson, 1980).

Thatcher, M., *The Downing Street Years* (New York, Harper/Collins, 1993).

Thompson, R., *Defeating Communist Insurgency: Experiences from Malaya and Vietnam* (London, Chatto and Windus, 1974).

Thompson, R., *Make for the Hills: Memories of Far Eastern Wars* (London, Leo Cooper, 1989).

Tirpitz, von, *My Memoirs by Grand Admiral von Tirpitz* (London, Hurst and Blackett, 1919).

Towle, P., *MPs and Defence: A Survey of Parliamentary Knowledge and Opinion* (London, Institute for European Defence and Strategic Studies, 1988).

———, *Enforced Disarmament from the Napoleonic Campaigns to the Gulf War* (Oxford, Clarendon, 1997).

———, *Democracy and Peacemaking: Negotiations and Debates 1815–1973* (London, Routledge, 2000).

———, *From Ally to Enemy: Anglo-Japanese Military Relations, 1900–1945* (Folkestone, Global Oriental, 2006).

────── and Kosuge, N. M. (eds), *Britain and Japan in the Twentieth Century: One Hundred Years of Trade and Prejudice* (London, I B Tauris, 2007).

Toynbee, A. J., *Survey of International Affairs 1920–1923* (London, Humphrey Milford/ Oxford University Press, 1925).

Trevelyan, G. M., *The Diaries of John Bright with a Foreword by Philip Bright* (London, Cassell, 1930).

──────, *The Life of John Bright* (London, Constable, 1930).

Trotter, W., *Instincts of the Herd in Peace and War* (London, Ernest Benn, 1916).

Ultey, M., (ed.), *Adapting to Conditions, War and Society in the Eighteenth Century* (Alabama, University of Alabama Press, 1986).

Vagts, A., *A History of Militarism Civilian and Military* (London, Hollis and Carter, 1959).

Vattel, E. de, *The Law of Nations and the Principles of Natural Law* (Washington, Carnegie Institution, 1916).

Vaux, T., *The Selfish Altruist: Relief Work in Famine and War* (London, Earthscan, 2001).

Vespa, A., *Secret Agent of Japan* (London, Victor Gollancz, 1938).

Veve, T. D., *The Duke of Wellington and the British Army of Occupation in France 1815–1818* (Westport, Greenwood University Press, 1992).

Waal, A. de, *Famine Crimes: Politics and Disaster Relief in Africa* (Bloomington, Indian University Press, 1997).

Walvin, J., *Slavery and British Society 1776–1846* (London, Macmillan, 1982).

Wark, W. K., *The Ultimate Enemy: British Intelligence and Nazi Germany, 1933–1939* (Oxford, Oxford University Press, 1986).

Wells, H. G., *Mr Britling Sees it Through* (London, Hogarth Press, 1984, first published 1916).

──────, *The Shape of Things to Come: The Ultimate Revolution* (Harmondsworth, Penguin, 2005).

Werner M., *The Military Strength of the Powers* (London, Victor Gollancz, 1939).

──────, *Battle for the World: the Strategy and Diplomacy of the Second World War* (London, Victor Gollancz, 1941).

──────, *The Great Offensive: the Strategy of Coalition Warfare* (London, Victor Gollancz, 1943).

Wilkinson, A., *The Church of England and the First World War* (London, SCM Press, 1996).

Williams, V., *The World of Action* (London, Hamish Hamilton, 1938).

Wilson, A., *More Thoughts and Talks* (London, Longmans Green, 1939).

Wilson, E., *The Wound and the Bow* (London, Methuen, 1961).

──────, *Patriotic Gore: Studies in the Literature of the American Civil War* (New York, Galaxy/Oxford, 1966).

Wilson, T., *Churchill and the Prof* (London, Cassell, 1995).

Winkler, H. R., *The League of Nations Movement in Great Britain 1914–1919* (Metuchen, New Jersey, Scarecrow Reprint Corporation, 1967).

Winnington, I. A. W., *The Church in Time of War* (London, Wells Gardener, 1915).

Winton J., *Convoy: The Defence of Sea Trade 1890–1990* (London, Michael Joseph, 1983).

Wood, A., *Nineteenth Century Britain: 1815–1914* (London, Longmans, 1960).

Woodburn-Kirby, S., *Singapore: The Chain of Disaster* (London, Cassell, 1971).

Woodforde, J., *The Diary of a Country Parson 1758–1802* (London, Oxford University Press, 1949).

Woodward, B., *The Commanders* (New York, Simon and Schuster, 1991).
———, *Bush at War* (New York, Simon and Schuster, 2002).
Woodward, D., *Sunk: How the Great Battleships were Lost* (London, George Allen and Unwin, 1982).
Woodward, A. S. and Robinson, P., *One Hundred days: The Memoirs of the Falklands Battle Group Commander* (London, HarperCollins, 1992).
Wrigley, E. A., *People, Cities and Wealth: The Transformation of Traditional Society* (Oxford, Basil Blackwell, 1987).
——— and Schofield, R. S., *The Population History of England 1541–1871* (London, Edward Arnold, 1981).
York, H., *The Advisors: Oppenheimer, Teller and the Superbomb* (San Francisco, Freeman, 1974).
Young, E., *A Farewell to Arms Control?* (Harmondsworth, Penguin, 1972).
Young, P. and Jesser, P., *The Media and the Military : From the Crimea to Desert Strike* (Basingstoke, Macmillian, 1997).
Zimmern Sir Alfred, *Spiritual Values and World Affairs* (London, Oxford University Press, 1939).
Zinsser, H., *Rats, Lice and History* (New York, Bantam, 1965).
Zuckerman, S., *Scientists and War: The Impact of Science on Military and Civil Affairs* (London, Hamish Hamilton, 1966).

Official Publications

The Armaments Year Book; General and Statistical Information in regard to Land, Naval and Air Armaments (Geneva, League of Nations, 1932).
Documents on Disarmament: 1957–1959 (Washington, Department of State, 1960).
Mac Isaac, D. (ed.), *The United States Strategic Bombing Survey* (New York, Garland Publishing, 1976).
The Disarmament Question 1945–1953 (London, Central Office of Information, 1953).
Statement on Defence Estimates 1956, Cmnd 9691 (London, HMSO, 1956).
Statement on Defence Estimates 1983, Cmnd 8951-1 and 8951-11 (London, HMSO, 1983).
Falkland Islands Review, Report of a Committee of Privy Counsellors, Cmnd 8787, (London, HMSO, January 1983).
Statement on Defence Estimates: Britain's Defence for the 1990s, Volume 1, Cm 1559-1 (London, HMSO, 1991).
Social Trends 1995 Edition (London, HMSO, 1995).
Statement on Defence Estimates 1996, Cm 3223 (London, HMSO, 2006).
Modernising Defence: Annual Report of Defence Activity 1998/99 (London, Ministry of Defence, 1999).
The 9/11 Commission Report: Final Report of the National Commission on Terrorist Attacks upon the United States (New York, W. H. Norton, undated).
House of Lords: Select Committee on the Constitution: *Waging War: Parliament's Role and Responsibility*, HL Paper 236-1 (London, Stationary Office).
Review of Intelligence of Weapons of Mass Destruction, Report of a Committee of Privy Counsellors, Chairman Lord Butler of Brockwell, HC 898, 14 July 2004.

Selected Periodical Articles

Quarterly Review

'The reform ministry and the reformed parliament', October 1833.
'*Journal of a West India Planter* and *Domestic Manners in the West Indies*', reviewed January 1834.
'Review of the history of the ancient Barony of castle Combe' by G. P. Scrope MP, March 1853.
Review of David Hume's *History of England from the Invasion of Julius Caesar to the Revolution of 1688*, June 1826.

Public Opinion Quarterly

'British institute of public opinion', 1940, pp. 77–81.
'Gallup and fortune polls', 1940, pp. 83–115, 357–393.
'Gallup and fortune polls', 1941. pp. 155–165, 319–333, 666–687.
'Gallup and fortune polls', 1942, pp. 149–171, 310–317, 660–665.
'Gallup and fortune polls', 1943, pp. 173–178, 329–335, 498–504.
'Public opinion polls', 1944–1945, pp. 151–161, 295–303, 447–457, 583–597.
Owen, J., 'The polls and newspaper appraisal of the Suez Crisis', Fall 1957, pp. 350–354.
Smith, T. W.,'The polls – a report – nuclear anxiety', Winter 1988.

History of Education

Betts, R., 'A new type of elementary teacher: George Collins 1839–1891', 1998, pp. 15–27.
Bowden, C., 'Women as intermediaries: an example of the use of literacy in the late sixteenth and early seventeenth centuries', 1993, pp. 215–223.
Charlton, K., 'Mothers as educative agents in pre-industrial England', 1994, pp 129–156.
Gibson, W., 'The social origins and education of an elite: the Nineteenth-century episcopate', 1991, pp. 95–105.
Gronn, P. C., 'An experiment in political education: V. G. Slimy and the Repton Sixth, 1916–1918', 1990, pp. 1–21.
Layton, D., 'The educational work of the parliamentary committee of the British Association for the advancement of science', 1976, p. 34.
Marsden, W. E., '"Poisoned history": A comparative study of nationalism, propaganda and the treatment of war and peace in the late nineteenth and early twentieth century school curriculum', 2000, pp. 29–47.
Motley, M., 'Educating the English gentleman abroad: the Verney family in seventeenth-century France and Holland', 1994, pp. 243–256.
Simon, J., 'The state and schooling at the reformation and after: from pious causes to charitable uses', 1994, pp. 157–169.
Smith, J. T., 'Punch and elementary education (1860–1900)', 1998, pp. 125–140.
———, 'Merely a growing dilemma of etiquette? The deepening gulf between the Victorian clergyman and Victorian schoolteacher', March 2004.

Taylor, T., 'Lord Cranborne, the church party and Anglican education 1893–1902: from politics to pressure', 1993, pp. 125–146.

Watts, R., 'Some radical educational networks of the late eighteenth century and their influence', 1996, pp. 1–14.

Encounter

'The American Crisis', January 1970.

Bell, D., 'Unstable America?' June 1970.

Fairlie, H. and Worsthorne, P., 'Suicide of a nation?' January 1976.

Shanks, M., 'The English sickness', January 1972.

Other Publications

Bull, J., 'The Rhine problem', and Augur, 'Germany in Europe', *Fortnightly Review*, Volume 121, 1927, pp. 310 and 577.

Daunton, M. J., 'How to pay for the war: state, society and taxation in Britain, 1917–24', *English Historical Review*, September 1996.

Khan, S., Shafi, M., and Khan, I., 'Insights into electoral history in Afghanistan', *Journal of Law and Society*, Peshawar, July 2006.

Okamoto, T., 'American-Japanese Issues and the Anglo-Japanese Alliance', *Contemporary Review*, 1921, Volume 119, p. 354.

Quirk, J., 'The anti-slavery project: Linking the historical and the contemporary', *Human Rights Quarterly*, 28 (2006).

Seligman, E. R., 'The cost of war and how it was met', *American Economic Review*, December 1919.

Simons, H., 'World-wide capabilities for production and control of nuclear weapons', *Daedalus*, Volume 88, Summer 1959.

Stibbe, M., 'Prisoners of War during the First World War', *German Historical Institute Bulletin*, November 2006.

On Line Opinion Polls

The Falklands War – Panorama Survey 1 by MORI in http://www.com/ polls/trends/falklands panorama1. shtml and The Falklands War – Trends – *Daily Star* Survey 26 April 1982/*Sunday Times* Survey 30 April 1982.

MORI, 'War with Iraq: Public view', 19 November 2002, 'The war with Iraq: The ideas of march poll', MORI 11/08/2003 at http://www.mori.com/polls/ 2003/Iraq3.

MORI, 'War with Iraq: Public view', 19 November 2002, http://www.mori.com/ polls/2002/Iraq-approval.shtml. MORI, 'End of the Baghdad Bounce', 8 June 2003, http://www.mori.com/polls/2003/t030526.shtml.

'Media coverage of Iraq conflict', MORI http://www.mori.com/polls/2003/ iraq-media.shtml.

Index

Note: the letters 'ff.' tagged along with locators indicate that the information continues in the following pages.

Abyssinia Italian attack in 1935 and British failure to protect, 160

Afghan war and media, 66, 67
and morality, 162
and public opinion, 140, 141, 144, 146

Aiken Frank initiates non-proliferation measures at UN, 77–8

American civil war, 157

Amritsar massacre 1919, 99

Angell Norman and economics of warfare, 83

Anglican Church and War, 24 ff.

Anti-Corn Law League founded, 47

Anti-slavery movement, 2, 43, 44, 45

Appeasement, 32, 33
criticism of, 160
and public opinion, 135, 136, 137, 140

Armchair strategists, 5, 80 ff., 228

Army British popularity of, 114, 146, 147

Ashdown Paddy, 7
and armchair strategists, 128

Asquith Herbert forced to resign, 7
and relations with Anglican Church in 1914, 30

Attlee Clement and public opinion, 137

Attorney General and Iraq War 2003, 149

Bacon Francis and causes of war, 26

Balance of power, 1, 3, 28, 49, 80
British support for, 161
and collapse of Soviet Union, 143, 144

effect on international relations, 158, 159

Balfour Arthur and war in 1914, 85, 86, 119, 128

Barnett Correlli and excessive moralism of British politics, 160

Belgium invasion of in 1914, 30, 31

Bell Bishop George and chemical weapons, 32
and bombing of Germany, 34, 35

Beresford Admiral Lord Charles attacks Churchill over Dardanelles, 120

Blackett P. M. S. and nuclear weapons, 96, 97

Blair Tony and George W. Bush, 24
and elected House of Lords, 154
and interventionism, 142, 164

Bloch Ivan and the future of war, 81, 82

Blockade naval, 83

Boer War and jingoism, 7
criticised by Nonconformists, 28
and reform of government machinery, 142

Bombing aircraft, 92, 93
United States Strategic Bombing Survey, 35
used against Germany, 34, 130

Bond Brian and literature of First World War, 72

Bonham Carter Violet wartime diaries, 63

Bosnia War and airpower, 56
and media, 65, 66

British Institute of Public Opinion (Gallup), 135

Burke Edmund and French Wars, 118

Bush President George W., 24, 32,
    34–5
    and balance of power, 143
Bush President George and war
    against Iraq 1991, 163
Butler Lord and review of Intelligence
    after Iraq War, 147, 148, 149
Byers Frank and lack of secrecy in
    Falklands War, 123
Bywater Hector and Pacific War, 88, 89

Cameron James and CND, 51
Carr E. H., 86, 95, 96
Castle Combe crimes in, 13
Casualties in war, 3, 18–19
Casus belli, 148, 154
Catholic views on wars, 37, 38
Censorship in the First World War, 63
    and Soviet Union, 156
Chamberlain Neville and reversal of
    policy of appeasement in 1939, 90
    declaration of war in 1939, 105
    and public opinion, 135, 161
Chamberlain W.H. and Japan, 87
Chaucer Geoffrey and description of
    Britain in 14ᵗʰ century, 14
Chemical weapons British use of First
    World War, 31
    Iraqi use of in 1980s, 163
    and Iraq War in 2003, 142, 145,
    150, 151
Chesterfield Lord and limitations on
    warfare, 16
Children and conflict, 13
Christianity and warfare, 13, 14
Churchill Winston and fear of nuclear
    war, 51
    and fall of France 1940, 113, 136
    and interest in warfare, 105
    recalls Parliament in 1941, 126
Clark Allen and Kosovo War, 125
Clarke I. F. and prophecies of war, 70
Clausewitz and declarations of war,
    104
CND, 20, 51, 52, 55, 91, 121
Cobbett William and hatred of
    Evangelical Movement, 43

Cobden Richard, 9
    and opposition to Crimean War, 47,
    48
    and slave trade, 46, 47
Cold War, 12, 19–20, 26
Committee of Imperial Defence, 165
Communications, 17, 18
Communists and causes of war, 156
Conservatives unpopularity of, 152
Convoys naval in First World War, 110
Corbett Sir Julian and naval
    blockade, 83
Costs of war, 18, 19, 20
Crimean War opposed by Cobden and
    Bright, 47

Dardanelles debate on, 120
Darwin Charles and Social
    Darwinism, 29
Davidson Archbishop Randall and
    First World War, 24, 30
    and imperialism, 162
    and League of Nations, 32
    life, 171
Debate in Parliament and Iraq war
    2003, 150
Debt British to United States, 19, 21
Declaration of war in 1914, 133
Defence and Overseas Policy
    Committee and Iraq war, 147, 151
Defence White Papers, 2, 3, 121–2
Douhet Giulio and bombing, 91, 92
Dunant Henry founds Red Cross
    1864, 48

Economics and warfare, 81, 83, 84,
    107
Eden Anthony and resignation, 36
    and military attitudes towards
    warfare, 129
    and public opinion, 136, 137
Education, 6, 12, 15, 16, 17
Elections declining voter turnout, 152
Enlightenment, 16
Esher Lord and Norman Angell, 83
Evangelical Movement and slavery,
    43, 44
Experts dependence on, 108

Falklands War and media, 65
    covert military support for islands,
        153
    and public opinion, 137
First World War, 1, 17
    outbreak of, 140
Fox Charles, James, 9
    and opposition to French Wars, 118
Foxton, 13
French Sir John and outbreak of war
    in 1914, 107
French Wars, 3, 27

Garden Lord Timothy and Afghan
    War, 125
General Belgrano sinking of and
    public opinion, 138
Germany and starvation after Second
    World War, 52
Golding William, pessimism about
    human nature, 78, 79
Goodhart Lord, 8
Gowing Nick and subjective
    reporting, 63
Grey Edward, 28
    and debate on war, 85, 103, 117
    and information to public, 116
    and motives, 11
Grotius Hugo, 16
Guerrilla warfare, 21, 98, 99, 107, 108,
        114, 165
    and Bosnian War, 66
    British defeats in, 144, 164
    and Duke of Wellington, 109
Gwynne Sir Charles and imperial
    policing, 98

Hague Peace Conference of 1899 and
    chemical weapons, 31
Haig Field Marshal and weapons in
    First World War, 111, 112
Halifax Lord and readiness for war
    1939, 117
Hardrada Harold and looting in
    wartime, 15
Harries Bishop Richard supports war
    1991, opposes 2003, 38
Hazlitt William and café society, 16

Healey Denis and civilian strategists,
    7, 100, 128, 129
Henry VIII King and warnings
    against war, 26
Hirst Francis and rearmament in the
    1930s, 89
Hobsbawn Eric and Falklands War, 65
Hobson J.A. and working class
    xenophobia, 7, 132, 133
    and Church support for war, 29
Holloway Admiral James and
    civil–military relations, 130
Homilies and war, 25, 26
Hoover Herbert and assistance to
    Belgium and Northern France in
    First World War, 52, 53
House of Lords reform of, 154
    Select Committee on the
        Constitution, 152, 153
Hulme T. E. and ingrained ideas, 41
Huntington Samuel and clash of
    civilisations, 54
Hurd Douglas and former Yugoslavia,
    124
Hussein Saddam removal from
    power, 41
    and Iraq War 1991, 163

Imperialism British, 2
India and British imperialism, 162
    economic growth and US policy
        towards, 158
Industrialists and War, 84
Intelligence and war in Iraq, 148, 149
Iraq War 1991 and oil interests, 163
Iraq War 2003, 8, 10, 24, 39, 66, 108,
        145
    and journalists, 64
    and public opinion, 155
Ironside Field Marshal William and
    declaration of war, 105
Israel US support for, despite its
    material interests, 163

Jesus of Nazareth, 13–14
Jewish people struggle for survival,
    13, 14
Just War, 15, 24, 37

Kennedy President John and
  civil–military relations, 130
King-Hall Sir Stephen and passive
  resistance, 97, 98
Kipling Rudyard and war and
  imperialism, 19
Kitchener Lord and First World War,
  107
Korchilov Igor and arms control, 77
Korean War and public opinion, 137
Kuwait Iraqi invasion of and recall of
  Parliament 1990, 123
  and UN Charter, 164

Lang Archbishop Cosmo and war, 33
Lansbury George opposes rearmament
  in 1930s, 50
Lansdowne Lord calls for negotiated
  end of First World War, 23
Leach Admiral Sir Henry and outbreak
  of Falklands War, 102
League of Nations, 3, 32
  sponsored by Union for Democratic
  Control, 49
Left Book Club, 86
Liberal MPs oppose war 1914, 118
Liddell Hart Sir Basil and prospects for
  war in 1930s, 90, 91, 92, 93
Lippmann Walter and Cold War, 20
  and establishment of NATO, 94, 95
  and public opinion, 134
Lloyd George David, 7
  and censorship, 63
  and war in 1914, 84
  and civil military relations, 110,
  111
  and disarmament of Germany, 87

MacArthur General Douglas and
  public opinion during Korean
  War, 137
Major Prime Minister John and
  interventionism, 142
Marx Karl and determinism, 157
Media and parliament, 127, 128
  and images of war, 147
Mill John, Stuart and education, 14
Milne A. A. and rearmament, 87
Milne Lord and war in 1939, 104

Milton John and education, 15
Moorehead Alan and reporting on
  Second World War, 61
More Thomas, Utopia, 68
Mozley J. B. and war, 27
MPs public opinion of, 154
Mugabe President and Western critics,
  161
Munich agreement 1938 criticism of,
  31, 160, 161
Muslim attitudes towards war, 12
Myanmar pressure to attack 2008, 160

NGOS British support for, 4, 36, 40 ff.
  and pressure for war, 160
Nott Sir John and Falklands War, 102
Nuclear weapons, 20, 36, 76
  attack on Japan 1945, 62
  tests and arms control, 62, 77
  debate on, 121

Olympic games revival of, 174
Orwell George, Nineteen Eighty Four,
  74–5
Owen Lord David and Saddam
  Hussein, 124
Oxfam, 52, 53

Palmerston Lord opposes slave trade,
  46
  supports opium trade with China,
  163
  and war in 1864, 103, 104
Parliament and war, 116 ff.
  and constitutional position, 152,
  154
Party loyalty and war, 134
Pascal Blaise and Christian view of
  war, 15
Peacekeeping forces, 37
Peace Pledge Union founded, 50
Percival Bishop of Hereford and war in
  1914, 30
Pitt the Younger, 6, 20, 22
  and British forces, 109
  and declaration of war against
  French, 28, 117
Playne Caroline assessment of public
  opinion, 133

Politicians and serving officers, 6, 7, 111, 115
    during Vietnam War, 130
Ponsonby Arthur opposes First World War, 48
Powell Colin and Iraq War 2003, 108
    on civilians and war, 130
Prisoners of war, 31
Public opinion, 4, 8, 23, 24, 34, 35, 55
    and appeasement in 1930s, 135
    and Falklands War, 138, 139
    and media, 58
    and war 1914, 118–19, 132 ff., 155, 164

Quarterly Review range of issues covered, 16

Ramsey Reverend James and slave trade, 46
Red Cross, 48
Rhineland remilitarised by Adolf Hitler, 37
Rose General Sir Michael and public opinion, 146
Roskill S. W. on Winston Churchill, 113, 114
Royal prerogative, 116
Runcie Archbishop supports 1991 war against Iraq, 38
Rural population and war, 134
Ruskin John and warfare, 70
Russell Bertrand, role in CND, 51
Russell William Howard and Crimean War, 58, 59, 61, 62
Russo-Japanese War and civilian casualties, 60
    and press, 59

St Peterburg Declaration on expanding bullets, 69
Seeley Sir John and British imperialism, 161, 162
Serbia invaded 1914, 30
    war in 1990s, 124, 125
Sharp Granville and abolition of slavery, 44
Sheppard Reverend Dick founds Peace Pledge Union, 50

Short Clare opposes Iraq war, 151
Shute Nevil and bombing in the 1930s, 74
    and nuclear weapons, 75, 76, 77, 78
Sierra Leone and anti-slavery movement, 46
Slavery movement to abolish, 42 ff.
    and US Civil War, 157
Smith Adam and funding for war, 82
Social Darwinism, 9, 29
    and media, 59
Soldiers and war-mongering, 129
Spaight J. M. estimates of effect of bombing, 91, 92, 93
Spanish-American war 1898, 148
Spender J. A., and British risk taking, 102
Spies for Soviet Union during Cold War, 22
Stirrup Sir Jock and Basra, 146
Submarines impact of, 83, 96, 110
Sudan atrocities alleged in, 40
Suez campaign and information to Parliament, 116, 121
    and Lord Mountbatten, 106
    and public opinion, 137
Suffrage universal, 6
Swift Jonathan satirises war, 68

Taleban and Afghan War, 144
Teller Edward and Nevil Shute, 76
    and P. M. S. Blackett, 97
Temple Archbishop William and bombing, 35
Tennyson Alfred Lord and Locksley Hall, 4, 69, 70
Terrorism and public opinion, 141
    motives for, 144
    pervasiveness of, 147
Thatcher Lady Margaret and Falklands task force, 102, 116, 122
    and war against Iraq 1991, 164
Thompson E. P. and Falklands War, 137
Thompson Robert on guerrilla warfare, 99, 100, 165
Tolstoy Leo and war, 157, 158
Tonkin Gulf incident and Vietnam War, 148

Toynbee Arnold and Royal Institute of International Affairs, 86
Trotter Wilfred and herd instincts in wartime, 159
Truman President Harry S. and science fiction, 71

Uncle Tom's Cabin and American Civil War, 157
Union of Democratic Control calls for democratic foreign policy, 48
United States public opinion and war, 139

Vagts Alfred and declaration of war, 103
Vattel Emmerich de and war, 16
Vietnam War and effect on public debate, 60, 73, 121, 130
Voting in elections, 152

Wars of choice, 153
Wellington Duke of, 21
and war in Spain, 109

Wells H.G. and description of First World War, 63
and 1930s, 73
and life, 179
and prophecy, 72
Werner Max and balance of power, 89, 90
Wilberforce William and slave trade, 7
and attacks on, 44
Williams Rowan Archbishop of Canterbury and war, 24, 38
Wilson Edmund and Kipling, 71
and causes of war, 156, 157
Wilson Harold and recall of Parliament 1968, 126
Wilson Sir Henry and outbreak of war in 1914, 103
Women and war, 49, 50
Woodward Admiral Sandy and Falklands losses, 66
Writers' support for First World War, 72

Zimbabwe pressure for Britain to invade in 2008, 160, 161
Zimmern Sir Alfred and Anglican view of war, 32, 33